SHADOW ON THE STEPS

Society of Biblical Literature

Resources for Biblical Study

Susan Ackerman
Editor (Old Testament/Hebrew Bible)

Number 64

SHADOW ON THE STEPS
Time Measurement in Ancient Israel

SHADOW ON THE STEPS

TIME MEASUREMENT IN ANCIENT ISRAEL

By
David Miano

Society of Biblical Literature
Atlanta

SHADOW ON THE STEPS
Time Measurement in Ancient Israel

Copyright © 2010 by the Society of Biblical Literature

All rights reserved. No part of this work may be reproduced or transmitted in any form or by any means, electronic or mechanical, including photocopying and recording, or by means of any information storage or retrieval system, except as may be expressly permitted by the 1976 Copyright Act or in writing from the publisher. Requests for permission should be addressed in writing to the Rights and Permissions Office, Society of Biblical Literature, 825 Houston Mill Road, Atlanta, GA 30329 USA.

Library of Congress Cataloging-in-Publication Data

Miano, David.
　　Shadow on the steps : time measurement in ancient Israel / by David Miano.
　　　p. cm. — (Resources for Biblical study / Society of Biblical Literature ; no. 64)
　　Includes bibliographical references.
　　ISBN 978-1-58983-478-1 (paper binding : alk. paper) — ISBN 978-1-58983-479-8 (electronic library copy)
　　1. Time in the Bible. 2. Time—Religious aspects—Judaism. 3. Bible. O.T.—Criticism, interpretation, etc. I. Society of Biblical Literature. II. Title.
　　BS1199.T5M53 2010b
　　221.8'529—dc22   2010007838

18 17 16 15 14 13 12 11 10   5 4 3 2 1
Printed on acid-free, recycled paper conforming to ANSI/NISO Z39.48-1992
(R1997) and ISO 9706:1994 standards for paper permanence.

This book is dedicated to the late Professor David Noel Freedman (1922–2008), who taught me the joys of scholarship.

Contents

Acknowledgments ix
Abbreviations and Terms xi
Figures and Tables xix

Introduction 1

1. Calendars 7
   1.1. Natural Units of Time   7
   1.2. The Day as a Unit of Measurement   7
      1.2.1. The Hebrew Word for Day   7
      1.2.2. When Did the Day Begin and End?   8
      1.2.3. Measurable Divisions of the Day   13
   1.3. The Month as a Unit of Measurement   19
      1.3.1. The Hebrew Words for Month   19
      1.3.2. The Naming and Numbering of Months   20
      1.3.3. When Did the Month Begin and End?   25
      1.3.4. Measurable Divisions of the Month   27
   1.4. The Year as a Unit of Measurement   29
      1.4.1. The Hebrew Word for Year   29
      1.4.2. When Did the Year Begin and End?   31
         1.4.2.1. The Agricultural Year   31
         1.4.2.2. The Civil Year   35
         1.4.2.3. The Liturgical Year   40
         1.4.2.4. The Regnal Year   42
   1.5. Lunar, Solar, and Lunisolar Calendars   47

2. Long-Time Reckoning 49
   2.1. The Counting of Time Units   49
   2.2. The Use of Eras   56
   2.3. Counting Generations   58

3. Genealogical Chronologies 63
   3.1. Dating Events by the Life of an Individual   63
   3.2. Genealogical Lists Containing Chronological Information   65
      3.2.1. Description   65
      3.2.2. List-Making in the Ancient World   65
      3.2.3. Textual Variants of Genesis 5 and 11 and Their History   67
         3.2.3.1. Genesis 5   67
         3.2.3.2. Genesis 11   76
   3.3. Sources of the Priestly Genealogical Chronology   83
      3.3.1. Preliminary Considerations   83
      3.3.2. Pedigrees   86
         3.3.2.1. Ancient Linear Genealogies in General   86
         3.3.2.2. The Life Spans of the Forefathers   88
         3.3.2.3. A Generational Pedigree in Genesis 5 and 11   91
      3.3.3. Conclusions   95

4. Rulership Chronologies 97
   4.1. Chronological Sources of the Deuteronomic History   97
      4.1.1. Time as Seen by the Deuteronomistic Historians
             and Their Audiences   97
      4.1.2. Chronological Sources for the Book of Jeremiah   98
      4.1.3. Chronological Sources Relating to the Judges   100
      4.1.4. Chronological Sources Relating to the Kings   106
         4.1.4.1. Preliminary Considerations   106
         4.1.4.2. King Lists   109
         4.1.4.3. Royal Chronicles   119
         4.1.4.4. Textual Difficulties in Kings   126
         4.1.4.5. Conclusions   141
   4.2. Historical Reconstructions   142

5. Conclusions and Implications 203

Appendix A: Chronographic Sources Incorporated into the
   Deuteronomic History 217
Appendix B: What Happened in the Fourteenth Year of Hezekiah? 221

Bibliography 245
Ancient Sources Index 257
Modern Authors Index 265

Acknowledgments

I wish to express my gratitude to the people who offered assistance to me in the writing of this book. When it was first taking shape as a doctoral dissertation, I received many helpful suggestions for improvement from the members of my doctoral committee: David Noel Freedman, Richard Elliott Friedman, David Goodblatt, Thomas E. Levy, Alden Mosshammer, and, most especially, my advisor William H. C. Propp, who provided me with a treasure trove of perceptive comments, thoughtful criticisms, and energizing encouragement, in the end even agreeing to contribute illustrations to the finished product. Throughout the writing process I also received constructive counsel from my friend and colleague Bradley Root, who has always been a willing sounding board for my ideas. Finally, many thanks to my editor, Susan Ackerman, for accepting my manuscript into the Resources for Biblical Study series and helping me to buff and polish it further, and to Bob Buller, Leigh Anderson, and the rest of the folks at SBL for preparing my work for publication.

Terms and Abbreviations

1. Terms and Regular Abbreviations

a	first part of verse
Aaronid	presumed descendant of Aaron, the first high priest of Israel
Adad-nirari III	king of Assyria (811–783 B.C.E.)
Africanus	Sextus Julius Africanus, a Christian traveler and historian (late second and early third century C.E.)
annals	record of events arranged in yearly sequence
antedating	system that counts the year of a king's accession as his first regnal year, even if he does not reign that entire year (cf. "postdating")
Akkadian	Semitic language of ancient Mesopotamia
Aramaic	Semitic language of Aram (ancient Syria)
archetype	a pattern or model of which several things of the same type are representations or copies
Ashurbanipal	king of Assyria (668–ca. 627 B.C.E.)
B.C.E.	Before the Common Era (equivalent to B.C.)
b	second part of verse
ca.	circa (approximately)
cardinal number	a number that refers to the size of a group
C.E.	Common Era (equivalent to A.D.)
cf.	confer (compare)
chronicle	an account of events arranged in order of time
chronology	(1) the science that deals with measuring time; (2) a table, list, or account arranged according to time
chronometry	the measuring of time
chronography	the recording of time
Codex Vaticanus	Greek Bible manuscript dating to the fourth century C.E. and housed in the Vatican library

col(s).	column(s)
cognate	etymologically related
consecutive *waw*	Hebrew conjunction signifying sequence of action in the past tense
corvée	mass forced labor
Court History of David	one of the hypothetical source documents of the books of Samuel
Covenant Code	legal text found in Exod 20:19–23:33 thought to be of northern origin and to have been embedded in the E source
Day of Atonement	a holy day of expiation in the Priestly legislation, occurring on the tenth day of the seventh month each year
Decalogue	the Ten Commandments
Demetrius	Demetrius the Chronographer, Jewish biblical commentator from Ptolemaic Egypt, third century B.C.E.
Deuteronomic	having the character of Deuteronomy, or the Deuteronomic Code
Deuteronomic Code	legal text found in Deut 12–26
Deuteronomic History	a multivolume work now found primarily in the books of Deuteronomy, Joshua, Judges, 1 and 2 Samuel, and 1 and 2 Kings, chronicling the histories of Israel and Judah from the perspective of the Deuteronomic Code.
Deuteronomist(s)	author(s) of the Deuteronomic Code
Deuteronomistic	having the character of the Deuteronomist(s)
Deuteronomistic Historian	author of the Deuteronomic History, presumed to have lived in Judah during the reign of Josiah (ca. 640–609 B.C.E.)
DH	Deuteronomic History
DH^1	first edition of the Deuteronomic History, produced ca. 622–610 B.C.E.
DH^2	second edition of the Deuteronomic History, produced ca. 560 B.C.E.
dittography	accidental duplication in textual copying
diurnal	pertaining to the daily cycle
divided monarchy, the	the period when the Israelites were divided into two separate kingdoms, Israel and Judah (ca. 930–720 B.C.E.)
Documentary Theory	theory that the Torah (and, by extension, the

	Primary History) was created through the combination of several written sources
E	writing of the Elohist(s), parts of which were incorporated into the Torah and perhaps also other books of the Primary History
Elohist(s)	author(s) of the E material in the Torah, believed to be of northern origin
Enuma Elish	Babylonian epic of creation
equinox	either of two points in the year when the sun is directly above the equator
Esarhaddon	king of Assyria (681–669 B.C.E.)
etymology	history of a word
Eusebius	Eusebius of Caesarea; Christian theologian and historian (third–fourth century C.E.)
exile, the	period when the Judahite nobility was deported to and resided in Babylon (586–538 B.C.E.)
exilic	pertaining to the Judahite exile in Babylon (586–538 B.C.E.)
exodus, the	departure from ancient Egypt of the Israelites under the leadership of Moses, as described in the Hebrew Bible.
Feast of Unleavened Bread	seven-day Israelite festival beginning the day after Passover in the spring month of Abib
Festival of Booths	also known as Feast of Tabernacles or Sukkot; the Priestly and Deuteronomic version of the Festival of Ingathering
Festival of Ingathering	Israelite autumn harvest festival
First Temple period	ca. 980–586 B.C.E.
gloss	explanatory textual insertion
GN	geographical name
haplography	accidental omission in textual copying caused by similarity of letters or words
harmonization	resolution of contradiction
hegemony	preponderant influence or authority over others
Hellenistic	of or relating to Greek culture
Hexaplaric	relating to the Hexapla, a six-column edition of the Bible prepared by Origen of Alexandria (third century C.E.), consisting of one Hebrew text, its transliteration in Greek characters, and four Greek translations
Holiness Code	legal text found in Lev 17–26

Hophra	biblical name for Apries, pharaoh of Egypt (589–570 B.C.E.)
Hyksos	a Semitic people from Western Asia who took control of Lower Egypt in the sixteenth century B.C.E.
Il.	Homer's *Iliad* (eighth century B.C.E.)
inclusio	framing of a text through repetition of words or phrases
intercalation	insertion into a calendar
J	narrative of the Yahwist, one of the sources of the Torah (and perhaps also of other books in the Primary History), presumed to have been written in Judah in the period of the divided monarchy (ca. 930–720 B.C.E.)
Josephus	Titus Flavius Josephus, Jewish historian (first century C.E.)
Jubilee	a special year of rest for the land in the Priestly legislation, occurring after the completion of seven seven-year cycles and during which property is returned to its original owner and slaves are released
Josianic	from the time of King Josiah of Judah (ca. 640–609 B.C.E.)
Kaige	an early revision of OG, which originated sometime in the first century B.C.E.
king list	list of the monarchs of a state, sometimes providing brief details about each, such as parentage and length of reign
Luc.	Lucianic text
Lucianic	manuscript family of the Greek Septuagint attributed to the work of Lucian of Antioch (late third–early fourth century C.E.)
LXX	Greek Septuagint, earliest translation of the Hebrew Bible (begun third century B.C.E.)
Marduk	storm god; chief deity of Babylon
Marduk-apla-iddina	Marduk-apla-iddina II (biblical Merodach-baladan), king of Babylon (722–710 B.C.E.)
Masoretic Text	medieval Hebrew manuscript family
MT	Masoretic Text

myth	a traditional story that uses the supernatural to explain a natural phenomenon, practice, or ideology
Nebuchadnezzar	Nebuchadnezzar II, king of Babylon (605–562 B.C.E.)
New Kingdom	Egypt ca. 1570–1070 B.C.E.
Nisan	first month of Babylonian calendar (spring)
northern	pertaining to the kingdom of Israel, north of Judah, in the period of the divided monarchy (ca. 930–720 B.C.E.) (cf. "southern")
Od.	Homer's *Odyssey* (eighth century B.C.E.)
OG	Old Greek; earliest manuscript tradition of LXX (third century B.C.E.)
Op.	Hesiod's *Works and Days* (Latin: *Opera et dies*) (eighth century B.C.E.)
ordinal number	a number that refers to a position in a series
P	the Priestly Source, one of the texts incorporated into the Torah
Passover	Israelite sacrificial meal observed in the spring month of Abib
Pentateuch	the first five books of the Bible (= Torah)
pericope	section of text
PN	personal name
postdating	system that counts a king's first *complete* civil year in office as his first regnal year, even if he begins reigning before that civil year begins (cf. "antedating")
postexilic	pertaining to the period after 538 B.C.E.
preexilic	pertaining to the period before 586 B.C.E.
Primary History	the continuous narrative found in the books of Genesis, Exodus, Leviticus, Numbers, Deuteronomy, Joshua, Judges, 1 and 2 Samuel, and 1 and 2 Kings
Ptolemaic	pertaining to Egypt during the rule of the Ptolemies (305–30 B.C.E.)
R	the redactor
redactor	final editor of the Torah (and perhaps also the Primary History)
rubric	a word or section of text used for emphasis or explanation

Sabbath	the holy day of rest on the seventh day of each week
Samaritan Pentateuch	medieval Hebrew version of the Torah having its origins in the community of Jews in Samaria in the early centuries C.E.
Sargon	Sargon II, king of Assyria (722–705 B.C.E.)
Second Temple period	ca. 515 B.C.E.–70 C.E.
Sennacherib	king of Assyria (704–681 B.C.E.)
Septuagint	earliest translation of the Hebrew Bible into Greek (begun third century B.C.E.)
Shalmaneser III	king of Assyria (859–824 B.C.E.)
Shalmaneser V	king of Assyria (727–722 B.C.E.)
Shamshi-Adad I	king of Assyria (eighteenth century B.C.E.)
Shoshenq I	pharaoh of Egypt (biblical Shishak) (ca. 945–ca. 925 B.C.E.)
southern	pertaining to the kingdom of Judah, south of Israel, in the period of the divided monarchy (ca. 930–720 B.C.E.) (cf. "northern")
solstice	either of two points in the year when the sun is farthest from the equator
SP	Samaritan Pentateuch
synchronic	concerned with events happening at the same time
synchronism	an indication of coincidence, coexistence, or simultaneousness
synchronistic	having the character of a synchronism
synodic	relating to the period between two identical phases of the moon
Targ.	Targums
Targum	Jewish Aramaic translation of the Bible
Tiglath-pileser III	king of Assyria (745–727 B.C.E.)
Torah	the first five books of the Bible (=Pentateuch)
trans.	translator(s)
tropical	relating to the time it takes for the sun to complete the cycle of seasons and return to the same position in the sky
united monarchy, the	the period when the Israelites were united under a single king (ca. 1020–930 B.C.E.)
Vulg.	Vulgate
Vulgate	translation of the Bible into Latin by Jerome (ca. 400 C.E.)

Yahwist	author of J, whose literary characters in stories set before the days of Moses know and invoke the name Yahweh

2. Bibliographical Abbreviations

4QIsa^a	an Isaiah scroll from Qumran found in Cave 4
AB	Anchor Bible
ABD	*Anchor Bible Dictionary.* Edited by David Noel Freedman. 6 vols. New York: Doubleday, 1992.
ANET	*Ancient Near Eastern Texts Relating to the Old Testament.* Edited by James B. Pritchard. 3rd ed. Princeton: Princeton University Press, 1969.
Ann.	Annal unit
ARAB	*Ancient Records of Assyria and Babylonia.* Daniel David Luckenbill. 2 vols. Chicago: University of Chicago Press, 1926–1927.
BA	*Biblical Archaeologist*
BASOR	*Bulletin of the American Schools of Oriental Research*
BHK	*Biblia Hebraica.* Edited by Rudolf Kittel. 3rd ed. Stuttgart: Deutsche Bibelgesellschaft, 1937.
BHS	*Biblia Hebraica Stuttgartensia.* Edited by Karl Elliger and Wilhelm Rudolph. Stuttgart: Deutsche Bibelgesellschaft, 1983.
Bib	*Biblica*
COHP	Contributions to Oriental History and Philology
diss.	dissertation
esp.	especially
ErIsr	*Eretz-Israel*
HSM	Harvard Semitic Monographs
HTR	*Harvard Theological Review*
HUCA	*Hebrew Union College Annual*
ibid.	ibidem (in the same place)
ICC	International Critical Commentary
IDB	*The Interpreter's Dictionary of the Bible.* Edited by George A. Buttrick. 4 vols. Nashville: Abingdon, 1962.
IEJ	*Israel Exploration Journal*
IOS	Israel Oriental Society
JANES	*Journal of the Ancient Near Eastern Society*
JAOS	*Journal of the American Oriental Society*
JARCE	*Journal of the American Research Center in Egypt*
JBL	*Journal of Biblical Literature*
JNES	*Journal of Near Eastern Studies*

JSOT	*Journal for the Study of the Old Testament*
JSOTsup	Journal for the Study of the Old Testament Supplement Series
JSS	*Journal of Semitic Studies*
LHBOTS	Library of Hebrew Bible/Old Testament Studies
NICOT	New International Commentary on the Old Testament
OTL	Old Testament Library
OtSt	*Oudtestamentische Studiën*
PAAJR	*Proceedings of the American Academy of Jewish Research*
RB	*Revue biblique*
RivB	*Rivista biblica italiana*
SAA	State Archives of Assyria
SAOC	Studies in Ancient Oriental Civilizations
SBLDS	Society of Biblical Literature Dissertation Series
SBLMS	Society of Biblical Literature Monograph Series
SBLWAW	Society of Biblical Literature Writings from the Ancient World
SBT	Studies in Biblical Theology
SHANE	Studies in the History of the Ancient Near East
SHCANE	Studies in the History and Culture of the Ancient Near East
SJOT	*Scandinavian Journal of the Old Testament*
STDJ	Studies on the Texts of the Desert of Judah
TDOT	*Theological Dictionary of the Old Testament.* Edited by G. Johannes Botterweck and Helmer Ringgren. Translated by John T. Willis, Geoffrey W. Bromiley, and David E. Green. 15 vols. Grand Rapids: Eerdmans, 1974–2006.
TSK	*Theologische Studien und Kritiken*
VT	*Vetus Testamentum*
VTSup	Vetus Testamentum Supplements
ZAW	*Zeitschrift für die alttestamentliche Wissenschaft*

Figures and Tables

Figure 1.1: The Cairo Shadow Clock — 15
Figure 1.2: A Drawing of the Cairo Shadow Clock — 16
Figure 1.3: Reconstruction of Hezekiah's Shadow Clock — 16
Figure 1.4: The Shadow Created on the Steps According to the Sun's Position — 18
Table 1.1: Priestly Dates That Include Months — 22
Table 1.2: Agricultural Activity in Modern Israel — 32
Table 2.1: The Count of Days — 51
Table 2.2: Time Covered by Solomon's Building Activities — 53
Table 3.1: Variant Readings of the Numbers in Genesis 5 — 70
Table 3.2: Variant Readings of the Numbers in Genesis 11 — 78
Table 3.3: Sources of the Ages in the Priestly Genealogy — 95
Table 4.1: Readings for Abijam, Asa, and Jeroboam — 129
Table 4.2: Readings for Baasha and Elah — 130
Table 4.3: Totaling the Years of Omri — 131
Table 4.4: Counts for Omri Assumed in the Manuscripts — 132
Table 4.5: Readings for Zimri, Tibni, Omri, and Ahab — 134
Table 4.6: Readings for Ahab, Jehoshaphat, and Ahaziah — 135
Table 4.7: Readings for Ahaziah, Joram, and Jehoram — 136
Table 4.8: Readings for Jehoram and Ahaziah — 136
Table 4.9: Readings for Amaziah and Azariah — 138
Table 4.10: Readings for Jotham, Ahaz, and Hoshea — 140
Table 4.11: Comparison of Extrabiblical Dates with Judahite King List Dates — 148
Table 4.12: Comparison of Extrabiblical Dates with Israelite King List Dates — 151
Table 4.13: Chronology of the Hebrew Kings Based Upon the Synchronisms — 155
Table 4.14: Comparison of Extrabiblical Dates with Chronicle Dates for the Kings of Judah — 200
Table 4.15: Comparison of Extrabiblical Dates with Chronicle Dates for the Kings of Israel — 201

Table 5.1: Chronology of DH²	210
Table 5.2: Chronology of DH¹	212
Table B.1: Name Patterns in 2 Kings 18–19	241
Figure B.1: The Reordering of 2 Kings 18–20	242

Introduction

How do you measure, measure a year?
In daylights, in sunsets, in midnights, in cups of coffee.
In inches, in miles, in laughter, in strife.
In 525,600 minutes—how do you measure a year in the life?
—"Seasons of Love," by Jonathan Larson (from the musical *Rent*)

The measurement of time often depends on the vantage of whoever is doing the measuring. How *does* one measure a year? Or any other period of time? There is a certain amount of arbitrariness to the whole process. What do the measurers think is important? People do not measure time because time demands it but because *they* demand it. The effort proves useful to them in some way. Thus we find that not all natural units of time are measured, nor are more arbitrary units of time devised, unless for some necessity, purpose, or convenience.

The reasons the ancients measured time were not unlike our own reasons. It was necessary for farmers to keep track of the parts of the year, so that they knew when to plant and when to harvest and could plan for the future accordingly. Religious observances and holy days took place at special times, and it was necessary to set these times according to some standard of measurement. Time was likewise often a key factor in tax collection, business transactions, and appointments. Finally, ancient societies were interested in keeping track of their histories, and time measurement helped to create chronologies by which they could orient themselves in relation to historical events in the past. It is the intention of this study to explore and analyze the methods used to do these very things.

The particular society with which this work is concerned is stated in the title as "ancient Israel," specifically the northern and southern Israelite kingdoms (Israel and Judah) in the period of their individual monarchies (ca. 930–586 B.C.E.), with attention also given to the earlier united monarchy (ca. 1020–930 B.C.E.). Recent scholarship has tended to be skeptical of the very possibility of recovering enough data from the ancient sources to reconstruct the time-measuring systems that were in use in ancient Israel.

James C. VanderKam, for instance, known for his expertise in the Jewish calendar of the Second Temple period, expresses a typical opinion about the First Temple period: "One may assume that the ancestors of Israel and the early Israelites themselves followed some sort of calendar (or calendars), but the extant sources do not permit one to determine what its (their) nature may have been."[1] I believe this statement is an exaggeration. The nature of ancient Israel's calendars and other time-keeping systems *are* recoverable, at least partially, with a relative amount of certainty. One of the aims of this work is to demonstrate just that and to show how far the evidence actually can take us.

To be sure, when dealing with any ancient society, evidence is much scarcer than it is for more recent societies. For ancient Israel, the written evidence is indeed limited (more limited for northern Israel than for southern Judah), the archaeological evidence, while able to shed light on various aspects of the culture, tells us almost nothing about Israelite time keeping, and the oral traditions are, by their nature, no longer accessible. However, we do have recourse to some of the major cultural documents of the period, which have been preserved in the pages of the Hebrew Bible. The documents to which I have paid the closest attention are those generally considered to contain material from before the Judahite exile in Babylon (586–538 B.C.E.): (1) the books of the early literary prophets: Amos (eighth century), Hosea (eighth century), Micah (eighth century), Isaiah (eighth century), Zephaniah (seventh century), and Jeremiah (seventh–sixth century); and (2) the Primary History (Genesis–2 Kings), recounting the history of the Israelite people from the creation of the world to the exile, which has proved to be the richest resource of knowledge in this area. Care had to be taken with these works, because certain parts of them also contain later (i.e., exilic and postexilic) material, added by subsequent editors.[2]

A few words should be said about the Primary History.[3] The final version of the work has had a complex editorial prehistory that needs to be taken into consideration when doing a historical study. It cannot be assumed that such a large work, which is composed of many parts written by different authors, is going to have a synoptic view of time measurement. Moreover, parts of the Primary History were written outside of the time period to which this study

---

1. James C. VanderKam, "Calendars, Ancient Israelite and Early Jewish," *ABD* 1:814.

2. The other lengthy historical narrative in the Bible (1 Chronicles–2 Chronicles–Ezra–Nehemiah) was not used for this study because of its late (postexilic) date. The chronological data of clear preexilic origin found therein are by and large a repetition of those found in the Primary History.

3. To the best of my knowledge, the term "Primary History" was coined by David Noel Freedman, "Pentateuch," *IDB* 3:711–27.

is limited. We are required to approach the sources one at a time, each on its own terms, before making any judgments in this regard. If they do exhibit a similar view, this will come out, but if we make the assumption beforehand and analyze the text holistically, our data could be contaminated.

While it is not always easy to separate the sources of the Primary History, and scholars themselves are divided over the particulars, we may use the standard Documentary Theory as a point of departure. According to that model, the main sources are as follows:

The work of the Yahwist.[4] The narrative commonly called J, although not concerned chiefly with matters related to time measurement, is an invaluable source of information for preexilic customs. The document is reputed to have originated in Judah in the period of the divided monarchy (ca. 930–720 B.C.E.).[5] Because of the close affinity between J and other early Judahite sources of the Primary History, such as the so-called Court History of David, I treat them together; indeed, a good argument has been made that the same author is responsible for these works.[6]

The Priestly source. The P document is full of data related to priestly interests and liturgical matters. Its author(s) are very interested in matters of time measurement. Law codes make up a significant part of this source, but there is historical narrative as well. Scholars are still divided over whether one or both of these parts derive from the preexilic or postexilic period. Because of the strong evidence for a preexilic date for much of the material,[7] I have

---

4. Even though this work was, in later times, incorporated into a historical narrative, I am hesitant to call it a "history," because on its own it contains no chronology to tie it to a historical timeline. Neither do I call it an "epic," because it is not a poem. Perhaps the best label for its genre is "legend," since it provides an account of the past and possesses certain qualities that give it verisimilitude but also is set in an undetermined time period, contains fantastical elements that resemble myth, and is presented in a conversational mode akin to oral stories.

5. For a survey of scholarship, see Albert de Pury, "Yahwist ("J") Source," *ABD* 6:1012–20. For recent discussions of the date of J, see Ernest Nicholson, *The Pentateuch in the Twentieth Century: The Legacy of Julius Wellhausen* (Oxford: Clarendon, 1998), 132–95; Richard M. Wright, *Linguistic Evidence for the Pre-exilic Date of the Yahwistic Source* (New York: T&T Clark, 2005).

6. See Richard Elliott Friedman, *The Hidden Book in the Bible* (San Francisco: HarperSanFrancisco, 1998). For a list of the passages attributable to this author, see p. 12 of the above work.

7. See Moshe Weinfeld, *Deuteronomy and the Deuteronomic School* (Oxford: Clarendon, 1972), 179–89; Avi Hurvitz, "The Evidence of Language in Dating the Priestly Code," *RB* 81 (1974): 24–56; Robert Polzin, *Late Biblical Hebrew: Toward an Historical Typology of Biblical Hebrew Prose* (HSM 12; Missoula, Mont.: Scholars Press, 1976); Menahem Haran,

chosen to include analysis of this source in the present study. One needs to be careful, however, to distinguish between P itself and the work of the priestly redactor (R) who edited P and other documents in the postexilic period.[8]

Temples and Temple Service in Ancient Israel: An Inquiry into the Character of Cult Phenomena and the Historical Setting of the Priestly School (Oxford: Clarendon, 1978); Gary A. Rendsburg, "Late Biblical Hebrew and the Date of P," *JANES* 12 (1980): 65–80; Richard Elliott Friedman, *The Exile and Biblical Narrative: The Formation of the Deuteronomistic and Priestly Works* (Chico, Calif.: Scholars Press, 1981); Menahem Haran, "Behind the Scenes of History: Determining the Date of the Priestly Source," *JBL* 100 (1981): 321–33; Avi Hurvitz, *A Linguistic Study of the Relationship between the Priestly Source and the Book of Ezekiel* (Paris: Gabalda, 1982); Ziony Zevit, "Converging Lines of Evidence Bearing on the Date of P," *ZAW* 94 (1982): 502–9; Avi Hurvitz, "Dating the Priestly Source in Light of the Historical Study of Biblical Hebrew a Century after Wellhausen," *ZAW* 100 (1988): 88–100; Jacob Milgrom, *Leviticus 1–16: A New Translation with Introduction and Commentary* (AB 3; New York: Doubleday, 1991), 3–35; Richard Elliott Friedman, "Torah," *ABD* 6:605–22; Jacob Milgrom, "The Antiquity of the Priestly Source," *ZAW* 111 (1999): 10–22. The reality appears to be that the Priestly source is the result of literary activity spanning many years, but the evidence presented in the above studies has inclined me to the opinion that P was more or less completed prior to the fall of Jerusalem.

8. See Friedman, *Exile and Biblical Narrative*, 77–80; Richard Elliott Friedman, *Who Wrote the Bible?* (Englewood Cliffs, N.J.: Prentice Hall, 1987), 217–33; Nicholson, *The Pentateuch in the Twentieth Century*, 215–18. The theory proposed by Israel Knohl (*The Sanctuary of Silence: The Priestly Torah and the Holiness School* [Minneapolis: Augsburg Fortress, 1995]) that a priestly editor from a "Holiness school" (whose work we call H or HS) edited and revised P need not overly concern us. If Knohl is correct in saying that the H editor redacted not only P but also the other pentateuchal sources, this scribe is to be equated with R, whom I have already taken into account. On the other hand, if the Holiness Code was, as he also proposes, written as a response to conditions in the preexilic period, then H must be set before the exile. Knohl wants it both ways. I cannot accept his argument that the work of a "Holiness school" began in the time of Ahaz and continued through the exile and into the postexilic period unscathed. Such a view does not account for the major upheaval that took place in the sixth century and the displacement of many people, including the priests. How could a priestly school of thought, particularly one that insisted on centralization of worship, continue through that time without there being any adjustments to its theology or language? If the H source is indeed to be equated with the postexilic redactor of the Pentateuch (and, it would seem, the entire Primary History), then this H source must be dated after the exile. However, if "the religious, social, and political conditions under the reign of Ahaz and Hezekiah in Judea most closely correspond to the picture that emerges in the Holiness Code" (Knohl, *Sanctuary of Silence*, 209), then the work of H must be from that time period. I am inclined toward the conclusion that the bulk of material Knohl considers to be H is preexilic. The most reasonable explanation for the similarity in language between the work of H and the work of R is that R is mimicking H (as he does with all of his sources). For that

*The Deuteronomic History.*⁹ This lengthy work (which, for convenience, I will abbreviate occasionally as DH), a historical narrative based upon the Deuteronomic Code of Deut 12–26, recounts the exploits and excesses of the leaders of the Israelite people, including Joshua, the judges, and especially the Judahite and Israelite kings. It contains a large amount of chronological data, some of which comes from contemporary sources and some from earlier times. One needs to be careful, however, to distinguish between the older Josianic edition of the history, which reflects preexilic customs, and the material added in the later exilic edition.¹⁰

---

reason, in this work I will include the Holiness Code in my examination of the chronographic data relating to P.

9. This history is variously referred to by scholars as the "Deuteronomic History" and the "Deuteronomistic History," with the latter being the current favorite. Although the term "Deuteronomistic" is a more faithful English equivalent to the German term coined by Martin Noth (*Deuteronomistische*), the "discoverer" of this history, I am of the opinion that "Deuteronomistic History" is a misnomer. While the adjective "Deuteronomistic" ("having the character of the Deuteronomist") is an appropriate description of the author(s) or editor(s) of this history, it is not a fitting description of the history itself, since the comparison (-ic) is not between the history and the Deuteronomist, but between the history and the writing that inspired it, the Deuteronomic Code. The designation "Deuteronomic History" therefore seems more appropriate.

10. This study accepts the two-edition theory of the Deuteronomic History. The evidence for an original edition during the reign of Josiah (seventh century B.C.E.) and an updated exilic edition (sixth century B.C.E.) is presented in the following: James A. Montgomery, *A Critical and Exegetical Commentary on the Books of Kings* (ICC New York: Scribner's Sons, 1951), 44–45; Wolfgang Richter, *Traditionsgeschichtliche Untersuchungen zum Richterbuch* (Bonn: Hanstein, 1963); idem, *Die Bearbeitung des "Retterbuches" in der deuteronomistischen Epoche* (Bonn: Hanstein, 1964); Frank Moore Cross, "The Structure of the Deuteronomic History," in *Perspectives in Jewish Learning* (Annual of the College of Jewish Studies 3; Chicago: Spertus College of Judaica, 1968), 9–24; John Gray, *I and II Kings* (Philadelphia: SCM, 1970), 6–9; Frank Moore Cross, *Canaanite Myth and Hebrew Epic* (Cambridge, Mass.: Harvard University Press, 1973), 274–89; I. Schlauri, "W. Richters Beitrag zur Redaktionsgeschichte des Richterbuches," *Bib* 54 (1973): 367–403; E. Cortese, "Problemi attuali circa l'opera deuteronomistica," *RivB* 26 (1978): 341–52, esp. 43–47; Richard Elliott Friedman, "From Egypt to Egypt: Dtr1 and Dtr2," in *Traditions in Transformation: Turning Points in Biblical Faith* (ed. B. Halpern and J. D. Levenson; Winona Lake, Ind.: Eisenbrauns, 1981), 167–92; Friedman, *Exile and Biblical Narrative*; Richard D. Nelson, *The Double Redaction of the Deuteronomistic History* (JSOTSup 8; Sheffield: JSOT Press, 1981); Pierre Buis, "Rois (Livres des)," *Supplément au Dictionnaire de la Bible* 10:728–31; H. G. M. Williamson, "The Death of Josiah and the Continuing Development of the Deuteronomic History," *VT* 32 (1982): 242–43; Norbert Lohfink, *Rückblick im Zorn auf den Staat, Vorlesungen zu ausgewählten Schlüsseltexten der Bücher Samuel und Könige* (Frankfurt: Privatdruck, 1984).

Northern materials in the Primary History. It is believed that stories from the northern Israelite kingdom made their way into the Primary History as well. The parts in the Torah attributed to an E source are usually considered northern (and perhaps it is equally appropriate to say that the parts of the Torah considered northern are usually attributed to the E source). There are similar narratives in Samuel and Kings. They are believed to be from the period of the divided kingdom (ca. 932–720 B.C.E.).[11]

***

The present work is divided into two main sections. The first deals with the yearly calendar and addresses questions pertaining to how the Israelites kept track of the astronomical cycles. The second is concerned with chronology, that is, the method of measuring intervals of time between events in order to understand how far removed these events were from the time of the measurers. It is hoped that a reexamination of the foundations of chronometric study will encourage us to reconsider common opinions held about Israelite timekeeping and enable historians more accurately to place events in the stream of time.

---

11. See A. W. Jenks, *The Elohist and North Israelite Traditions* (SBLMS 22; Missoula, Mont.: Scholars Press, 1977); Friedman, "Torah," 605–22; A. W. Jenks, "Elohist," *ABD* 2:478–82.

1
Calendars

1.1. Natural Units of Time

The natural intervals of time that commonly come into play in the construction of calendars are the day, the synodic month, and the tropical year. Most societies are interested in keeping track of all three phenomena, but the three are not quite compatible with one another, so calendars are forced either to ignore one of them (usually the second or third) or to accommodate them all by some sort of artificial manipulation.

For purposes of measurement, the full day may be taken as a constant unit, and so may the tropical year, but it is clear from the length of the latter (365 days, 5 hours, 48 minutes, and 46 seconds) that an even number of days will not fit into it. The synodic, or lunar, month averages 29 days, 12 hours, 44 minutes, and 2.78 seconds, but varies in length (up to 13 hours) and is not often divisible by an even number of days, nor is an even number of months able to fit into a tropical year.

The ancients, while not able to measure all of these time intervals with precision, were nevertheless well aware of their approximate lengths and of the difficulties associated with constructing calendars that took all of them into consideration. Length of days was determined by observation of the sun (its rising and setting), length of months by observation of the moon (its waxing and waning), and length of years also by observation of the sun (the solstices and equinoxes).

1.2. The Day as a Unit of Measurement

1.2.1. The Hebrew Word for Day

The term used throughout the Hebrew Bible to refer to a 24-hour period is יוֹם (*yôm*). This word has several other meanings as well, which may indicate more general periods of time, some greater and some lesser than one day,[1] but when it comes to quantitative measurement of time יוֹם is used only to refer to a 24-hour span.

Occasionally in quantitative measurement יוֹם is used along with the coordinate term לילה ("night") to refer to one complete day. Thus, for example, we are told that the length of the period of rainfall during the flood was "forty days and forty nights" (or better, "forty daytimes and forty nighttimes"). In these cases, יוֹם represents not the complete diurnal period, but only the part of the day during which the sun is up. However, daytimes are never *counted* without nighttimes.

1.2.2. WHEN DID THE DAY BEGIN AND END?

Although it is obvious that a day is made up of a complete period of daylight and a complete period of night, it is necessary, for calendrical purposes, to choose a specific point for the change of date. Observation of the sun would have been important for this determination in antiquity. The Egyptians began their official day at dawn,[2] and the Mesopotamians and Athenian Greeks at sunset.[3]

A subject of debate over the years has been when the ancient Israelites understood the day to have begun. Two main camps exist: those who believe the Israelite day began in the morning, and those who believe it began in the evening. When addressing this problem it is important to keep in mind that we cannot assume that every source in the Bible agrees in this regard, so we

---

1. Gershon Brin, *The Concept of Time in the Bible and the Dead Sea Scrolls* (ed. F. Garcia Martinez; STDJ 34; Leiden: Brill, 2001), 52–57, 142–45.

2. Kurt Sethe, "Die Zeitrechnung der alten Ägypter im Verhältnis zu der der andern Völker," in *Nachrichten von der Königlichen Gesellschaft der Wissenschaften zu Göttingen, Philologisch-historische Klasse aus dem Jahre 1920* (Berlin: Weidmann, 1920), 130–38; Richard A. Parker, *The Calendars of Ancient Egypt* (SAOC 26; Chicago: University of Chicago Press, 1950), 9–23; Marshall Clagett, *Calendars, Clocks, and Astronomy* (vol. 2 of *Ancient Egyptian Science: A Source Book*; Independence Square, Pa.: American Philosophical Society, 1995), 22; Eric Hornung, Rolf Krauss, and David A. Warburton, "Methods of Dating and the Egyptian Calendar," in *Ancient Egyptian Chronology* (ed. Eric Hornung et al.; Handbook of Oriental Studies 1.83; Leiden: Brill, 2006), 49–51.

3. Richard A. Parker and Waldo H. Dubberstein, *Babylonian Chronology, 626 B.C.–A.D. 75* (3rd ed.; Providence, R.I.: Brown University Press, 1956), 26; Elias J. Bickerman, *Chronology of the Ancient World* (Ithaca: Cornell University Press, 1968), 13–14; Alan E. Samuel, *Greek and Roman Chronology: Calendars and Years in Classical Antiquity* (Munich: Beck, 1972), 13.

will consider each of the sources separately.[4] To be sure, we should expect that any given ancient society would hold a general and prevalent view, but every society is composed of factions with their own needs, views, and concerns. Moreover the documents in our possession do not all derive from the same time period, and ideas may have changed over the centuries. Also important to note is that none of the authors of these texts see any need to explain when the day begins. Their audiences already know that, and so we can only attempt to ascertain what the *assumptions* are regarding the beginning of the day in these documents.[5]

(1) J. The evidence is fairly clear that in J (a southern source) the day begins in the morning. For example, in the story of the aftermath of Lot's escape from Sodom, his daughters intoxicate him and have sex with him at night, and the next morning is said to be the *next* day (Gen 19:33–34).[6] Such could not have been the case if the day began at sundown because the following morning would have been considered the *same* day. The assumption is that the day begins at dawn or sunrise. In the DH's early monarchic sources akin to J, we find similar evidence. In the story of the dismembered concubine, the father of the young woman views the nighttime as the close of the day, rather than the beginning of a new one, and the morrow begins early in the morning (Judg 19:9). Similarly, when the Israelites build an altar to Yahweh after the decimation of Benjamin, they do it early in the morning, when the next day begins (Judg 21:4). When Saul tries to kill David in the nighttime, David's wife Michal refers to the morning as the next day (1 Sam 19:10–11).[7]

---

4. Unless otherwise indicated, I follow the source divisions of Richard Elliott Friedman, *The Bible with Sources Revealed: A New View into the Five Books of Moses* (San Francisco: HarperSanFrancisco, 2003).

5. Most of the observations that follow have been made by others (though in most cases without distinction between sources). See Julian Morganstern, "Supplementary Studies in the Calendars of Ancient Israel," *HUCA* 10 (1935): 1–148; Roland de Vaux, *Ancient Israel: Its Life and Institutions* (London: Darton, Longman, & Todd, 1961), 180–83; H. R. Stroes, "Does the Day Begin in the Evening of Morning? Some Biblical Observations," *VT* 16 (1966): 460–75; Shemaryahu Talmon, "Whence the Day's Beginning in the Biblical Period and in the Beginning of the Second Temple Period?" in *The Bible in the Light of Its Interpreters: Sarah Kamin Memorial Volume* [Hebrew] (ed. Sara Japhet; Jerusalem: Magnes, 1994), 109–29; Roger T. Beckwith, *Calendar and Chronology, Jewish and Christian: Biblical, Intertestamental, and Patristic Studies* (Leiden: Brill, 1996), 6–7; Brin, *Concept of Time*, 153–64.

6. Although Heb. מחרת (an adjective) is often used by itself, the implied noun is יום (cf. Gen 30:33). See G. André, "מחר," *TDOT* 8:237–41.

7. See also 1 Sam 5:2–4.

(2) E. Not much evidence is available for the beginning of the day in E (a northern source). However, it would seem that the day also begins in the morning. In the account about the gathering of quail by the Israelites in the desert, the people are said to have gotten up to gather the birds "all that day and all night, and all the next day" (Num 11:32). It is probable that the first "day" mentioned is limited to the daytime, that is, the sunlight hours, since it is used side-by-side with "night" (the usual idiom). The second use of "day," however, is not used in conjunction with "night;" instead we find the adjective המחרת ("the morrow"), which is commonly used when יום refers to a complete calendar day (as in the J examples cited above). The second יום therefore must refer to the entire diurnal period. In other words, the next day is not the next daytime, but the next full day. If so, E's day begins at the conclusion of the nighttime, that is, at dawn or sunrise. Also worthy of mention is one of the DH's sources for the story of Gideon (Judg 6:34–40; 7:2–11, 13–25).[8] A fleece is laid out overnight, and the next morning is considered the next day (6:37–38).

(3) The Deuteronomic History. Very little can be found in the DH to assist us in ascertaining when the Historian understood the day to begin. The most significant passage is Josh 5:10–12, which is a reference to the Passover and based upon legislation in the Deuteronomic Code (Deut 16:1–9). The historian states that the Passover was celebrated in the evening.[9] The reason given for the commemoration in the evening is not because the day begins in the evening, but because the evening was the "time of [their] coming out of Egypt" (Deut 16:6). In Joshua, reference is made to "the day after the Passover," on which the people eat from the produce of the land. The implication is that their eating of the land's yield occurs on the following morning and

---

8. The tribe of Ephraim plays the heroic role, so the story may be of northern origin. For evidence that the Gideon passages are not authored by the Deuteronomistic Historian, but are independent, see J. Alberto Soggin, *Judges: A Commentary* (Philadelphia: Westminster, 1981), 103–5.

9. The word ערב ("evening") comes from a root meaning "to enter" and refers to the sun's retiring into its resting place beneath the horizon, as is shown by the frequent combination of ערב with בא השמש (e.g., Deut 16:6; 23:12[11]; Josh 8:29; 10:26–27). When referring to a point in time, it has the meaning "sunset," and when to a general time, the period following sunset. See H. Niehr, "ערב," *TDOT* 11:335–41. The statement that the Passover was celebrated on the 14th of the month may be an addition to bring the account into harmony with the priestly legislation. The Deuteronomic law specifies the month, but not the day, of the Passover. It does, however, say the sacrifice should be made in the evening (Deut 16:4). On the other hand, perhaps the message in Joshua is that the tradition for celebrating the Passover on the 14th is to be traced to this occasion; it was the day the Israelites celebrated it after entering the Promised Land.

afternoon. Those who would argue for a day beginning in the evening would have to assume that, since the following morning and afternoon are still part of the same day on which the meal was eaten, then the gathering of the produce from the land did not occur until at least 24 hours from the evening that the Passover was celebrated, but probably even later, since the gathering would not have been done in the dark, but would have been delayed until daylight. However, since the eating of unfermented cakes is commanded to take place over *six* days (Deut 16:8), the gathering of the produce to make those cakes *must* be understood to occur on the morning following the Passover celebration, when the people would have been instructed to return to their tents (Deut 16:7). The morning after the Passover sacrifice is therefore considered the next day by the Deuteronomistic Historian.

(4) P. The evidence from P is more plentiful, but sometimes appears contradictory. Nevertheless, it would seem that the priests too understood the day normally to begin at dawn or sunrise. When the Sabbath is instituted during the desert wanderings, Moses says, "Tomorrow is a ceasing, a holy Sabbath to Yahweh" (Exod 16:23), and when the following morning arrives, Moses says, "Today is a Sabbath to Yahweh" (Exod 16:24–25). The new day clearly begins in the morning. In the Law, Yahweh commands, "The meat of [the priest's] peace-offering shall be eaten *on the day* of his offering. *He shall not leave any of it until morning*" (Lev 7:15). The morning here is understood to be on the following day (see also Lev 22:30).[10]

Some have argued that P's creation account, now in the first chapter of Genesis, suggests that the priests counted the beginning of the day from the evening.[11] The repeated refrain, "and evening came, and morning came," on each creative day suggests to some that the author is stating the order of the day. A few considerations should lay this argument to rest.

(1) The combination ערב ("evening") and בקר ("morning") is not equivalent to לילה ("nighttime") and יום ("daytime"), and in fact does not add up to a complete day, but amounts only to two lesser parts of one day. We cannot, therefore, understand the two-fold refrain as constituting some kind of summation of two parts of an entire day of creation.

(2) The appearance of the consecutive *waw* before the refrain suggests that the evening and morning are part of a sequence of events. We should

---

10. One might also look at the evidence from the priestly redactor of the Primary History, who, although writing at a later time, includes a source document in Num 33, which also suggests that the day begins at dawn or sunrise. It is stated therein that the 15th day of the 1st month was on the morning after the Passover that was observed on the 14th day of the month (Num 33:3).

11. E.g., Morganstern, "Supplementary Studies in the Calendars of Ancient Israel," 19.

not therefore understand them in isolation from the rest of the events mentioned on any given creative day. The sequence is as follows: (1) act or acts of creation; (2) evening; (3) morning. The evening clearly follows the creative activity that occurs during the day.

(3) If the evening follows God's creative acts on any given day, the evening cannot be the beginning of the day, but rather would be the concluding part of it. It is the morning that would signal the transition from one day to the next.[12]

Far from demonstrating the day to begin in the evening, P's creation account adds further support to the conclusion that P assumes a day that begins in the morning.[13]

Another set of evidence used to demonstrate a day beginning in the evening in the priestly material is that related to the holy days. The Sabbath runs from evening to evening (Lev 23:32). The Feast of Unleavened Bread lasts from the evening of the fourteenth day of the first month of the year until the evening of the twenty-first day of the month, seven days from evening to evening (Exod 12:18–19). This evidence seemingly points to a day that begins in the evening. Suggestive also is the fact that the paschal offering on the first of those days is to take place "between the evenings" (Exod 12:6; Lev 23:5; Num 9:3, 5, 11), an expression that appears to mean the time between sunset and full night.[14] Some sacrifices are also to be made "between the two evenings" (Exod 29:39, 41; 30:8).

However, the very fact that the law has to specify that observances and special performances take place in the evening or run from evening to evening suggests that such was not normally the case. If the day began at sundown, then the only necessary information would be the date of the observance (e.g., that the Sabbath is on the seventh day of the week). It would already be understood that such days begin and end in the evening. Yet the law makes a point to highlight that such observances must commence in the evening. This evidence actually implies a day that does *not* usually begin at such a time.[15] In other words, a liturgical day is not identical with a secular day.

---

12. Note especially the first day of creation, in which the appearance of light begins the day.

13. See Jacob Milgrom, *Leviticus 23–27: A New Translation with Introduction and Commentary* (AB 3B; New York: Doubleday, 2001), 1967–68, 2025–26.

14. See discussion in William H. C. Propp, *Exodus 1–18: A New Translation with Introduction and Commentary* (AB 2; New York: Doubleday, 1999), 390–91.

15. See also Propp, *Exodus 1–18*, 390–92; Milgrom, *Leviticus 23–27*, 1967–69.

As the preceding survey demonstrates, all of the main sources in the Primary History (J, E, DH, and P), both northern and southern, assume a day that begins and ends in the morning. The broad agreement suggests that this was a general view for a long period of time. P, however, appears to have a different system of reckoning the day when it comes to rituals of the cult. Indeed, it would seem that P makes an effort to impose its liturgical day onto the existing system (cf., for example, the problem of naming the date of the Day of Atonement, which is to take place between evenings; Lev 23:27, 32). We cannot therefore interpret P's regulation as evidence of a *change* in the reckoning of the day's beginning. Its liturgical day presupposes, and therefore exists side by side with, the secular day.

A question we might ask is: Is a day beginning in the evening an innovation of the priests (or something borrowed from another culture), or is P incorporating or preserving an older system? Rituals tend to have long lives, so it is certainly possible that the priests are preserving an ancient practice, but we have no evidence for an evening-to-evening day in any source older than P. Both P's liturgical year (as we will see) and P's festival day begin at different times than in the other biblical sources (including the P narrative), and they both appear to imitate foreign custom. It therefore seems more probable that the liturgical calendar was based on foreign systems than on an early Israelite one.

1.2.3. Measurable Divisions of the Day

The Bible writers do not often divide the day into measurable parts. Although general designations exist, like בקר ("morning"), צהרים ("midday"), ערב ("evening"), and חצי הלילה ("the middle of the night"), these are not clock times, nor are they used in chronological measurement. There is, however, limited evidence of quantifiable divisions of the day from which we may draw some educated conclusions.

Several writers use the term אשמורה (*ašmûrāh*) to designate a fixed period of time during which a guard keeps watch, and it would seem that over time the word, which originally came from a military context, carried over into everyday language.[16] Each watch seems to have borne a name, but the Bible does not provide us with the names of all of the watches. The "morning watch" (אשמרת הבקר) is spoken of in two places (Exod 14:24; 1 Sam 11:11, both J), and once we hear of a "middle watch" (האשמרת התיכונה) (Judg 7:19,

---

16. Cf. Greek φυλακαι and Latin *vigiliae* (Bickerman, *Chronology of the Ancient World*, 14).

the DH or one of its sources). All of the watches appear to be associated with the nighttime, including, it would appear, the morning watch, in which daybreak seems to have occurred (cf. Pss 63:6; 90:4; 119:147–148). However, Lam 2:19 suggests that תוראש האשמר ("the start of the watches") occurred in the morning and therefore that watches were kept all throughout the day.[17]

Since one of the night watches is referred to as the "middle" watch, we are justified in assuming an odd number of night watches, most likely three. These would consist of an early evening watch, the middle watch, and probably the morning watch. This three-fold division was also the practice of the Babylonians[18] and the Greeks in Homer's time.[19] In a night twelve hours long, each watch would have been approximately four hours in duration. As was also the custom in those lands, we would expect in Israel a similar division of the daytime, with three watches of about four hours each. However, for reasons that will be outlined below, it is possible that Israel had *four* watches during the daytime, rather than three. Whatever the case, as the length of daylight changed throughout the year, the length of the watches would no doubt have been affected, with the night watches being longer in the winter and shorter in the summer. Time would have been measured during the day by the position of the sun, and during the night by the position of the stars. Customs may have varied from place to place, but it is impossible with the scanty information the Bible provides to make any further judgments.

Apart from the אשמרת, the only other reference to measured divisions of the day occurs in a narrative about Isaiah and King Hezekiah. When the king asks the prophet for a sign that he will recover his health, the latter performs a miracle that suggests the turning back of time: he causes a shadow on a flight of steps, which had been moving forward, to recede (2 Kgs 20:8–11 = Isa 38:7–8, 22).

The steps upon which the shadow moves are of particular interest to us, because it would appear that they are to be understood as part of some sort of timekeeping device that was set up at the king's palace to measure the passing of the day by the sun's shadow. They are called מעלות אחז ("the steps of Ahaz") in the Masoretic Text (MT), a name that suggests that the clock was installed by Hezekiah's father. There is a good chance, however, that the phrase has been shortened accidentally through a scribal error (haplography). In the Isaiah text, several witnesses (LXX, 1QIsaa, Vulg., Targ.) testify to an additional word (עלית) between the two nouns (i.e., מעלות עלית אחז

---

17. Lamentations 2:19 happens to be another source of evidence for a day beginning in the morning.
18. Bickerman, *Chronology of the Ancient World*, 14.
19. *Il.* 10.253; *Od.* 12.312.

instead of זחא תולעמ).²⁰ The similarity between the two words תולעמ and תילע could easily have led a scribe's eye astray, so that the second word was skipped during the copying process in the Masoretic scribal tradition. A parent reading of זחא תילע תולעמ ("the steps of the roof chamber of Ahaz") is likely. The reference to זחא תילע ("the roof chamber of Ahaz") elsewhere (2 Kgs 23:12) establishes the existence of such a place and adds further credence to the longer reading.²¹ The attribution of the roof chamber to Ahaz may be an allusion to the alterations he had made to the palace complex earlier in the narrative (2 Kgs 16:17–18), alterations which seem to have included cultic innovations borrowed from Assyria. The steps may have been part of the new design. In a study of this subject, Yigael Yadin draws attention to Egyptian shadow clocks, one type of which consisted of two flights of stairs (one set facing east and one facing west), upon which the sun's shadow fell, and this may be the closest equivalent we can find.²² One example of this type

Figure 1.1. The Cairo shadow clock

---

20. LXX has "your father" instead of "Ahaz."

21. See Samuel Iwry, "The Qumran Isaiah and the End of the Dial of Ahaz," *BASOR* 147 (1957): 27–33.

22. Yigael Yadin, "זחא תולעמ," *ErIsr* 5 (1958): 91–96.

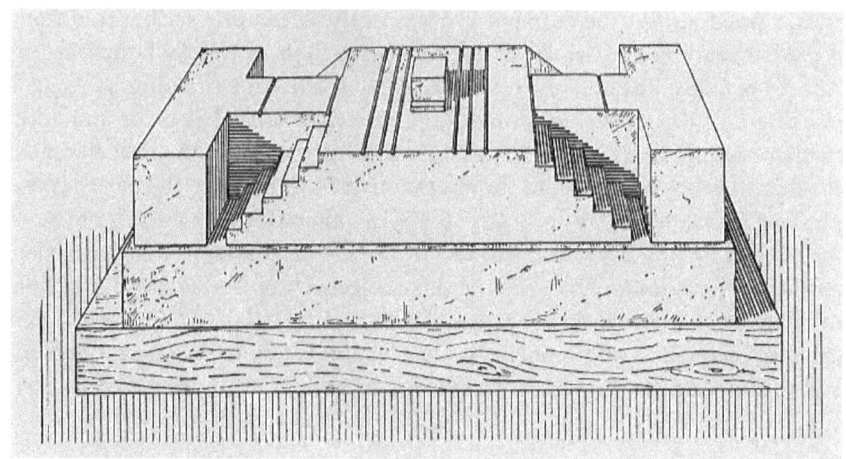

Figure 1.2. A drawing of the Cairo shadow clock

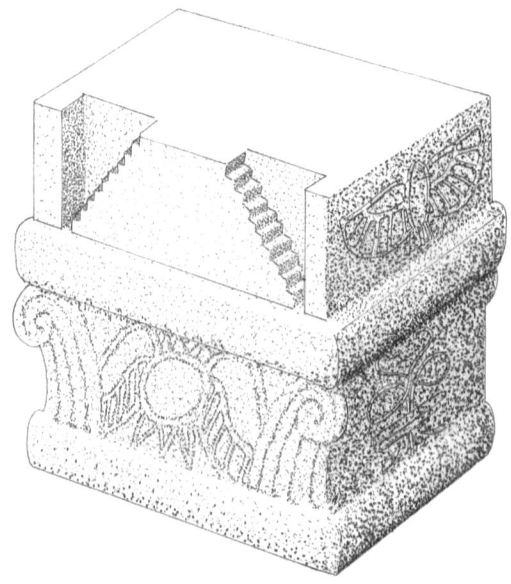

Figure 1.3. Reconstruction of Hezekiah's Shadow Clock.
Illustration by William H. C. Propp.

is part of a clock now in the Cairo Museum (No. 33401) and generally dated to the later New Kingdom period.[23] A photo and drawing appear in figs. 1.1 and 1.2.[24] Based on this model, the roof chamber of Ahaz may have looked something like fig. 1.3.

The Cairo model was small enough (34 cm × 10 cm) that it could be adjusted to be directly in line with the sun, no matter the time of year.[25] A permanent fixture on Ahaz's roof, as theorized by Yadin, would not have allowed for this. It may be that the clock was smaller than Yadin suggests and movable.

The text of Isa 38:8 in LXX, which is the fullest, gives some clues as to how the clock may have worked. It reads as follows:

[ιδου εγω στρεφω][26] την σκιαν των αναβαθμων ους κατεβη ο ηλιος τους δεκα αναβαθμους του οικου του πατρος σου αποστρεφω τον ηλιον τους δεκα αναβαθμους και ανεβη ο ηλιος τους δεκα αναβαθμους ους κατεβη η σκια.

"Behold! I shall bring the shadow of the steps, the ten steps of the house of your father that the sun went down. I shall bring back the sun the ten steps." And the sun went up the ten steps that the shadow went down.[27]

The account provides us with several pieces of information. First, after Yahweh says that he will make the sun *go back*, the sun *goes up*. The two expressions, "go back" and "go up," are equivalent. In other words, the sun, which had been in the process of setting, is made to return to a higher place in the sky. So the story must take place late in the day, towards evening. Second, we are told that, as time went backward and the sun went up, the shadow descended the steps. This would mean that in normal time, as the sun began to set, the shadow would ascend the steps. As it moved over them, it would create more light and less shadow, so the shadow must have increased in size as the sun moved down the steps.

This fixes the place of the object creating the shadow. It must be at the bottom of the stairs, and high enough to create a shadow over all of the steps as the sun sets. Finally, we are told that there are ten steps. If the clock mea-

---

23. Clagett, *Calendars, Clocks, and Astronomy*, 93–94.

24. Taken from Ludwig Borchardt, *Die Altägyptische Zeitmessung* (Berlin: de Gruyter, 1920), 37, 38.

25. Clagett, *Calendars, Clocks, and Astronomy*, 93.

26. The opening words are missing in the major LXX manuscripts but are restored here from variant manuscripts in conformity with MT.

27. For a discussion of the textual history of this passage, see Iwry, "The Qumran Isaiah and the End of the Dial of Ahaz," 32–33.

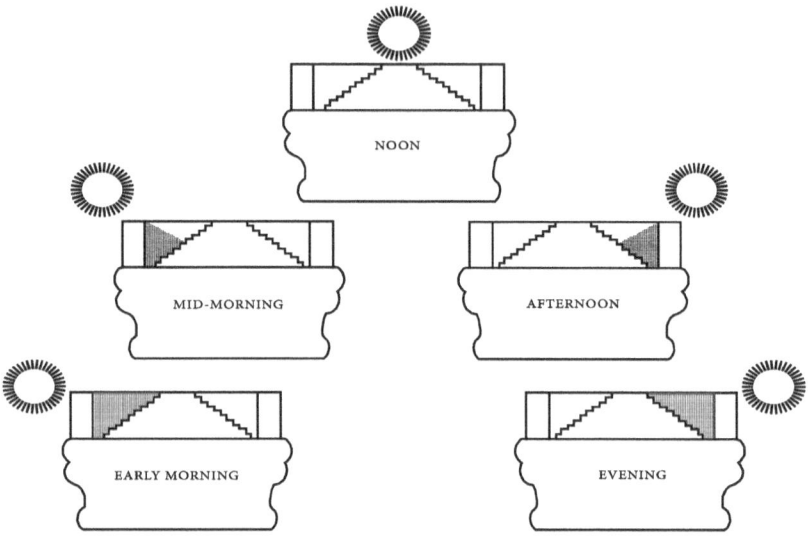

Figure 1.4. The shadow created on the steps according to the sun's position. Illustration by William H. C. Propp.

sured the movement of the sun throughout the entire day, we must presume there are ten steps on the other side as well. The stairway would have been running east–west.

Each step would represent a division of time. Ten steps on one side for the first half of the day (shadow moving down), and ten on the other for the second half of the day (shadow moving up), indicate twenty units total. Keep in mind that this would be for daylight time only. Each step would represent approximately thirty-six minutes, that is, at times of the year when daytime and nighttime were equal, but would have been shorter during the winter and longer during the summer, as in the case of Egyptian shadow clocks.[28] A division of the daytime into twenty units is unattested in the sources of any other ancient culture. If so, we may have here a uniquely Judahite clock.

Alternately, we might suppose that it would take some time after sunrise for the shadow to drop down the first step on the eastern stairway. In early Egyptian flat-surfaced shadow clocks, for example, it took two hours for the shadow to reach the first mark.[29] Since the clock seems to be based on an

---

28. Cf. also Greece in Robert R. Hannah, *Time in Antiquity* (New York: Routledge, 2009), 74.

29. Clagett, *Calendars, Clocks, and Astronomy*, 85–86.

1. CALENDARS 19

Egyptian model, we might surmise that it was an hour after sunrise before the shadow began to move (the equivalent of two steps), and likewise an hour before sunset when the shadow reached the top of the steps on the other side, which would yield twelve units on one side and twelve on the other, thus suggesting a daytime divided into twenty-four parts in harmony with both the Egyptian and Babylonian twelve-hour system.[30] On the other hand, the step clock appears to have been different than the flat-surfaced shadow clock. The Cairo model has a number of steps *equal* to the number of hours in the Egyptian daytime (12), so perhaps we should expect that the Ahaz clock, if the same type of step-clock, had a number of steps that equaled the number of hours in the day (20). If that were the case, it is unlikely that only three watches were kept during the daytime, because in order for the hours and the watches to be consistent with one another, twenty hours would need to be divided by an even number of watches. It may be, then, that while the night consisted of three watches determined by the position of the stars, the day consisted of four watches determined by the position of the sun, for a total of seven watches.

1.3. The Month as a Unit of Measurement

1.3.1. The Hebrew Words for Month

There are two words in Hebrew that can mean "month." One, יֶרַח (*yeraḥ*), is a derivative of the word יָרֵחַ ("moon"), which comes from a root meaning "to wander, travel," and no doubt is meant to evoke the thought of the moon as a wanderer or traveler.[31] It is the term of choice in the Gezer Calendar, in Phoenician inscriptions, and in the Ugaritic texts.[32] The word is not used frequently in the Bible. It occurs six times in the Deuteronomic History, three of which are in the citation of Phoenician month names (1 Kgs 6:37, 38; 8:2), once in the blessing of Moses (Deut 33:14), once in the Deuteronomic Code (Deut 21:13), and once in reference to the length of the reign of an Israelite king (2 Kgs 15:13). It occurs once in J (Exod 2:2), four times in the poetry of Job (3:6; 7:3; 29:2; 39:2), and once in the book of Zechariah (11:8). The second term, חֹדֶשׁ (*ḥōdeš*), appears forty-four times and is used by all of the major

---

30. Stephen S. Langdon, *Babylonian Menologies and the Semitic Calendars* (London: Oxford University Press, 1935), 54–64; Bartel L. van der Waerden, *Science Awakening II: The Birth of Astronomy* (New York: Oxford University Press, 1974), 69, 86–89.
31. R. E. Clements, "ירח," *TDOT* 6:355–62.
32. Ibid., 356.

sources. It comes from a root meaning "new" and no doubt is meant to evoke the thought of the rebirth of the moon at the beginning of each month.[33]

1.3.2. THE NAMING AND NUMBERING OF MONTHS

Months in the Bible are rarely named. Exceptions are found chiefly in the accounts of Solomon's building projects (1 Kgs 6:1, 37–38; 8:2), where the months Ziv, Bul, and Ethanim are mentioned. Two of these names, Bul and Ethanim, appear in Phoenician inscriptions.[34] Because the month names in 1 Kings are limited to this context, it is quite possible that the accounts are based, at least partially, on Phoenician records or on contracts with the Phoenicians (King Hiram of Tyre is said to have supervised the contruction work). It is therefore not certain that the Israelites employed these names on a regular basis. On the other hand, the month name Abib (a name not found in any Canaanite texts) is attested in the law codes of E (Exod 13:4; 23:15), J (Exod 34:18), and the DH (Deut 16:1), so there is reason to believe that this was a name commonly used in Israel in early times. Although some have argued that Abib is no month name at all, but rather a descriptor of some agricultural or seasonal event,[35] Abib has no features that set it apart from other month names. Many months of the ancient Near Eastern calendars were named after agricultural or seasonal events and sometimes carry the definite article (e.g., "the month of the Ethanim" in 1 Kgs 8:2).[36] It therefore seems likely that the Israelites named their months at one time.[37]

---

33. J. L. North, "חדש," *TDOT* 4:225–44.

34. Mark E. Cohen, *The Cultic Calendars of the Ancient Near East* (Bethesda, Md.: CDL, 1993), 384–85.

35. E.g., Franz X. Kugler, *Von Moses bis Paulus: Forschungen zur Geschichte Israels* (Münster: Aschendorff, 1922), 12–17; Jan A. Wagenaar, *Origin and Transformation of the Ancient Israelite Festival Calendar* (Wiesbaden: Harrassowitz, 2005), 25–31. Wagenaar argues that use of the term חדש for "month" is a late development and that the word meant "season" in the preexilic period. He therefore concludes that Abib is not a month name. However, he dismisses the many instances in which preexilic authors clearly use the word חדש to mean "month" (e.g., Gen 38:24; 1 Sam 27:7; 2 Sam 24:8; 1 Kgs 5:7 [4:27]; 2 Kgs 23:31) and instead supports his understanding of the word with a single passage in Jeremiah (2:23–24) in which חדש appears to mean something like "season."

36. See Jeremy Hughes, *Secrets of the Times: Myth and History in Biblical Chronology* (ed. David J. A. Clines and Philip R. Davies; JSOTSup 66; Sheffield: JSOT Press, 1990), 161.

37. Auerbach draws attention to an interesting passage in Exod 9:31–32, which appears to name two other Israelite months: Gibeol and Aphilot (Elias Auerbach, "Die

The custom of referring to months by number is evident in both P and the DH. While monthly references permeate the priestly text, the Deuteronomic History contains month references only in three small sections: in its final chapter (2 Kgs 25), in the account of Solomon's building projects (1 Kgs 6:1, 37–38 and 8:2), and in the account of Jeroboam's shrine dedication festival (1 Kgs 12:32–33). The last chapter of the DH was written during the exile. The month references in 1 Kgs 6 and 8 also contain month *names*, and the numbered months are marked off by the independent pronoun הוא, an indication that they are glosses. The similar use of היא in 2 Kgs 25:8 raises the possibility that the glosses in 1 Kgs 6 and 8 were added by the reviser of the DH during the exile. The date provided in the pericope concerning Jeroboam also appears to be a late addition because it assumes knowledge of the priestly legislation for the harvest festival (see the discussion below on the civil year). For these reasons, use of the DH as evidence for numbered months in preexilic times would be problematic.[38]

If P existed in some form in preexilic times (and the evidence is strong that it did), it is the only biblical text that demonstrates a preexilic usage of numbered months. However, some priestly data were contributed by the redactor in later times. Is it possible to separate P chronological data from R chronological data in order to determine who numbered months and who did not?

When the priestly texts provide dates with reference to months, they do so for two purposes. One is to specify the times at which rituals are to be performed; the other is to date events in the narrative. For the reader's convenience, all thirty-one of these references in the priestly texts are divided according to purpose and listed in two columns below.

---

babylonische Datierung im Pentatuech und das Alter des Priester-Kodex," *VT* 2 [1952]: 334–35). Like Abib, these are unattested as month names outside the Bible.

38. A partially preserved inscription from late-eighth century B.C.E. Jerusalem carries two numbered elements, "in the seventh" and "in the fourth," both without nouns (see Frank Moore Cross, "A Fragment of a Monumental Inscription from the City of David," *IEJ* 51 [2001]: 44–47). Cross takes both of these as synchronisms, the first to refer to a seventh *year*, and the second to a fourth *month*. If his interpretation is correct, we would have extrabiblical evidence for the numbering of months in administrative documents from late-monarchic Judah. However, given the ambiguity of the text as a result of its fragmentary condition, there simply is not enough here to support any sort of argument on this point.

TABLE 1.1. PRIESTLY DATES THAT INCLUDE MONTHS

Dates of Yearly Rituals	Dates of Historical Events
Sheep taken for Passover: 1/10–1/14 (Exod 12:2, 3, 6)	Beginning of flood: 2/17 in the 600th year of Noah's life (Gen 7:11)
Eating of unfermented bread: 1/14–1/21 (Exod 12:18)	Ark rests on Mt. Ararat: 7/17 in the 600th year of Noah's life (Gen 8:4)
Day of Atonement: 7/10 (Lev 16:29)	Tops of mountains appear: 10/1 in the 600th year of Noah's life (Gen 8:5)
Passover: 1/14 (Lev 23:5)	Water is drained from the ground: 1/1 in the 601st year of Noah's life (Gen 8:13)
Festival of Unleavened Bread begins: 1/15 (Lev 23:6)	The earth is dried and Noah leaves ark: 2/27 in the 601st year of Noah's life (Gen 8:14)
New Year's observance: 7/1 (Lev 23:24)	Israelites come to wilderness of Sin: 2/15 after leaving Egypt (Exod 16:1)
Day of Atonement: 7/9–7/10 (Lev 23:27,32)	Israelites come to Sinai: 3rd month after leaving Egypt (Exod 19:1)
Festival of Booths: 7/15–7/21 (Lev 23:39,41)	Tabernacle set up: 1/1 in 2nd year after leaving Egypt (Exod 40:2,17)
Sounding of horn in Jubilee year: 7/10 (Lev 25:9)	Census taken: 2/1 in 2nd year after leaving Egypt (Num 1:1,18)
Make-up Passover: 2/14 (Num 9:3,5,11)	God institutes make-up Passover: 1st month in 2nd year after leaving Egypt (Num 9:1)
Passover: 1/14 (Num 28:16)	Israelites leave Sinai: 2/20 in 2nd year after leaving Egypt (Num 10:11)
Festival of Unfermented Cakes: 1/15–1/21 (Num 28:17)	Israelites come to Qadesh in Zin and Miriam dies: 1st month [in 3rd year?] after leaving Egypt (Num 20:1)
New Year's observance: 7/1 (Num 29:1)	Israelites leave Egypt: 1/15 (Num 33:3)

1. CALENDARS

Day of Atonement: 7/10 (Num 29:7)	Aaron dies: 5/1 in the 40th year after leaving Egypt (Num 33:38)
Festival of Booths: 7/15–7/21 (Num 29:12)	Moses delivers law on plains of Moab: 11/1 in the 40th year after leaving Egypt (Deut 1:3–4)
	Israelites cross the Jordan: 1/10 [in the 41st year?] after leaving Egypt (Josh 4:19)

The ritual schedule is provided three times in the priestly material, once in P proper (first part of the year in Exod 12, second part in Lev 16, and a supplement in Num 9), once in the "Holiness Code" (Lev 23, 25), and once in the work of R (Num 28, 29).[39] If the date legislation of P is preexilic, we possess evidence for numbered months before the exile. (Under these circumstances, they would be numbered according to the liturgical calendar; see below.)

When it comes to the actual dating of historical events, however, we cannot be certain of preexilic practice among the Aaronid priests. There appears to be unity of authorship in the second column. Someone is clearly interested in laying out a comprehensive chronology of the wilderness events, and the flood chronology exhibits some of the same characteristics. Textual analysis has shown that the list of the wilderness stations of Israel's journeys (Num 33) probably was incorporated into the Torah by the redactor. R used this list to organize the stories he combined, and he set twelve station headings within the newly formed narrative to coincide with the list.[40] Two important dates are included in Num 33, the date that the Israelites left Egypt, and the date of Aaron's death. Four of the station headings within the wilderness narrative *also contain dates* (Exod 16:1; 19:1–2; Num 10:11–12; 20:1–2), so they are likely redactorial as well (all are in the right-hand column in the table above).[41] If six of the nine wilderness dates in the table are R's, it

---

39. Knohl argues that Num 28–29 has priority over the present version of Lev 23 (Knohl, *The Sanctuary of Silence*, 8–14), but accepting this argument would not require us to date Num 28–29 any earlier if we assume, with Knohl, that Lev 23 has been tampered with by later editors. For evidence that Num 28–29 is from the hand of R, see Friedman, *The Bible with Sources Revealed*, 296–97.

40. For the evidence, see Cross, *Canaanite Myth and Hebrew Epic*, 308–17. Cross, however, while demonstrating a priestly redactor, does not distinguish between P and R.

41. A claim could be made that the headings are composite and that therefore the

makes little sense to assign the other three (Exod 40:2, 17; Num 1:1, 18; 9:1) to P. It appears R is responsible for the entire chronology. Regarding the date found in Deuteronomy (1:3–4), it appears likewise to be a part of R's wilderness chronology, because it continues to date events by the exodus, follows precisely six months after the previous date (suggesting a connection between the two), and makes an effort to include the Deuteronomic speeches on the plains of Moab (absent in P) in the wilderness journey (cf. Num 33:48–49). R, not the author of P, had knowledge of the Deuteronomic material. Moreover, Deut 1:3–4 is clearly an intrusion in the Deuteronomic text. I would also venture to say that the date at Josh 4:19 is by R as well, because it is the final (and only other) date in the wilderness trek (the crossing of the Jordan would be the natural terminal point), and the editor wants to make it clear that the Israelites got to the other side by the tenth of the first month, so that they could observe the ritual of Exod 12:2–6 [P].

That the flood chronology also derives from R makes sense, as it exhibits the same characteristics as the rest of the chronology. The dates having to do with the flood stand out as very specific, naming both the month and the day that an event takes place:

> In the 600th year of Noah's life, in the 2nd month, on the 17th day of the month, on this day, all the springs of the great deep were burst, and the gates of the skies were opened (Gen 7:11).

> And the ark came to rest, in the 7th month, on the 17th day of the month, on the mountains of Ararat. And the water lessened until the 10th month. In the 10th [month], on the first of the month, the tops of the mountains appeared (Gen 8:4–5).

> And it came to be, in the 601st year of Noah's life, in the first [month], on the first of the month, that the water dried from on the earth (Gen 8:13–14).

This specific form of dating can be found elsewhere in the Torah *only* in R's wilderness chronology. Note that the expression ביום הזה in Gen 7:11 appears also in Exod 19:1 [R].[42]

---

dates might not be from R, but I have yet to see evidence of multiple authorship here, and the presence of the dates in the headings is difficult to ignore.

42. Knohl asserts that בראשון used as an abbreviation for בחדש הראשון is found only in exilic and postexilic texts (Knohl, *The Sanctuary of Silence*, 19). Although this argument would lend further support to my conclusion about the lateness of the date notations for the flood because Gen 8:13 uses בראשון, there simply is insufficient evidence for customary preexilic usage to make a judgment on the matter.

Although P's month references are limited to the ritual calendar, they are a clear indication that, at the very least, the priests began numbering months in their liturgical calendar sometime in the late preexilic period. We cannot safely assume this convention began earlier than the late eighth century B.C.E. (that is, prior to the fall of the northern kingdom of Israel).[43]

1.3.3. WHEN DID THE MONTH BEGIN AND END?

In the preparation of a calendar, a choice needs to be made whether to count actual synodic months based on observation of the moon, in which case the lengths of months will fluctuate, or whether to arbitrarily assign a certain number of days to a month, regardless of the position of the moon (as we do in our calendar), in which case the lengths of the month will remain constant. The question is: what did the ancient Israelites do?

It has sometimes been argued that the very name חֹדֶשׁ for a month makes it clear that the month is based on the observation of the new moon.[44] However, we should be careful not to put too much emphasis on etymology. The word "month" in any language is related to the word for moon or a phase of the moon, but not all months are measured by observation of the moon. Even if originally a month denoted the passage of the moon, we cannot assume it always did.[45] Nevertheless, the occasional use in the Bible of חֹדֶשׁ to denote an actual new-moon celebration, the date of which was not known ahead of time (Amos 8:5), points to a custom that kept track of the phases of the moon. There are references to new-moon celebrations, often alongside Sabbath observances, in some of the books of the earlier prophets, both northern and southern (Amos 8:5; Hosea 2:13 [11]; Isaiah 1:13), in the Deuteronomic History (1 Sam 20:5, 24; 2 Kgs 4:23), and in the Psalms (Ps 81:4 [3]). The association of these observances with activities of kings suggests that the observations of the moon were connected with the civil calendar. P, too, appears to assume that the moon was watched to keep track of time

---

43. See Bernard R. Goldstein and Alan Cooper, "The Festivals of Israel and Judah and the Literary History of the Pentateuch," *JAOS* 110 (1990): 23.

44. See, e.g, Sigmund Mowinckel, *Zum israelitischen Neujahr und zur Deutung der Thronbesteigungspsalmen* (Oslo: Dybwad, 1952), 22; Solomon Gandz, "The Calendar of Ancient Israel," *Homenaje a Millás Vallicrosa* 1 (1954): 630.

45. In Egypt, for example, the hieroglyph for "month" was written with a crescent moon, even in the civil calendar, which had a set length for the month, regardless of the waxing and waning of the moon (Clagett, *Calendars, Clocks, and Astronomy*, 7). See also Sacha Stern, *Calendar and Community: A History of the Jewish Calendar, Second Century BCE–Tenth Century CE* (Oxford: Oxford University Press, 2001), 3.

when it states that, as one of the luminaries, the moon's primary purpose is to mark time (Gen 1:14).[46] The implication of Gen 1:14, then, is that the liturgical calendar, like the civil one, was based on actual observation of the moon.

On the other hand, evidence could be cited to demonstrate that months may have been assigned a set number of days, regardless of the actual phases of the moon. In the flood narrative of Genesis, the priestly chronology informs us that five months separated the beginning of the flood and the landing of the ark on Mt. Ararat, and that this period comprised 150 days (Gen 7:11; 8:3–4). The clear inference is that each month lasted an even 30 days.[47] In a system in which direct observation of the moon determined the length of months, this could never happen. This schematic representation of the months is similar to that found in Daniel (12:7, 11), in which 3½ years is equated with 1,290 days (42 months of precisely 30 days). These figures are idealized numbers of the type found in the schematic calendar of Babylon, which was used for astronomical purposes but not as a real calendar. It consisted of 12 months of 30 days each for a total of 360 days per year.[48] Regardless, the flood chronology was created by the redactor of the Primary History (see above) and cannot therefore be used as evidence of preexilic custom.

When a calendar is intended to measure the actual length of months (i.e., the course of the moon), rather than create an arbitrary length for convenience, the most useful phenomena to observe are the moon's phases. A month is the interval of time between two successive observations of the same phenomenon. Since this period fluctuates slightly with no apparent pattern, there would have been little opportunity for prediction. Conjunction (when the sun, earth, and moon are in line) is the natural line of demarcation of the synodic month.[49] A common beginning point for a

---

46. The word מועדים, often translated "seasons" refers more generally to "appointed times."

47. Cooper and Goldstein see a preexilic priestly calendar here and posit Egyptian influence (Alan Cooper and Bernard R. Goldstein, "The Development of the Priestly Calendars (I): The Daily Sacrifice and the Sabbath," *HUCA* 74 [2004]: 6–7).

48. See Gandz, "The Calendar of Ancient Israel," 623–46; John P. Britton, "Calendars, Intercalations and Year-Lengths in Mesopotamian Astronomy," in *Calendars and Years: Astronomy and Time in the Ancient Near East* (ed. J. M. Steele; Oxford: Oxbow, 2007), 117–18.

49. See the helpful discussion in Samuel, *Greek and Roman Chronology*, 5–10. The month can also be measured by its position in reference to a star, but the length of time the moon takes to travel around the earth and back to the same place (27⅓days—a sidereal month) is actually two days shorter than a synodic month and not commonly used for calendar purposes.

month was the evening in which the crescent first became visible. The Mesopotamians and Greeks counted months this way, because their days began at sunset.[50] The Egyptian lunar calendar, both the earlier and the later form, seems to have marked the months by the last visibility of the crescent in the morning.[51] This makes sense, since the Egyptian day began at dawn. (In other words, we should expect the beginning of a month to coincide with the beginning of a new day.) Because the Israelites followed the Egyptian practice of counting their days from morning, it is likely that, if they did count the months by observing the moon, they would have marked the months by morning observation rather than evening observation.

The synodic month averages about twenty-nine and a half days (+/- 13 hours), so in a calendar a lunar month can be only twenty-nine or thirty days—never more and never less. According to the Egyptian system, if the moon crescent were no longer visible in the eastern sky just before sunrise on the morning of the thirtieth day of any given month, that day would be the first of the new month (the length of the preceding month would be determined to have been twenty-nine days). Sometimes poor visibility would make it impossible to tell, so the month might last another day, but the month would end at thirty days no matter what the atmospheric conditions were the next morning. If the observers made an error (counting a 29-day month as 30 days), it would automatically be corrected by the next clear observation of the crescent (so sometimes a 29-day month might end up being 28 days as a result).

1.3.4. Measurable Divisions of the Month

Apart from being divided into days, months apparently were not divided into anything else for calendar purposes in ancient Israel. The week, a convenient short period of time greater in length than a day, and lesser in length than a month, is not a natural unit of time. Four weeks (28 days) come close to the length of a synodic month (29½ days), but not close enough to maintain accordance between weeks and months over any lengthy period of time. The ancient Egyptians had a ten-day week, arbitrarily created to fit neatly

---

50. Francesca Rochberg-Halton, "Calendars, Ancient Near East," *ABD* 1:810; John M. Steele, "The Length of the Month in Mesopotamian Calendars of the First Millennium BC," in Steele, *Calendars and Years*, 133–37; Samuel, *Greek and Roman Chronology*, 14.

51. Parker, *The Calendars of Ancient Egypt*, 9–23; idem, "The Beginning of the Lunar Month in Ancient Egypt," *JNES* 29 (1970): 217–20; Clagett, *Calendars, Clocks, and Astronomy*, 22–28.

into the thirty-day month of its civil solar calendar.[52] The Athenian Greeks also divided their months into three ten-day weeks, though because the length of their months was determined by moon observation, the final week sometimes was only nine days long.[53] The seven-day week, though attested earliest among the Israelites, nevertheless was based on a number commonly regarded as significant or sacred in many ancient Near Eastern cultures and probably having its origin in the observation that seven heavenly bodies (sun, moon, Mercury, Venus, Mars, Jupiter, and Saturn) were known to move against the fixed background of the stars. The organization of days into groups of seven, in honor of these heavenly bodies, was convenient.[54] By the first century B.C.E. the days of the week would be named after these bodies.

On the other hand, it is possible that seven-day weeks were based on the phases of the moon. In the Enuma Elish, when Marduk creates the moon "to mark out the days," he says:

> At the month's very start, rising over the land,
> You shall have luminous horns to signify six days,
> On the seventh day reaching a half-crown.
> So shall the fifteen-day period be like one another—two halves for each month.
> When the sun overtakes you at the base of heaven,
> Diminish your crown and retrogress in light.
> At the time of disappearance approach the course of the sun,
> And on the thirtieth you shall again stand in opposition to the sun.
> (V:12–22)

In this scheme, the week plays an important role. The first seven days cover the period from the new moon to the half-moon. Another period of seven days covers the period from the half-moon to the full moon. Day 15 is the middle of the month. Then the reverse happens. Seven days cover the period from the full moon to the half-moon, and seven days the half-moon to the new. Day 30 may be the last day of the month, or the first day of the next. To be sure, this delineation of the days may simply be an attempt to harmonize the week with a lunar month, but it is also possible that the idea of a seven-day week came from this scheme.

---

52. Clagett, *Calendars, Clocks, and Astronomy*, 49–50.

53. Hannah, *Time in Antiquity*, 19–20.

54. Solomon Gandz, "The Origin of the Planetary Week or the Planetary Week in Hebrew Literature," *PAAJR* 18 (1949): 213–54.

1. CALENDARS

The word for week in Hebrew is שבוע, which comes from the word for "seven;" it appears infrequently in the Bible.[55] Most often we find it as part of the expression "Festival of Weeks," a feast that received its name because it occurred at the culmination of a series of seven weeks commencing at harvest.[56] The earliest reference to this festival is in J's Decalogue (Exod 34:22). We also find it in the Deuteronomic Code (Deut 16:9–12) and in the priestly laws, but without the name (Lev 23:15–16). Interestingly, the only time we find weeks being *counted* in the Bible is in conjunction with the Festival of Weeks. Only in J do we find the word "week" used in a secular sense (Gen 29:27–28). Nevertheless, because of the Sabbath observance, the week is an important part of Israelite society, usually called a period of "seven days" rather than "one week." Though not often employed this way, the word for Sabbath (שבת) is sometimes used by P as a parallel designation for a week (e.g., Lev 23:15).[57] The days of the week are of particular interest to P and are usually numbered. An apparent innovation of P is not only to organize *days* into weeks, but *years* into weeks as well (Lev 25:8), although there is a possible instance of this usage in J (Gen 29:26–27).

1.4 The Year as a Unit of Measurement

1.4.1. The Hebrew Word for Year

The Hebrew word for year, שנה (*šānāh*), once thought to come from a root meaning "to change" or "to repeat," probably is a primary noun.[58] It is found in all of the Semitic languages, except for Old South Arabic and Ethiopic. Ancient farmers were well aware of the change in seasons, and such knowledge would have governed their idea of what constituted a year. The annual cycle marked by seasons is assumed in many preexilic texts (e.g., Gen 8:22; 17:21). More exact observation of the movement of the sun revealed the times of the year when the period of daylight and period of night were equal (the equinoxes on about September 23 and March 20), as well as the days when the daylight was shortest (December 21) and longest (June 21; the solstices).[59]

---

55. Brin, *Concept of Time*, 167–68; Eckart Otto, "שבע," *TDOT* 14:336–67.
56. James C. VanderKam, "Weeks, Feast of," *ABD* 6: 895–97.
57. Interestingly, the Mesopotamians used what appears to be a cognate word, *šabattu/šapattu*, to designate the 15th day of a month, as well as half of a month. See Langdon, *Babylonian Menologies and the Semitic Calendars*, 90–97.
58. F. J. Stendebach, "שנה," *TDOT* 15: 324–25.
59. The equinoxes occur when the sun crosses the equator and equally irradiates the north and south poles, and the solstices when the sun seems to stand still as it is travel-

The length of the tropical year therefore was well known among the ancients to be approximately 365 days.[60]

There is no natural beginning point of a year (i.e., a place where the sun naturally begins its journey), so ancient societies would establish the first day of a year as they preferred. This could be done by selecting a seasonal change, an important anniversary date, or a natural astronomical phenomenon. Calendars that took into account the phases of the moon tended to choose the latter (the beginning of a natural month), and calendars that disregarded the moon's phases would usually pick an arbitrary date. Civil and cultic calendars tended to select the first day of the month closest to either the spring or autumnal equinox to commence the year, whereas agricultural calendars often began with a seasonal occurrence or farming task. A single society might have more than one sort of calendar in use. Assyria had at least two calendars operating at the same time (before its adoption of the Babylonian calendar), one solar and one lunar. The solar year began around the time of the autumnal equinox. The lunar year began at a different point in the solar year each year.[61] Egypt had two co-existing calendars. The civil year was 365 days long, consisting of 12 months of 30 days, plus 5 extra days. This calendar was one-quarter of a day short of a solar year and so each year began one-quarter of a day earlier than it had the previous year. The religious calendar was lunar and used for fixing festival days but was linked to the solar year, through intercalation, to the rising of the Dog Star Sirius, so that it began in the summer at the onset of the Nile inundation.[62] In ancient Syria, we find that there were three separate calendars in use—one civil, one royal, and one cultic—in addition to Assyrian and Babylonian ones.[63] They appear to have been luni-solar.

---

ing northward and then again as it is traveling southward. Another way of calculating the equinoxes and solstices is by measuring the sun's shadow.

60. The Egyptians were counting a 365-day year as early as the third millennium B.C.E. (Parker, *The Calendars of Ancient Egypt*, 54; Leo Depuydt, "Calendars and Years in Ancient Egypt: The Soundness of Egyptian and West Asian Chronology in 1500–500 BC and the Consistency of the Egyptian 365-Day Wandering Year," in Steele, *Calendars and Years*, 70–74). In the Bible, the number of years in the lifespan of Enoch (Gen 5:23) may be a symbolic figure based on the length of the tropical year.

61. Cohen, *Cultic Calendars*, 237–47.

62. J. W. S. Sewell, "The Calendars and Chronology," in *The Legacy of Egypt* (ed. Stephen R. K. Glanville; Oxford: Clarendon, 1942), 1–9.

63. Daniel E. Fleming, *Time at Emar: The Cultic Calendar and the Rituals from the Diviner's Archive* (Winona Lake, Ind.: Eisenbrauns, 2000), 196–213.

1.4.2. When Did the Year Begin and End?

1.4.2.1. The Agricultural Year

That Israelite farmers saw the year generally as comprising two main parts, seedtime (winter) and harvest (summer), is seen in J (Gen 8:22; 45:6; Exod 34:21) and in E's Covenant Code (Exod 23:10). Seedtime would have run from mid-November to mid-April, and harvest (almost twice as long) from mid-April to mid-November (see table 1.2).

In J, Isaac is said to have planted and harvested in the same year (Gen 26:12), an impossibility if the year began with the harvest. Moreover, the legislation that the land was to lie fallow every 7th year (Exod 23:10–11; Lev 25:1–22 [P]) can hardly be understood to occur in anything but an agricultural year, divided between seedtime and harvest.[64] The year referred to in Deut 11:12, in context, also appears to be the agricultural year, beginning with the sowing of seed. Jeremiah, equating the harvest with the summer (Jer 8:20; cf. also Amos 8:1–2), implies that the second of the two seasons was over (and therefore the year itself) when the harvest was over.

Agriculturalists in ancient cultures marked important points in the year by astronomical observation and weather conditions. The Greek farmer Hesiod (eighth century B.C.E.), in his poem *Works and Days*, provides us with some of our earliest evidence for the timing of agricultural activities.[65] For

---

64. Hughes (Hughes, *Secrets of the Times*, 168) argues, following Morgenstern (Morganstern, "Supplementary Studies in the Calendars of Ancient Israel," 83–86), that the Sabbath year reflected in Lev 25 begins in the spring, because, in vv 20–22, God says he will ensure that the harvest of the sixth year will produce enough food for three years (sixth, seventh, and eighth). The reasoning goes as follows: In an autumn-based calendar, there would be no need to have produce from the sixth year feed people in the eighth, because the harvest of the eighth year would provide food for the eighth year. In a spring-based calendar, on the other hand, the harvest of the sixth year would *commence* a new year, rather than end one, and so, although there would be planting at the conclusion of the sixth year, no one would be permitted to harvest the crops in the beginning of the seventh. So the sixth year harvest would provide, not only for the sixth year, but also the seventh and the eighth (for there would be no harvest at the beginning of the eighth year). However, to assume that there would be planting in the sixth year with the full knowledge that those crops would not be harvested is ludicrous. Why would the farmers go through all that work for nothing? The autumn-based calendar presents no problem to the understanding of these verses. The produce of the sixth year would provide (1) for the second half of the sixth year, (2) for the entire seventh year, and (3) for the first half of the eighth year. The three years are counted inclusively.

65. *Op.* 383–688.

TABLE 1.2. AGRICULTURAL ACTIVITY IN MODERN ISRAEL
(Based on Borowski, *Agriculture in Iron Age Israel*, 34, 37)

	Nov	Dec	Jan	Feb	Mar	Apr	May	Jun	Jul	Aug	Sep	Oct
Wheat	Sow	Sow					Reap					
Barley	Sow	Sow				Reap						
Oats	Sow	Sow					Reap					
Vetch	Sow	Sow				Reap	Reap					
Flax		Sow							Reap			
Peas		Sow	Sow			Reap	Reap					
Lentils		Sow				Reap	Reap					
Vegetables			Sow	Sow	Sow							
Chickpeas				Sow				Reap				
Millet					Sow	Sow			Reap	Reap		
Sesame						Sow			Reap			
Grapes								Reap	Reap	Reap	Reap	
Figs										Reap	Reap	
Pomegranates										Reap	Reap	
Olives	Reap										Reap	Reap

him these activities are governed by the movement of the stars,⁶⁶ the movement of the sun, the weather, and the condition of the crops. He makes it clear that the commencement of planting often was an individual decision. Moreover, when referring to periods of time, he often rounds his figures, thus showing that they are approximations. Practices were probably very similar in ancient Israel. The husbandman's calendar was not very precise, because climatic factors varied from year to year and would sometimes affect visibility of the heavens. It therefore is not likely that the beginning of the agricultural year occurred on a specific fixed day for all farmers. Because of this fact, such a calendar would have been of minimal value in administrative or priestly circles, which required precise time measurement that could be applied to large communities as a whole.

The longer period in the agricultural year, harvest (seven–eight months), is approximately twice as long as planting time (four–five months) and in some sources is separated into two equal parts: threshing time and vintage (Lev 26:5 [P]; Amos 9:13), so that, for the agriculturalist, the year would be divided into three equal seasons of four months, the first of which, the planting season, would have commenced around November 15. A case has been made that the plural form of the Hebrew word for day (ימים) may be used at times to refer to a four-month season.⁶⁷ In support of this position, Judg 19:2 and 1 Sam 27:7 are cited, both of which appear to contain an explicative gloss ("four months") for the word ימים. This understanding makes good sense in many biblical passages (e.g., Gen 1:14; 24:55; 40:4; Lev 25:29; Num 9:22; Judg 17:10; 1 Sam 29:3; 2 Sam 14:26; Isa 32:10; 2 Chr 21:15, 19). Such a division into three seasons of four months each, based on climatic and agricultural factors, was the custom in Egypt.⁶⁸ The Egyptian seasons were: 1) *peret* ("coming forth"), when the planting and tilling of crops took place, 2) *shemu* ("deficiency"), the time of harvest and the dropping of the waters of the Nile, and 3) *akhet* ("indundation"), when the Nile rose and overflowed the fields. The Israelite seasons would not be exactly parallel, but there is nothing equivalent to the Nile-based agriculture in the Levant, and any system of seasons would naturally reflect the climatic and agricultural conditions found in a given locality.

---

66. Waerden, *Science Awakening II: The Birth of Astronomy*, 11–13. The length of a "star year" (technically called a sidereal year), which is measured by observing the apparent passage of the sun across each of the constellations, is only 20 minutes and 23 seconds longer than a solar year. The ancients would have noticed no difference. See Hannah, *Time in Antiquity*, 14–15, 42–43, 72.

67. F. S. North, "Four-Month Seasons of the Hebrew Bible," *VT* 11 (1961): 446–48.

68. Clagett, *Calendars, Clocks, and Astronomy*, 4–5.

Alternately, it has been suggested that the Israelite agricultural year was divided into four seasons of three months each.[69] Such a subdivision of the year is implied by the description of Solomon's corvée system in the DH (1 Kgs 5:27–28), in which three contingents of men are called up to work for one month, after which they receive two months off. Neat units of three months are therefore implied. However, this labor schedule does not appear to be connected with the agricultural year at all.

It has sometimes been argued that the placement of the Festival of Ingathering at the "exit of the year" (צאת השנה) in E's Covenant Code (Exod 23:16) provides evidence for the termination of the agricultural year. All one would have to do, therefore, is pinpoint the date of the harvest festival, and then the time of the beginning of the agricultural year would become apparent. However, simply because the harvest festival is a seasonal agricultural activity, this does not mean the expression "exit of the year" points to the agricultural calendar. Both the Deuteronomic and Priestly sources place the festival in the seventh month counting from the onset of spring (1 Kgs 8:2; Lev 23:39, 41; Num 29:12), which would be late September/early October according to our calendar, and this would contradict what we know about agricultural activity in the region. The harvest season would not yet be over at this time. Besides, the Festival of Ingathering was timed to occur at the height of the vintage, not at the tail end of the agricultural year when the last remnants were coming in.[70] In none of our sources is there any indication that *all* ingathering work was finished by the time of the festival. To be sure, the collection of olives had already commenced (cf. Deut. 16:13), but surely once the week-long feast had passed, the farmers returned to gathering up their olives.[71] Neither is the year mentioned in Exod 23:16 likely to be the

---

69. See Shemaryahu Talmon, "The Gezer Calendar and the Seasonal Cycle of Ancient Canaan," in *King, Cult and Calendar in Ancient Israel: Collected Studies* (Jerusalem: Magnes, 1963), 101.

70. Cf. the similar festival at Ugarit, which began on the first day of the month called r'is yn ("First of the Wine"). See Johannes C. de Moor, *New Year with Canaanites and Israelites* (2 vols.; Kampen: Kok, 1972), 1:6, 2:13.

71. It is sometimes asserted that crops in northern Israel matured slightly later than in Judah and that this may account for the statement by the Deuteronomistic Historian that Jeroboam of northern Israel celebrated the Feast of Gathering "on the fifteenth day of the eighth month" (1 Kgs 12:32–33). However, the differences between north and south are somewhat exaggerated. In fact, there is a greater difference between Hebron and the Shephelah (both in the south) in the time of the maturation of the crops than there is between the Shephelah and the Valley of Jezreel (in the north) (see Oded Borowski, *Agriculture in Iron Age Israel* [Winona Lake, Ind.: Eisenbrauns, 1987], 41–42). It is very likely that the agricultural season in both the north and the south were approximately the same.

standard civil year, which, if it commenced in autumn, would do so at the new moon signaling the beginning of the seventh month. The harvest festival would have to take place *before* that date in order for the festival to come at the end of an autumn-based civil year. If we were to take into account the context of this verse, we would find that it sits in the midst of a festival schedule based on a cultic year beginning in spring. The schedule opens with the words "Three times in the year you shall celebrate a festival to me" (14) and ends with "On three occasions in the year every male of yours shall appear before the face of the Lord Yahweh" (17). A presumption of consistency would demand that the word "year" in 23:16 (the only other appearance of the word in this passage) carry the same meaning as in these two verses. That would mean that the year referenced is the festal or liturgical year in all three instances. Perhaps a reason for the confusion is a misunderstanding of the expression צאת השנה, which, instead of meaning the final days or weeks of the year, may mean the final *half* of the liturgical year, from the autumnal equinox to the vernal equinox. We might surmise that there was a parallel term באת השנה to signify the first half of the liturgical year. (For more on the liturgical year, see below.)

1.4.2.2. The Civil Year

The earliest evidence we have discovered for a description of the ancient Israelite year is some writing on a limestone slab that was found in 1908.[72] The inscription is popularly known as the Gezer Calendar, although it is more accurately a list of agricultural activities arranged by months than it is a calendar. The document was written in the lowlands somewhere between 950 and 925 B.C.E. and has been interpreted variously as an administrative document drawn up for the purpose of tax collections and as some kind of mnemonic ditty for children.[73] Whatever its purpose, the Gezer Calendar divides the year into one-month and two-month periods and assigns an agricultural activity to each one.

> Its two months are [olive] harvest,
> Its two months are planting [grain],
> Its two months are late planting,

---

72. Published by Robert A. S. Macalister, *The Excavation of Gezer* (2 vols.; London: Palestine Exploration Fund, 1912), 2:24.
73. William Foxwell Albright, "The Gezer Calendar," *BASOR* 92 (1943): 16–26; Talmon, "Gezer Calendar," 89–91.

Its month is grass-cropping,[74]
Its month is barley harvest,
Its month is harvest and measuring,[75]
Its two months are grape harvesting,[76]
Its month is summer fruit.

The first thing to note is that the list does not begin at the beginning of planting season, but at the time the olive harvest commenced (late September, around the autumnal equinox). Had the months been arranged strictly according to the farmer's schedule, we would have found the olive harvest at the conclusion of the list, so that the eight months of harvest would have been together, and the four months of sowing would have headed the list.[77] Since the agricultural year began with planting season (end of autumn/beginning of winter), an independent, non-agricultural (i.e., civil) calendar must be influencing the order of months in the Gezer Calendar. Moreover, the division into months is reflective of a lunar calendar, which is not the calendar of a farmer. If this document was created for purposes of tax collection, it makes sense to see it as the work of a scribe or administrator who was calibrating the work of the peasants with the civil year. Comparable is the Sumerian "Farmer's Almanac," another document describing yearly agricultural activities, which coincides with the standard Mesopotamian year.[78] P's statement that the spring month Abib should become the first of the months (Exod 12:2) makes it likely that this arrangement reflects an innovation,[79] and thus

---

74. On the translation of פשת, see Talmon, "Gezer Calendar," 92–100; Borowski, *Agriculture in Iron Age Israel*, 34–36.

75. Reading the last word as וכיל; see Borowski, *Agriculture in Iron Age Israel*, 36.

76. On the translation of זמר, see Borowski, *Agriculture in Iron Age Israel*, 36, 38.

77. It is difficult to agree with Clines's assertion that the beginning of the year for a farmer in ancient Palestine would be, not the time of planting, but the autumn, on the ground that it was "the most conspicuous transitional point in the seasonal year" (David J. A. Clines, "The Evidence for an Autumnal New Year in Pre-exilic Israel Reconsidered," *JBL* 93 [1974]: 38). What makes it the most conspicuous transitional point for a farmer?

78. Cohen, *Cultic Calendars*, 384. Another comparable text is found on the second tablet of the ^{mul}APIN series (section XIV), the oldest extant copy being from seventh-century Assyria. Here we find the year divided into four three-month periods, which are calibrated both with the climatic changes of the year and the movement of the sun. See Waerden, *Science Awakening II: The Birth of Astronomy*, 70, 80–83.

79. Goldstein and Cooper argue that Exod 12:2 indicates a change in the new year of only one month (Goldstein and Cooper, "Festivals of Israel and Judah," 22–25). In their view, the New Year and Passover originally were celebrated one month later, but P's legislation moved them to the previous month. To support their claim for the New Year, they cite Amos 5:8 as an indication that the heliacal rising of the Pleiades marked the beginning of

1. CALENDARS 37

we should expect that a calendar beginning on the other side of the year (in the autumn) would have preceded, and possibly also coexisted with, the one beginning in spring.[80] The Gezer Calendar confirms this conclusion.

A civil calendar beginning in the autumn seems not to have been the Canaanite custom, though our data is scanty. At Ugarit the first month of the civil year was *ibʻlt*, which corresponds to March/April. During this month a seven-day kingship festival was celebrated, which suggests that this was also the time of the beginning of regnal years.[81]

It has sometimes been argued that the phrase "summer and winter" found in Gen 8:22 and Ps 74:17 specifies the order of the Judahite civil year.[82] However, Ps 74:17 appears to have been written after the Babylonian desolation of Jerusalem (see vv. 7–8), so we should hesitate to use it as a source for monarchic Judahite custom, and even if it happens to be preexilic, who is to say the expression "summer and winter" is to be equated with the civil year, rather than the priestly festival year, which we are certain commenced in the spring? With regard to Gen 8:22 (J), it is worthwhile to note the order it provides for the year in two other expressions: "planting and harvest" and "cold and heat." The order of these phrases implies the very opposite of "summer and winter." Perhaps the author refers loosely to three different calendars here: 1) the agricultural calendar ("planting and harvest"), 2) the civil calendar ("cold and heat"), and 3) the priestly festival calendar ("summer and

---

the year. However, while Amos 5:8 praises God for the creation of the Pleiades (among other things), I cannot find any reason to take this passage as a calendrical statement. Because Exod 12:2 concerns a change in the year and not a change of Passover date, an argument for a presumed original month of the Passover need not be addressed here. Perhaps the Passover was indeed observed a month later in earlier times. However in such a case it is not likely to have coincided with the beginning of either the agricultural or civil new year.

80. It is sometimes argued that expressions such as "autumn rain and spring rain" (note the order) are found in the preexilic portions of the DH and the early sections of the book of Jeremiah (Deut 11:12, 14; Jer 5:24) and that these imply a year beginning in the autumn. The idea is that a year beginning in spring would encourage the reverse expression, "spring rain and autumn rain." However, while an autumn New Year was probably the reality, because there are not two rainy seasons in the Levant, but only one, which begins in the autumn and ends in early spring, it is highly unlikely that the expression "spring rain and autumn rain" would ever be used, even in a spring-based calendar. Therefore, I do not see this as a valid argument for an autumnal calendar.

81. Cohen, *Cultic Calendars*, 377–78. The Ugaritic cultic year, however, did begin in the autumn.

82. See, e.g., Goldstein and Cooper, "Festivals of Israel and Judah," 22.

winter"). Whatever the case, this instance of the phrase "summer and winter" by itself is insufficient reason to presume a spring-based Judahite civil calendar.

The book of Jeremiah contains the earliest unambiguous references to a civil year beginning in the spring. In the account about Baruch's reading of Jeremiah's scroll to Jehoiakim (written sometime between 605 and the exile), the "ninth month" is clearly set in the wintertime, because the king is in his winter home and has a fire burning to keep him warm (36:22). Unfortunately, because we do not know precisely when this account was composed (it is entirely possible that it was written after the fall of Jerusalem), we cannot say for certain that the spring year was used in preexilic Judah. If the account were written prior to the fall of Jerusalem, it still would have been composed during the period of Babylonian suzerainty, when the Babylonian spring-based calendar would have had a great influence on Judah and therefore is not necessarily a piece of evidence reflective of traditional Judahite custom.

It is true that the Deuteronomic History contains month references that suggest a spring-based year, but these occur only in three places:

(1) *The final chapter of the History* (2 Kgs 25). This, however, is an exilic addition and therefore cannot be used as evidence of preexilic practice.

(2) *The account of Solomon's building projects* (1 Kgs 6:1, 38; 8:2). This account provides both actual month names *and* month numbers. The latter, which do indicate a spring-based year, are probably added by way of explanation. For example, it is stated that, in Solomon's reign, the ark of the covenant was brought to the temple in the month of Ethanim, and then it is added that this was the seventh month (1 Kgs 8:2). However, it would be a mistake to conclude that in Solomon's time, Ethanim was, in fact, the seventh month according to the calendar then in use. The historian apparently needed to add a gloss (marked off by the independent pronoun הוא) explaining to his readers that Ethanim corresponded to month seven because they were not familiar with the old month names. All we can say for sure is that in the *editor's* time, Ethanim corresponded to the seventh month. The month-numbering system that he used might not have corresponded to Judah's civil calendar at all.[83] The same procedure is used in 2 Kgs 25:8, which separates the notice of the month and day from Nebuchadnezzar's regnal datum with the independent pronoun היא. The similarity of the glosses in 1 Kgs 6 and 8 to the data in 2 Kgs 25 suggests that both sets of glosses were added by the reviser of the DH in the exile. The month numbers therefore would not reflect preexilic custom.

(3) *The account of Jeroboam's religious reforms* (1 Kgs 12:32–33). There are indications that these references too are additions. The passage reads:

---

83. And as we shall see below, it did not.

And Jeroboam held a festival **in the eighth month, on the fifteenth day of the month**, like the festival that was in Judah, and he offered upon the altar that he made in Bethel a sacrifice to the calves that he had made, and he put in attendance in Bethel the priests of the high places that he had made. So he offered upon the altar that he made in Bethel, **on the fifteenth day of the eighth month**, in the month he invented for himself, and he held a festival for the Israelites, and he offered upon the altar sacrificial smoke.

As in the case of Solomon's building projects, there is an original, though ambiguous, month reference ("the month he invented for himself") that may have needed further explication for a later audience. However, a version lacking the numbered month references would have read quite smoothly. Indeed the phrase, "on the fifteenth day of the eighth month, in the month he invented for himself," seems somewhat redundant. Further raising our suspicion is the realization that the specific date seems not to carry any significant meaning in the context of the Deuteronomic History. It is only P that provides the day for the Judahite festival (15th day of the 7th month) with which to contrast this one (Lev 23:39, 41; Num 29:12). Only readers familiar with the priestly legislation would note that Jeroboam's festival was precisely one month later. Why would the Deuteronomistic Historian place the exact date here for the northern Israelite festival, but not do the same for the southern Judahite one? It seems unlikely that he would have. The date may therefore have been added by the redactor of the Primary History.

With the above considerations in mind, we should at least acknowledge the possibility that the numbered month references are secondary and that the first edition of the DH did not assume a spring-based civil calendar.

Some have taken the passage in 1 Kgs 12:32–33, regarding Jeroboam, as evidence that, during the divided monarchy, the northern Israelites celebrated their civil new year one month later than did the southern Judahites.[84] However, while it is common to take this passage as a reference to the institution of *permanent* calendar reform, we should be cautious about making such an assumption. These words open a lengthy narrative that continues all the way through the next chapter. All we are told in the present version of the text is that Jeroboam held a festival in the eighth month, and the details of that festival are then recounted: Jeroboam makes an offering upon the altar at Bethel, a man of God prophesies that the altar will be destroyed, Jeroboam orders his guards to seize the prophet, the prophet freezes the king's arm, Jeroboam apologizes, his arm is restored, etc. So it seems we are being told details of

---

84. See, e.g., Shemaryahu Talmon, "Divergences in Calendar-Reckoning in Ephraim and Judah," *VT* 8 (1958): 48–74; Hughes, *Secrets of the Times*, 164–65.

a specific event, rather than a repeating custom. According to the text, this festival was designed to celebrate the inauguration of Jeroboam's new holy places in Bethel and Dan, and the festival in Judah upon which it would be based is the one held a short time earlier by King Solomon to inaugurate his newly-constructed temple (1 Kgs 8). What we have here appears to be a blasphemous, mirror-image version of the temple dedication celebration held in Judah. Essentially Jeroboam is presented as Solomon's evil twin. While it is possible that it was accompanied by a harvest feast,[85] there is no explicit indication of this in the text, much less a New Year celebration. The common practice in the Near East was to commence the civil and regnal years on the new moon closest to one of the equinoxes. A New Year in the late fall, well past the autumnal equinox, would have been strange indeed. So, even if we put trust in the "eighth month" date provided, it may not be particularly significant for a discussion about calendar reform, because this celebration would have happened only once, in Jeroboam's first year, for the probable reason that, in the seventh month, the new shrines had not yet been completed. The delay would have been due to extenuating circumstances.

Another interesting expression, possibly related to the civil year, is תשובת השנה ("the return of the year"). Because the expression is concerned with the time when kings go to war (2 Sam 11:1; 1 Kgs 20:22, 26) and not with agricultural or cultic activity, it seems more likely a civil designation. If so, then because indications are that the civil year began at the new moon closest to the autumnal equinox, this phrase would not refer to the time when the civil year ends and the next begins, but to the time when the year has reached its furthest point and begins its journey back.

1.4.2.3. The Liturgical Year

P's assertion that the spring month of Abib (Mar/Apr) should be the first of the months (Exod 12:2) clearly reveals when the priestly year began. The Passover and the Feast of Unleavened Bread (spring observances) begin the priestly calendar of holy days (Lev 23:4–8). (Neither of these feasts, however, is to be considered a New Year's celebration.)[86] Even in earlier material, in the codes preserved by E (Exod 23:15) and J (Exod 34:18), the festal calendar commences in the spring, so it would seem that, even prior to P, the priests of North and South began their cultic years at the same time, that is, on the

---

85. There seems to have been a connection between the harvest feast and temple dedication. See J. van Goudoever, *Biblical Calendars* (2nd rev. ed.; Leiden: Brill, 1961), 30–35.

86. Norman H. Snaith, *The Jewish New Year Festival* (London: SPCK, 1947), 18–20; Propp, *Exodus 1–18*, 386–87; Milgrom, *Leviticus 23–27*, 2012–18.

new moon nearest the vernal equinox.⁸⁷ One interesting difference between the two codes is that E (Exod 23:16) places the Festival of Ingathering בצאת השנה ("in the exit of the year"), while J (Exod 34:22) has it תקופת השנה ("at the coming around of the year"). As discussed above (in reference to the agricultural year), צאת השנה may refer to the period between the autumn and spring equinoxes, the latter half of the liturgical year. What, however, about תקופת השנה? That it is intended to be an equivalent term is confirmed by the fact that the two passages from which they come are clearly parallel.⁸⁸ The Judahite editor, however, has adapted his version to his own audience. Perhaps צאת השנה had fallen out of use or was not the common expression in the South, and was liable to be misunderstood.⁸⁹ Yet he has not chosen an expression with the same precise meaning, because his term apparently refers to a narrower time period, when the roll of the months reaches the furthest part of the year and begins to come back. It is thus closer in meaning to תשובת השנה (see above on the civil year) than it is to צאת השנה. The only difference is that תשובת השנה is used in connection with the autumn-based civil year, whereas תקופת השנה is employed with reference to the spring-based liturgical year.

The priests were clearly aware of other calendars. In P, the Sabbath and Jubilee laws are based on the agricultural calendar, which begins the year with planting season (Lev 25). The proclamation of the Jubilee at the end of the harvest festival in the seventh month is an accommodation of the civil year, which began with the seventh month.⁹⁰ The holiday calendar from the Holiness Code, in fact, doubly insists that the harvest Festival of Booths *must* be

---

87. This stands in contrast to the material we possess representing northern Canaanite custom. A Phoenican festal calendar is briefly alluded to in an 8th century B.C.E. inscription, and it appears to begin in the autumn. See Moor, *New Year with Canaanites and Israelites*, 2:29–30.

88. Cf. E. Kutsch, "'...am Ende des Jahres': Zur Datierung des israelitischen Herbstfestes in Ex 23,16," *ZAW* 83 (1971): 15–21; see also Wagenaar, *Origin and Transformation*, 9–11.

89. Wagenaar suggests that the reason Exod 34 (which appears to be the later version) reads תקופת השנה is because the civil year no longer ended in the autumn and the earlier expression בצאת השנה was no longer appropriate (Wagenaar, *Origin and Transformation*, 11, 21–22). However I can find no evidence that, in monarchic Judah, the civil calendar *ever* began in the spring. Moreover, because there similarly is no evidence that the civil year ever began after the harvest festival, I cannot accept that the civil year even is being referenced here.

90. The Jubilee itself is both an agricultural and a civil observance (see Hughes, *Secrets of the Times*, 167–68). On the preexilic date of the Jubilee, see Lisbeth S. Fried and David Noel Freedman, "Was the Jubilee Year Observed in Preexilic Judah?" in Jacob Mil-

celebrated in the seventh month (Lev 23:39–41). A concentration of festivals in the seventh month, largely parallel to those in the first month, clearly shows the priests' recognition of the calendric importance of the seventh month, an acknowledgment of the civil year. On the first day there is even a call to blow the trumpets, offer a sacrifice, and rest from labor (Lev. 23:23–25; Num. 29:1–6). We thus see that the priestly cultic calendar, while probably younger than the administrative civil calendar, nevertheless existed side-by-side with it.

1.4.2.4. The Regnal Year

So far it has been determined that the beginning of the civil year in Judah commenced on the new moon closest to the autumnal equinox (Sept. 23), and that, at least in the early period, the year in northern Israel began at the same time. (We have not established, however, the beginning of the civil year in northern Israel after the kingdoms split.) It has also been demonstrated that the agricultural year in both kingdoms began approximately two months later (November 15 or so). The liturgical year began on the new moon nearest the vernal equinox (March 20), but our priestly sources still acknowledge the existence of a civil year beginning in the autumn. What effect do these conclusions have upon our understanding of the regnal year? We should not take it for granted that the regnal year and civil year coincided, but it is likely.

At Babylon and Aššur, the ritual of coronation and renewal of the king's sovereignty seems to have been associated with the New Year's festival and purification of the temple of Marduk.[91] Parallels between the Babylonian purgation of the temple in the spring, at the beginning of its civil year, and Israel's Yom Kippur in the autumn, at the beginning of its civil year, are readily apparent (cf. Ezek 45:18).[92] In Mesopotamia there apparently was a direct connection between the celebration of the assumption of kingship by Marduk and that of the mortal king. We might presume a connection similarly between the liturgical psalms celebrating the enthronement of Yahweh (Pss

---

grom, *Leviticus 23–27: A New Translation and Commentary* (New York: Doubleday, 2001), 2257–70; Milgrom, *Leviticus 23–27*, 2241–48.

91. See Henri Frankfort, *Kingship and the Gods* (Chicago: University of Chicago Press, 1948), 313; Henry W. F. Saggs, *The Greatness that Was Babylon* (New York: Mentor, 1968), 364; Thorkild Jacobsen, "Mesopotamian Gods and Pantheons," in *Toward the Image of Tammuz and Other Essays on Mesopotamian History and Culture* (ed. William L. Moran; Cambridge, Mass.: Harvard University Press, 1970), 16–38, esp. 36–37; Baruch Halpern, *The Constitution of the Monarchy in Israel* (Chico, Calif.: Scholars Press, 1981), 51–61.

92. Milgrom, *Leviticus 1–16*, 1067–71.

47, 93, 95–100) and the enthronement of the Davidic king. Such a celebration is likely to have occurred during the autumnal New Year's festival, and late prophetic material appears to confirm this (e.g., Zech 14:16).[93]

Independent of this argument, we might examine some other evidences of the regnal year. Of the two kingdoms, Judah leaves us with more clues. Most of them come from the period after the fall of the northern kingdom of Israel (ca. 720). At first glance we might conclude that the evidence unambiguously points to a spring-based calendar. One significant text is 2 Kgs 25:8 (= Jer 52:12), which dates the destruction of Jerusalem's temple to the fifth month. Since we know from the Babylonian records that the city fell in the month of August, there is no doubt that, according to the system used here by the historian, the year began in the spring. Another significant text, the context of which is in the reign of King Jehoiakim, is Jer 36:22 (mentioned earlier), which clearly places the "ninth month" in the wintertime. This piece of evidence also points to a system governed by a spring regnal new year.[94] However, these evidences are based on the assumption that the calendar by which the historian was dating these events was Judah's *regnal* calendar. We should be reluctant to put too much weight on these data. The historian's information does not always derive from government sources, and his point of view shifts frequently. He may also speak on occasion (or even often) from the context of his own times. We thus are unable to use the datum at Jer 36:22 as evidence that the beginning of the regnal new year in Judah in Jehoiakim's reign was in the spring. The most we can say is that, by the calendar to which the scribe himself was accustomed at the time of writing, the year began in the spring. That calendar may not have been, and, as we shall see, in all likelihood was not, the regnal calendar of Judah. It more probably was the civil calendar of Babylon.

All other indications, to my knowledge, point to a regnal year beginning in the autumn in the latter days of Judah. For example, the data in 2 Kgs 22 and 23 place the beginning of King Josiah's temple reparations and religious reforms and the subsequent Passover celebration all within his eighteenth regnal year. Since the Passover would have fallen on the fourteenth day of

---

93. For full discussions, see Sigmund Mowinckel, *Psalmenstudien* (2 vols.; Amsterdam: Schippers, 1966); Halpern, *The Constitution of the Monarchy in Israel*, 61–109; C. L. Seow, *Myth, Drama, and the Politics of David's Dance* (HSM 44; Atlanta: Scholars Press, 1989); Goldstein and Cooper, "Festivals of Israel and Judah," 26–27; J. J. M. Roberts, "Mowinckel's Enthronement Festival: A Review," in *The Book of Psalms: Composition and Reception* (ed. P. W. Flint and P. D. Miller Jr.; VTSup 99; Leiden: Brill, 2005), 97–115.

94. E.g., Gershon Galil, *The Chronology of the Kings of Israel and Judah* (SHANE 9; Leiden; New York: Brill, 1996), 9–10.

the presumed first month, the assumption of a spring regnal new year would require us to believe that the work of the repair and all involved with it was accomplished in a two-week span. It is more reasonable to conclude that the repairs began prior to the first day of that month, in which case that month could not have been the first one of the year, and we would then have to posit that Josiah's eighteenth year began in the autumn.[95]

We have additional indications of an autumn-based regnal year from the reign of Zedekiah. The historian's sources place the fall of Jerusalem in Zedekiah's eleventh year (2 Kgs 25:2) and in Nebuchadnezzar of Babylon's nineteenth year (2 Kgs 25:8). In the book of Jeremiah, in a description of events associated with the Babylonian siege, Baruch connects Zedekiah's tenth year with Nebuchadnezzar's eighteenth (Jeremiah 32:1). Seemingly, then, the regnal years of these two kings coincided exactly, and it is well known that Nebuchadnezzar's regnal years began in the spring, on the 1st day of Nisan.[96] However, additional data do not support this presumption and suggest that their regnal years merely overlapped in the summertime. Jeremiah 32 recounts the visit of Hanamel, Jeremiah's cousin, to Jeremiah in the court of the guard sometime after the defeat of Pharaoh Hophra's forces by the Babylonians and the resumption of Nebuchadnezzar's siege of Jerusalem. When was this? An oracle of Ezekiel, recounted in the third month of the eleventh year (by Babylonian reckoning) of the captivity of King Jehoiachin, mentions the defeat of the Egyptians as having happened recently, probably a few months before (Ezekiel 31). Jehoiachin's captivity began on the first day of the Babylonian year, Nisan of 597. Therefore the eleventh year of his captivity ran from Nisan 587 to Adar 586. Since Zedekiah was placed on the throne immediately after Jehoaichin, if his regnal years were counted from Nisan, then the years of his reign and the years of Jehoiachin's captivity would correspond precisely. However, if Zedekiah's eleventh year ran from Nisan 587 to Adar 586, it would coincide with Nebuchadnezzar's eighteenth year, not his nineteenth, as the data in 2 Kings 25 indicate. If, on the other hand, Zedekiah began counting his reign in the autumn after the captivity began (597), his eleventh year would run from the autumn of 587 to the autumn of 586, and there would be an overlap with Nebuchadnezzar's eighteenth *and* nineteenth years. All of the chronological pieces would fall into place. It seems best, therefore, to understand the Judahite regnal new year as begin-

---

95. Argument also in Edwin R. Thiele, *The Mysterious Numbers of the Hebrew Kings* (3rd ed.; Grand Rapids: Eerdmans, 1983), 29–30.

96. Francesca Rochberg, "Astronomy and Calendars in Ancient Mesopotamia," in *Civilizations of the Ancient Near East* (ed. Jack M. Sasson; New York: Scribner's Sons, 1995), 1931.

ning in the autumn, rather than in the spring, at least in the later monarchic period (Josiah through Zedekiah).[97] The custom of counting the kings' years from the autumn was certainly not in keeping with the Babylonian or Assyrian systems. The implication is that the Judahite system was a preservation of a system that had been in use for some time before Assyria and Babylon had gained influence in the area.[98]

How far back did Judah count its regnal years from the autumn? We cannot say for certain, but it is worth noting that the Deuteronomistic Historian assumes an autumnal regnal year even as far back as the reign of Solomon. According to 1 Kgs 6:37–38, Solomon began the temple construction in the month of Ziv (April/May) of his fourth regnal year and finished the work in the month of Bul (October/November) of his eleventh regnal year. If the regnal year began in the spring, then each building season, which lasted from spring to autumn while the weather was friendly, would have been contained in a single regnal year. The total number of years taken up by this project, then, would be eight: (1) fourth year; (2) fifth year; (3) sixth year; (4) seventh year; (5) eighth year; (6) ninth year; (7) tenth year; (8) eleventh year.[99] On the other hand, if the regnal year began in the autumn, then each building season would cover part of two regnal years. The total number of years taken up by this project, then, would be seven: (1) fourth–fifth year; (2) fifth–sixth year; (3) sixth–seventh year; (4) seventh–eighth year; (5) eighth–ninth year; (6) ninth–tenth year; (7) tenth–eleventh year. The Historian, gives the total time as seven years (6:38), thus assuming an autumnal

---

97. See Julian Morganstern, "The New Year for Kings," in *Occident and Orient: Being Studies in Semitic Philology and Literature, Jewish History and Philosophy and Folklore in the Widest Sense* (ed. Bruno Schindler; London: Taylor's Foreign Press, 1936), 448–50; Fried and Freedman, "Was the Jubilee Year Observed in Preexilic Judah?," 2259–61.

98. Hayes makes the argument that, because the Babylonian chronicles assign Nebuchadnezzar's first Akitu festival to his accession year, rather than to his first regnal year, it was customary for the Babylonians to begin the regnal year after the Akitu festival (mid-Nisan). He then suggests that Israel and Judah likewise began their regnal years after their festivals (John H. Hayes, "The Beginning of the Regnal Year in Israel and Judah," in *The Land That I Will Show You: Essays on the History and Archaeology of the Ancient Near East in Honour of J. Maxwell Miller* [ed. John A. Dearman and Matt P. Graham; JSOTSup 343; Sheffield: Sheffield Academic Press, 2001], 92–95). However, another Neo-Babylonian source, the Chronicle of Nabonidus, indicates in several places a regnal year beginning prior to the festival. It is unlikely that the beginning of a year would not coincide with the beginning of a month.

99. Years were counted inclusively. See full discussion in ch. 2 below.

regnal year.[100] Although we cannot say for certain that he counted the years according to early monarchic custom, without any evidence to the contrary, it is best to assume some consistency between the earlier and later periods and between the civil and regnal calendars.

There is no direct evidence in the biblical text whether the northern kingdom of Israel counted its king's reigns from the autumn or spring. We should be inclined to think that the northern kingdom followed past custom from the united monarchy and began the civil and regnal year in the autumn. However, there is evidence to suggest that Israel's regnal new year did *not* coincide with that of Judah. If we take a look at the Deuteronomic History's chronology for the reign of King Zechariah of Israel, we observe that he began to rule in the thirty-eighth year of Azariah of Judah and ruled for only six months (2 Kgs 15:8). Yet his reign ended in the thirty-ninth year of Azariah (2 Kgs 15:10). For this to be true, the regnal new year in Judah would have passed during that six-month period, but not the regnal new year in Israel. Otherwise, Zechariah would have been assigned a full regnal year by the chronographers.[101] A different regnal calendar year in Israel, therefore, would appear likely. To be sure, this argument assumes chronological agreement between the synchronisms and the reign total—in other words that the data would have to derive from the same source or from sources employing an identical method of calculation. As I will argue in ch. 4, there is strong evidence to suggest that the synchronisms and the reign totals come from two different sources. However, other factors, discussed in ch. 4, indicate that the northern Israelite reign totals reflect the same system of counting as the synchronisms (antedating). So this piece of evidence does seem to be a clear indicator of a regnal year in Israel that *did not begin in the autumn*, at least in the time of Zechariah. This leads us to believe that the civil and regnal year began in the spring, the most common time to begin a year in the ancient Near East. I will therefore tentatively assume the Israelite regnal year began in the spring. We do not know how long it would have been the custom there, but with no other compelling evidence either way, it seems best to assume consistency and that there was a difference between Israel and Judah's regnal calendars for most of Israel's history.

---

100. Thiele, *Mysterious Numbers of the Hebrew Kings*, 28–29. Remember that the month numbers in this part of the text are probably secondary (see above).

101. Hayim Tadmor, "The Chronology of the First Temple Period: A Presentation and Evaluation of the Sources," in *Age of the Monarchies: Political History* (ed. Abraham Malamat and Israel Eph'al; Jerusalem: Massada, 1979), 50–51.

1.5. Lunar, Solar, and Lunisolar Calendars

Because it is much shorter than the tropical year, and because its beginning and end were more obvious and determinable with precision than that of the tropical year, the lunar month was often the benchmark of ancient calendars. In a strictly lunar calendar, time is simply measured month by month, and observation of the moon's phases settles the length of each month (twenty-nine or thirty days). A whole number of synodic months does not fit into a tropical year. The number that comes closest to 365¼ days is twelve, but twelve lunar months amount to only 354 days on the average (29.5 × 12), which is eleven days short of the tropical year. Thus, if a society were to employ a strictly lunar calendar, satisfied with twelve lunar months per "year," there would be little correlation between the months and the seasons of the year. A month that at one time came in the summer would, within the lifetime of one person, come also in the winter. This is the result of the eleven-day discrepancy between a tropical and a lunar year, building up year after year.[102] Any religious observances connected with seasonal phenomena would be thrown off. For this reason, most ancient calendars were not strictly lunar.

Attempts were almost always made to adjust the cycle of lunar months to coincide with the tropical year. The most common technique for harmonizing a lunar calendar with the solar year is intercalation, which is the insertion into the calendar of an extra month every so often, or, perhaps to phrase it more accurately, delaying the beginning of a new year by one month.[103] So, for example, after three lunar years, the lunar calendar would be about thirty-three days short of the point in the tropical year at which it began, but another month could be added in that third year that would bring the calendar within three or four days of its original starting point. Calendars that employ intercalation of this sort are technically lunisolar calendars, although "lunar calendar" is still an appropriate term.

Solar calendars keep track only of the natural day and the tropical year. The month may be included in a solar calendar, but if so, is merely assigned an arbitrary number of days and has no relation to the actual phases of the

---

102. The Assyrian calendar from the second millennium B.C.E. would fall into this category (Cohen, *Cultic Calendars*, 17, 239).

103. This was the custom in ancient Babylon before a more precise system was developed (Parker, *Babylonian Chronology, 626 B.C.–A.D. 75*, 1; Rochberg, "Astronomy and Calendars in Ancient Mesopotamia," 1931–32; Britton, "Calendars, Intercalations and Year-Lengths," 119–21, 124–30). See also Fleming, *Time at Emar*, 214–18. The Greeks also practiced this system for a time (Hannah, *Time in Antiquity*, 22, 31–32).

moon. Nevertheless, because a whole number of days does not fit into a tropical year, a solar calendar has problems of its own. The incompatibility between days and years would not pose a serious problem in the short term (365 days is only one-quarter of a day short of an actual tropical year), but over a long period of time the discrepancy would become more and more noticeable. In 730 years, the seasons would be completely reversed.[104]

It is not difficult to determine which sort of calendar was used in ancient Israel. The agricultural year, based on the seasons, would necessarily be solar in nature and not connected to any lunar cycle. Because of the evidence that the phases of the moon were observed by both officials and priests (see above), the civil, regnal, and liturgical years must have begun always on the first day of a lunar month. However the time of year was also important. In a strictly lunar calendar, the New Year would not be fixed to any season. Yet the Gezer Calendar assumes a civil year that consistently begins with the olive harvest, thus presupposing harmonization with the solar year. We can confidently assume that a lunisolar civil calendar was in place.[105] We have no direct evidence from the Bible, but the Israelites probably would have used the common ancient Near Eastern system of intercalation: each year contained twelve months (cf. 1 Kgs 4:7–19), and every three years or so, the new year would be delayed so that one more month could pass. What about the liturgical year? Can the same be said for the priestly calendar? Its first month, Abib, is named for a seasonal occurrence (the new grain, the ripening of the barley) and must have coincided with that season year after year. Since the moon appears to have been observed by priests (Gen 1:14) and seasonal festivals are precisely dated, there is little doubt that the priestly calendar too, although beginning at a different time of year, also was lunisolar in character.

---

104. As in the Egyptian solar calendar (Clagett, *Calendars, Clocks, and Astronomy*, 28–37).

105. See J. B. Segal, "Intercalation and the Hebrew Calendar," *VT* 7 (1957): 250–307; de Vaux, *Ancient Israel: Its Life and Institutions*, 188–90; Hughes, *Secrets of the Times*, 161–65.

2
Long-Time Reckoning

2.1. The Counting of Time Units

A once popular theory was that, whereas we moderns tend to think of time as moving in a line, the ancient peoples thought of it as moving in a circle.[1] This rather tidy view is unsupported by the facts. It is evident that by the first millennium B.C.E. most societies maintained *both* a cyclic and a linear understanding of time. Festivals and rituals observed in response to predictable and repeating natural phenomena are attuned to the cycles of time, while an interest in tying events of the past to those of more immediate recollection depends on a linear understanding of time, in which events succeed one

---

1. An idea made famous in Mircea Eliade, *Cosmos and History: The Myth of the Eternal Return* (trans. Willard K. Trask; New York: Harper & Row, 1959). Eliade rightly calls attention to the various rites in ancient societies through which cosmic myths are relived year after year, but note his far-reaching conclusions:
 What is of chief importance to us in these archaic systems is the abolition of concrete time, and hence their antihistorical intent. This refusal to preserve the memory of the past, even of the immediate past, seems to us to betoken a particular anthropology. We refer to archaic man's refusal to accept himself as a historical being, his refusal to grant value to memory and hence to the unusual events (i.e., events without an archetypal model) that in fact constitute concrete duration. In the last analysis, what we discover in all these rites and all these attitudes is the will to devalue time. Carried to their extreme, all the rites and all the behavior patterns that we have so far mentioned would be comprised in the following statement: "If we pay no attention to it, time does not exist; furthermore, where it becomes perceptible—because of man's 'sins,' i.e., when man departs from the archetype and falls into duration—time can be annulled." Basically, if viewed in its proper perspective, the life of archaic man (a life reduced to the repetition of archetypal acts, that is, to categories and not to events, to the unceasing rehearsal of the same primordial myths), although it takes place in time, does not bear the burden of time, does not record time's irreversibility; in other words, completely ignores what is especially characteristic and decisive in a consciousness of time. Like the mystic, like the religious man in general, the primitive lies in a continual present.

another and are related through cause and effect. A system for measuring cyclic time is the calendar. Linear time was measured in the ancient world as well. How? The answer may seem obvious, but it bears articulating: by counting units of time in sequence. The very act of counting is a linear function, and the counting of non-recurring time units is practiced in all societies.[2] In relating one event to another in linear time, the space is measured by the number of units between one occurrence and another. This space can be measured in small or large units: days, weeks, months, seasons, years, etc. Thus in the Bible, for example, the ark was in the hands of the Philistines for seven months (1 Sam 6:1) and in Kireath-jearim for twenty years (1 Sam 7:2); Nabal dies ten days after David decides to spare his life (1 Sam 25:38), and Menahem reigns ten years (2 Kgs 15:17); the Israelites are in the wilderness for forty years (Num 14:34), and the census taken by David takes nine months and twenty days (2 Sam 24:8) (cf. also Num 11:19–20; Deut 1:2; 1 Sam 30:13). Note that these are not measurements of the length of repeated yearly observances, but of historical events—they happen just once in time, and then they are over.

The system of counting used in the sources is a bit different from our own, and it is important to have an understanding of this system whenever one is working in biblical chronology. Their use of ordinal numbers (first, second, third, etc.) conforms to our modern understanding. The unit counted first was called the first, the second was called the second, and so on. We are always situated in a particular unit of time, whether that is a day, a month, a year, and, if we count forward or backward, we consider that unit to be the first in the sequence. Thus if I am counting days forward (using ordinal num-

---

2. Note the difference between "non-recurring" and "non-cyclical." Jean-Jacques Glassner asserts that "Mesopotamia did not know linear time," because even when concerned in matters of historical chronology, the chronographers measured by units of time that were cyclical—years, months, and days (Jean-Jacques Glassner, *Mesopotamian Chronicles* [SBLWAW 19; Atlanta: Society of Biblical Literature, 2004], 7). However, use of a cyclical unit does not make the measurement itself cyclical. Under such an assumption, there would be no such thing as linear time in *any* culture. A unit of measurement, such as a year, may be cyclical, but in linear measurement the unit is not repeated. That the Mesopotamians knew linear time is shown in B. Albrektson, *History and the Gods: An Essay on the Idea of Historical Events as Divine Manifestations in the Ancient Near East and in Israel* (Lund: Gleerup, 1967), see esp. 94–95. Further observations are made in Fleming, *Time at Emar*, 218–21. On the Greeks, see Arnaldo Momigliano, "Time in Ancient Historiography," in *History and the Concept of Time* (History and Theory 6: Middletown, Conn.: Wesleyan University Press, 1966), 12–14. See also Astrid Möller and Nino Luraghi, "Time in the Writing of History: Perceptions and Structures," *Storia della Storiografia* 28 (1995): 6–7.

bers), today is the first day, tomorrow the second, and so on. The Israelites counted the same way.

Cardinal numbers (1, 2, 3, etc.), however, are another matter entirely. The ancient Israelites employed an *inclusive* system of counting, reflected in all of the sources. An inclusive system assigns each and every unit a number; the first unit counted is called both "one" and "first" (cf. Gen 1:5, which could be translated either way). Occasionally we do this too: for example, when I say, "I was sick for three days," I am probably counting inclusively (e.g., Tuesday, Wednesday, and Thursday). However, we moderns do not always assign the number one to the first unit in a sequence. When it comes to *measuring the distance between two points in time*, we count the units exclusively. In an exclusive count, the first unit is assigned no number.[3] For example in measuring the distance between today and a day in the future, we do not count today at all, but start with tomorrow. Thus tomorrow is *one* day from now, the day after that is *two* days from now, and so on. This is not how the Israelites counted. They counted inclusively, even when measuring the distance between two points in time. *Today* they would call *one* day, tomorrow two days, the day after tomorrow three days, etc. According to their point of view, exactly one week from now would be eight days, while for us it would be only seven days.

TABLE 2.1. THE COUNT OF DAYS

Exclusive count		1	2	3	4	5	6	7
	Sun	Mon	Tue	Wed	Thu	Fri	Sat	Sun
Inclusive count	1	2	3	4	5	6	7	8

Evidence for this custom is all over the Bible. So, for example, in J and E we have numerous occasions where the "third day" and "three days" are used to refer to the passage of the same amount of time (Gen 30:36 and 31:22; 40:19–20; 42:17–18; Exod 19:15–16). In the DH, we find identical usage (Josh 9:16–17; Judg 14:14–15; 1 Kgs 12:5, 12). Also, "third year" and "three years" mark equal lengths of time (Deut 14:28 and 26:12; 1 Kgs 22:1, 2; 2 Kgs 18:9–10), and so do "seventh year" and "seven years" (Deut 15:1, 9; Judg 14:17). In

---

3. Or a zero. The ancient Israelites, however, had no zero.

P, "seventh day" and "seven days" are employed similarly (Exod 12:15; Lev 13:4–6), as are "fiftieth day" and "fifty days" (Lev 23:16). To put this point another way, we might say that, for the Israelites, cardinal and ordinal numbers did not reflect two different ways of counting, but only two different points of reference. A cardinal number signified the entire period that had passed, whereas an ordinal number marked only the end-point of that period.

It is not true that inclusive counting is reserved only for small numbers (less than ten).[4] Although larger figures are scarcer in the text, we find that, when they do appear, inclusive counting is still the rule. Thus in Gen 14, Chedorlaomer is served by the cities up until the twelfth year, and this is counted as "twelve years" (Gen 14:4). The prophet Jeremiah counts twenty-three years from the thirteenth year of Josiah to the fourth year of Jehoiakim (Jer 25:3). With Judah on an accession-year system (postdating),[5] this can only be possible if the count is inclusive. By our count it is only twenty-two years. P's Jubilee Year seems to be counted the same way as its Jubilee Day (thus the fiftieth year would be counted as fifty years). Although R is later than P, when P says that Noah was six hundred years old at the flood (Gen 7:6), R understands that to mean Noah's six hundreth year (Gen 7:11). I have not, as yet, been able to find a single exception to this system of counting in any preexilic text.

Persons who are familiar with ancient Israelite inclusive counting might become confused when they become aware of the manner in which two time periods, each containing multiple units, are added together. In biblical reckoning, if a period of three years is added to another period of three years, the total number of years is six. This seems perfectly normal. It is simple math. However, what happened to the inclusive count? Remember that, in an inclusive count, the first and last units in a sequence are understood to be incomplete, because the count starts somewhere within that first unit, and not necessarily at its beginning, and ends somewhere within the last unit, and not necessarily at its end. So in a period of three years, Year 1 and Year 3 might not be full years, and we might estimate that only two years had passed. So some might believe that when another inclusively-counted period of three years is tacked on, there would be only four years accounted for, and this would be reckoned by the Israelites as five years inclusive.[6] However, further examination will lay this notion to rest.

---

4. As implied in Clines, "The Evidence for an Autumnal New Year," 30.
5. This will be demonstrated in ch. 4.
6. Clines makes this error ("The Evidence for an Autumnal New Year," 30–31).

The implication of this sort of reasoning is that somehow Year 3 of the first group of years (being incomplete) and Year 1 of the second group (also being incomplete) would together form a complete year. All together we would then have:

(1) a partial Year 1,
(2) a full Year 2,
(3) a partial Year 3 and a partial Year 1, together making one full year,
(4) a full Year 2, and
(5) a partial Year 3.

Yet this is not how the count is made. The ancient Israelites did not take the final unit in one time segment and combine it with the first unit in a succeeding time segment to consider them one unit. Indeed, a count by itself does not make explicit how long the partial years are; two of them together could very well add up to more than twelve months. Even if not, the final unit in the first segment of time is already accounted for; it has a number, and it stands alone. The same can be said of the first unit in the second segment of time; it also has a number and stands alone. The two are never counted as one, even if both are incomplete.

Perhaps this point is best illustrated by the case involving the twenty years that Solomon is said to have taken to build the temple and the king's palace. The twenty years is the sum of two lesser periods: the seven years it took to build the temple (1 Kgs 6:38), and the thirteen years it took to build the palace (1 Kgs 7:1). An inclusively-reckoned seven years and an inclusively reckoned thirteen years, if the final year of the first segment and the first year of the second were together counted as one, would total nineteen inclusive years, not twenty.[7] However that is not the case, and this makes sense if we consider the nature of the construction work.

TABLE 2.2. TIME COVERED BY SOLOMON'S BUILDING ACTIVITIES

Exclusive Year Count	Inclusive Year Count	Description of Project	Correct Inclusive Count of Each Period	Incorrect Inclusive Count of Each Period
0	1	Temple work	1	1
1	2	Temple work	2	2

---

7. This is what Clines maintains (Clines, "The Evidence for an Autumnal New Year," 31).

2	3	Temple work	3	3
3	4	Temple work	4	4
4	5	Temple work	5	5
5	6	Temple work	6	6
6	7	Temple work	7	7/1 (temple and palace)
7	8	Palace work	1	2
8	9	Palace work	2	3
9	10	Palace work	3	4
10	11	Palace work	4	5
11	12	Palace work	5	6
12	13	Palace work	6	7
13	14	Palace work	7	8
14	15	Palace work	8	9
15	16	Palace work	9	10
16	17	Palace work	10	11
17	18	Palace work	11	12
18	19	Palace work	12	13
19	20	Palace work	13	

The season of building occurs once every year. When the work ends, it goes on hiatus until the following year. So the last year of temple work was not likely also to have been the first year of palace work; the seventh year of temple building would conclude one year, and the palace project would commence the following year. What we have here are two periods (seven years and thirteen years) reckoned inclusively, but there is no merging of years, so they add up to twenty. Another example occurs in Joshua, where Caleb says forty-five years have passed since Moses sent him to spy the land (Josh 14:10). Because he is counting inclusively, he means forty-five different years (we would measure this as forty-four years). The first forty years of his life (14:7), also counted inclusively, refers to forty different years (we would measure this as 39). Yet, because the first year of the forty-five-year segment comes *after* the fortieth year of his life (they each are different years), he thus can say the total is eighty-five inclusive years (eighty-four in our own reckoning). We find a similar example in P. In the genealogy of Gen 5, each entry consists of two periods of time, the years from a man's birth until the birth of his son, and the period from the birth of his son to his own death. The second period begins the year *after* the first period ends, and so we can add together the two figures normally. These examples illustrate the way time units are counted in all situations: each unit carries one, and only one, number.

This being the case, how might we understand compound designations, such as "one year and four months" (1 Sam 27:7)? "One year" would refer to the "first year." The "four months," then, which cannot overlap with the first year, must occur in the second year, but, because of an inclusive count, would refer to a period of time between three and four months. In other words, the expression "one year and four months" is equivalent to saying: "from the first year until the fourth month of the second year," or perhaps, "all the first year, and up until the fourth month of the second year." It would depend upon whether the writer was referring to calendar years or actual time. Since months were probably not numbered by the Deuteronomistic Historian, we should probably assume this measurement is in actual time, and therefore the second interpretation is most likely.

To review the principles of counting, we note three important points:

(1) All individual units of time (day, months, years, etc.) are added inclusively, so in translating into our own system of counting, we should subtract one unit from the total to make an Israelite cardinal number into one of our cardinal numbers.

(2) When adding together two or more segments of time, the Israelites did not overlap them. When converting to our own system of measurement, this is actually convenient for us, because we can add the numbers together normally, remembering simply to subtract one unit from the total ($[X + Y + Z]-1$). Alternately, to be more precise, because the nature of the difference between their custom and ours has to do with when the count starts, we could subtract one unit from the first figure and add the rest normally ($[X-1] + Y + Z$).

(3) In keeping with this understanding, when encountering compound figures (e.g., ten years and six months), we should realize that each part is inclusive, but there is no overlap (in this case, ten years and six months is equivalent to saying: "until the sixth month of the eleventh year").

Fortunately, the inclusive counting practice is of importance chiefly when we are in the realm of applied chronology, converting the dates of the sources into units of our own reckoning. When dealing with ancient Israelite chronography on its own, we need not get bogged down in conversions (and we won't).

2.2. The Use of Eras

The counting of years is a prominent feature of two of the ancient histories of Israel (P and the DH). Units are always counted individually (1, 2, 3, 4…) and measured from an important date (the birth of a famous person, the accession of a ruler, or a significant event), and end at an important date. Interestingly the span of time between these two dates is quite short, usually only a handful of years. P employs a system of chronology based on the births of important people (genealogical in nature), which will be explored in the following chapter. The dates of events are not counted from a point in time in the distant past, but rather associated with a contemporary figure. The DH similarly dates events within the terms of judges and kings, which will be explored in ch. 4. It is rare to find, in these histories, events dated according to an *era* (a lengthy succession of years proceeding from a fixed point in time or *epoch*). Nevertheless, there are a few instances in which this method is used.

Eras in any civilization were not always generated immediately when a great event occurred. More often they were created retrospectively as aids to the study of historical chronology. Such was the case with the era by which we count years today (c.e.), and such appears to be the case in both P and the DH.

The DH dates the building of the temple by the Israelites' exodus from Egypt: "And it was in the 480th year after the Israelites came out from the land of Egypt, in the fourth year, in the month of Ziv, that is, the second month, after Solomon became king over Israel, that he built the house to Yahweh" (1 Kgs 6:1).

The number 480 in the DH is a multiple of 12 and 40, the number of months in a year (12) and the length of a Deuteronomic generation (40 years).[8] This does not necessarily mean that the editor was saying that 12 generations passed between the exodus and Solomon. The two numbers may

---

8. On generations, see below.

have been chosen simply because they were symbolically meaningful. The parts of that 480 years are laid out in the DH rather explicitly.[9]

> 45 years for the exodus and Conquest (Josh 14:10)
> 70 years for the periods of oppression (Judg 3:8, 14; 4:3; 6:1; 10:8)
> 200 years for the periods of rest (Judg 3:3, 11; 5:31; 8:28)
> 76 years for the minor judges (Judg 10:1–4; 12:7–15)
> 3 years for the reign of Abimelech (Judg 9:22)
> 40 years for the Philistine oppression (Judg 13:1)[10]
> 2 years for Saul (1 Sam 13:1)[11]
> 40 years for David (1 Kgs 2:11)
> 3 years for Solomon (1 Kgs 6:1).[12]

The symbolic significance of the 480 years makes it more likely that the periods within the larger period were arranged so that they added up to 480 years than that these smaller periods were simply added up and happened to equal 480 years. Keep in mind that the number 480 is ordinal, and so the period measured would, by our reckoning, equal 479 years. Even without having the total figure, we could count the parts inclusively (one year would be subtracted from the first block of time), and the total would be 479 years.

The DH refers to this era only once, and no other events in the work are dated by it. Neither does any work prior to the DH date by this era. This

---

9. A similar count is made in Wolfgang Richter, *Die Bearbeitung des "Retterbuches" in der deuteronomistischen Epoche* (Bonn: Hanstein, 1964), 132–41, but Richter ignores the figures in Judg 9:22, 10:8, and 13:1.

10. This would include the terms of Samson and Samuel. The note at Judg 15:20 states a term of twenty years for Samson, which is placed "in the days of the Philistines" and thus assumes the period of Philistine oppression mentioned in 13:1 and must be included in the forty years. A term for Samuel is conspicuously absent from the text, but it most likely was understood to coincide with the final years of the Philistine oppression. The oppression clearly ends when Samuel is judge (1 Sam 7:13). The narrative could be interpreted to mean that his judgeship continues *after* the oppression is over, but the statement that "the hand of Yahweh was against the Philistines all the days of Samuel" suggests that the chronographer was counting the full term of Samuel in the oppression period.

11. Normally thought of as a scribal mistake, the short reign of Saul seems to fit just right into the 480-year period. Was the length of his reign shortened deliberately by the Deuteronomistic editor? Or is the figure original? See Klaas A. D. Smelik, "Saul, de voorstelling van Israëls eerste koning in de Masoretische tekst van het Oude Testament" (Ph.D. diss., Universiteit van Amsterdam, 1977), 69–71.

12. In an accession-year system of counting regnal years, Solomon's fourth year would have marked four actual years from his accession, but the Deuteronomistic editor seems not to have taken this into consideration and counted normally.

makes it highly likely that the era is the DH's own creation. Interestingly, the redactor of the Primary History also dates the events of the wilderness wanderings from the exodus in his waystation notices. Perhaps he does so simply because it is a logical date from which to count, but R's knowledge of the DH makes it quite possible that he purposefully is dating according to the era created by the DH. R, however, does not continue dating past the 41st year.

P places its own epoch at the entry of the Israelites into Egypt: "And the dwelling of the Israelites, who had dwelt in Egypt, was 430 years. And it was at the end of the 430 years, and it was on this day exactly that all the armies of Yahweh went out from the land of Egypt" (Exod 12:40–41).

Because no events are dated according to this period of time (i.e., nothing is placed X years from the entry into Egypt), apart from the exodus itself, it seems probable that the era is a creation of P. The number 430 has tended to defy attempts to give it symbolic meaning. It may simply be an educated guess but is almost certainly an inflation of the oppression period, which if historical, was probably much shorter. The priests may have inherited a tradition that the time of Joseph lay some 400 years into the past. However, the precise figure of 430 years may indeed be a priestly creation. It makes more sense when considered a part of P's larger chronological framework. P's genealogical chronology puts the birth of Jacob exactly 130 years before the entry into Egypt (Gen 47:7–9), and the Israelites' entry into the Promised Land exactly 40 years after the exodus (Num 14:33–34). With the oppression 430 years long, the period from the birth of Jacob (Israel) to the entry into the Promised Land (Israel) would amount to exactly 600 years, a multiple of the numbers 12 and 50. The significance and sacredness of the number 12 in Israelite and Jewish literature is well known. The number 50 is also a special number in the priestly material (cf. Lev 23:15; Lev 25:10). The choice of 430 years may have been governed by the desire to make the total time, from the appearance of Israel as a man to the appearance of Israel as a country, equal 600 years.

2.3. Counting Generations

The Hebrew word דור (*dôr*) has the basic sense of "circle," with specific reference to a circular hut, and the meaning "assembly" is an extension of this basic sense.[13] It is unclear from which sense of the word the Bible's most

---

13. Frank J. Neuberg, "An Unrecognized Meaning of Hebrew *dôr*," *JNES* 9 (1950): 215–17; Peter R. Ackroyd, "The Meaning of Hebrew דור Considered," *JSS* 13 (1968): 3–10; David Noel Freedman and Jack R. Lundbom, "דור," *TDOT* 3:169–81.

common meaning of דור ("generation") derives (is it a "circle" of time, or an "assembly" of people?). A generation in ancient Israel was, as it is today, a group of individuals constituting a single step in the line of descent from an ancestor (cf. Exod 20:5).[14] When used as a measurement of time, it would naturally refer to the period between a point in one man's life and the same point in the life of his offspring, for example, from a man's birth until the birth of his son(s). Since the age of a man at the birth of his children can vary, so the lengths of the generations may vary. Job was able to see his descendants to the fourth generation and himself lived 140 years (Job 42:16). If five generations (i.e., four generations plus Job himself)[15] encompass 140 years, the assumption is that a generation is equivalent to 28 years. Sometimes an author may use an average figure for a generation to make approximate calculations. The Deuteronomistic Historian, for example, assumes 40 years for a generation (Jos. 5:6–7) and uses this figure frequently (see ch. 4).

One biblical example is sometimes provided to show that דור may, when used as a length of measurement, also mean "life span."[16] Genesis 15:16 (J) states that the Israelites will return from their oppression "in the fourth *dôr*" (דור רביעי). This statement appears to be supported by the redactor's genealogy of Exod 6:16–20, which recounts the immediate ancestors of Moses: Levi, Kohath, and Amram. Since Levi's generation is the one that entered Egypt, and Moses's generation is one that left, we find four generations covering the period of the Israelites' residence in Egypt. However, both Gen 15:13 (J) and Exod 12:40 (P) state that the period of the Israelites' residence in Egypt amounted to at least 400 years. This seems far too long for four *generations*. This has led some to conclude that that the דורות (*dôrôt*) mentioned in Gen 15:16 are, in fact, life spans rather than generations.[17] The life spans of Levi, Kohath and Amram add up to 407 years (137 + 133 + 137 = 407), approximately equal to the period of Egyptian residence. So it might seem that whoever calculated the length of the period did so by adding up the life spans of these men (or, alternately, by dividing the 400 odd years roughly by three and assigning each part to a generation).

Such a conclusion, however, assumes that the data in Exod 6 must harmonize with Exod 12:40 and Gen 15:16, and that the chronographer deliberately ignored the fact that Levi, Kohath, and Amram are grandfather,

---

14. The word may also be used in a general sense to refer simply to a population belonging to a single stratum of time (see Brin, *Concept of Time*, 58–61).

15. On the counting of generations, see below.

16. As in William Foxwell Albright, "Abram the Hebrew: A New Archaeological Interpretation," *BASOR* 163 (1961): 50–51.

17. See, e.g., Freedman and Lundbom, "דור," 174.

father, and son by placing the three men's life spans back-to-back. To be sure, the fact that Gen 15:13 and 15:16 are in the same source and in such close proximity suggests that the 400 years equals four דורות, and therefore a דור would have to equal 100 years here. Since a generation would never be that long, but a life span would, it must be that the word דור sometimes can refer to a life span. It should be remembered, however, that a figure of 100 years for a life span does not match J's fixed number for the full length of a person's life: 120 years (Gen 6:3). Propp makes a better case, noting that the number of generations is not cardinal, but ordinal. We are therefore to count the period as three full generations, plus part of another. He speculates that the 400 years equals three of J's life spans (120 × 3 = 360) plus 40 years (part of a fourth).[18]

The case of Gen 15:13–16 does present an interesting puzzle, and the data can be interpreted several ways:

1) The 400 years is being equated with a number of life spans.
2) The 400 years is being equated with a number of generations.
3) The 400 years and the דור רביעי do not refer to the same period.
4) The two data contradict one another.

Militating against the first possibility is the fact that there are no other instances in the Bible where דור refers to a person's full life span, and there is scanty evidence outside the Bible for the term used in that sense. An example sometimes cited as evidence is an inscription of Shamshi-Adad I of Assyria, wherein the king claims that seven *dārū* had elapsed between the *šulum Akkadîm* (the foundation of Akkad) and his own time.[19] The word *dārū* is cognate with Hebrew דור and is likewise normally understood as "generation." In this inscription it is understood by some to mean "life span," because seven generations before Shamshi-Adad would be too recent to place the event to which he refers. However, it would be a mistake to put too much stock in this reference. Even if Shamshi-Adad were measuring a period of time by life spans in this inscription, we would expect that he would be using a standard life span (a single fixed figure) as a yardstick by which to measure. He would not be referring to a sequence of seven life spans assigned to specific individuals in a linear genealogy, for the simple reason that, in reality, life spans are not sequential, but overlap. Moreover, the often symbolic number seven is not likely to be literal. A better interpretation is that the king is refer-

---

18. Propp, *Exodus 1–18*, 415.

19. See Percy E. Newberry, *Annals of Archaeology and Anthropology* 19 (Liverpool: Institute of Archaeology of the University of Liverpool, 1931), Pl. 81, i:18. The Akkadian word *šulum* can mean either the full realization of a state or its complete ruin, but the former seems to be meant here. See Glassner, *Mesopotamian Chronicles*, 5–6.

ring to seven ideal *generations* (using the word *dārū* in its usual sense), the last and perfect of which is identified with his own.[20] In other words, there is no correlation between the actual length of time covered and the number of *dārū* cited. It is simply a form of elevated speech. With no other evidence of דור being used to mean "life span," we may discount the first possible interpretation of the meaning of Gen 15:13–16.

The third solution, which posits that the two data are referring to different periods, is also unlikely. The concluding points of both time periods are the same: the end of the oppression. That much is clear. The beginning point of the four hundred years is the start of the oppression, and the beginning point of the four דורות must be understood to be either the start of the oppression or the present moment in the narrative (i.e., Abraham's time). However, if the count of time begins immediately, then the problem is only exacerbated (the four דורות would have to cover a period longer than four hundred years). It is best to take the passage at face value and consider both data as referring to the same period of time: the length of the oppression.

Militating against the fourth conclusion (that the data contradict one another) is the fact that the two pieces of information are textually very close to one another. This fact makes it likely that, even if they each are the creation of a different author or editor, the person responsible for the most recent datum was aware of the first and would not likely deliberately contradict it.

This leaves us with possibility 2, which, although it has its problems (a generation normally covers less than fifty years), is the least objectionable. While long generations are uncommon in the text, and unheard of in later times, they are still attested.[21] The patriarchs in Gen 5 all have sons at very old ages. After that, Noah has his three sons at five hundred, Shem has Arpachshad at one hundred, Terah has Abram at seventy, and Abraham has Isaac at one hundred. The best solution to the difficulties associated with this passage is to assume that דור is to be understood in its usual sense (always the first and best option unless facts force a different interpretation), but nevertheless to acknowledge a tension between verses 13 and 16 that was not intended by the original author. J does not assume lengthy generations; P does. The datum of Gen 15:16 (J), which makes the period of Egyptian residence rather short,

---

20. Cf. "tenth generation" (Deut 23:2–3) and "thousandth generation" (Exod 20:6; Deut 5:10) in the Bible, which are not likely to be literal. Other extrabiblical examples are sometimes cited as evidence of measuring time by life spans, but they are few and come from times far removed from the biblical period.

21. Cf. Shemaryahu Talmon, "»400 Jahre« oder »vier Generationen« (Gen 15,13–15): Geschichtliche Zeitangaben oder literarische Motive?" in *Die Hebräische Bibel und ihre zweifache Nachgeschichte* (Neukirchener: Neukirchener Verlag, 1990), 13–25.

would have posed a problem to someone accustomed to a longer figure (R was well aware, not only of P's lengthy generations in Genesis, but of P's figure of 430 years for the oppression period in Exod 12:40). How could the difficulty be fixed without eliminating the reference altogether? Fortunately, verse 16, while referring to generations, does not specify a length of time for each generation. This allowed the redactor some freedom to play. Although equating four generations with four hundred years is a stretch (and the redactor no doubt knew this), the length of a generation in the Bible is never precise; it is always estimated. Something had to be done to rectify the contradiction with Exod 12:40, and the four-hundred-year figure was still passable (rounded down from 430). So he added the gloss ארבע מאות שנה ("four hundred years").

Generations seem to have been counted differently in ancient Israel than they are today. When looking forward in time, we normally begin counting with the generation of the parents. Thus, I would consider myself part of the first generation, and my children the second, and so on. Bible writers use a different system.[22] The famous formula of Exod 34:6–7, which was included in J, reckons *children* as the first generation, grandchildren as the second, etc. E counts similarly, reckoning Joseph's great-grandchildren as the third generation (Gen 50:23). The DH places King Zechariah of Israel, the great-great-grandson of Jehu, in the fourth generation of Jehu's family (2 Kgs 10:30; cf. 15:12). Ironically, when it comes to generations, we abandon our exclusive system of counting, and the Israelites abandon their inclusive system. Thus, when we consider Gen 15:16, "the fourth generation" must be the great-great-grandchildren of the generation in which the Egyptian oppression begins.

---

22. See Freedman and Lundbom, "דור," 174–75.

3
Genealogical Chronologies

3.1. Dating Events by the Life on an Individual

In the Hebrew Bible, only the priestly writer(s) (and the Deuteronomistic editor[s] to a limited degree) seem interested in constructing chronologies based on genealogical information. The Aaronid priests turn it into a science, and their chronology is based *primarily* on genealogies. This dating system forms a significant part of the narrative of the Torah as it now stands, especially the book of Genesis.

The priestly chronology dates events that occur prior to the exodus by placing them within a specific year in the lifetime of an individual. Most of the events concern only the activities of the individual to whose life the events are dated.[1] Not all of the events are genealogical in nature, but the births of sons are of particular interest to the author(s), and history is presented according to the passing of time in individuals' lives, rather than to regnal years of kings or judges or to dates of other notable events.

The priestly material occasionally refers to larger, broader events that are of relevance to a greater community, but nevertheless dates them according to the years of a specific person's life. In P, the universal flood occurs in Noah's

---

1. "And Abram was a son of 75 years when he left Haran" (Gen 12:4); "And Abram was a son of 86 years when Hagar bore Ishmael to Abram" (Gen 16:15); "And Abram came to be a son of 99 years, and Yahweh appeared to Abram" (Gen 17:1); "And Abraham was a son of 100 years when his son Isaac was born to him" (Gen 21:5); "And Isaac came to be a son of 40 years when he took Rebekah the daughter of Bethuel, the Aramean from Paddan-aram, the sister of Laban the Aramean, for a wife" (Gen 25:20); "And Isaac was a son of 60 years when she gave birth to them" (Gen 25:26); "And Esau came to be a son of 40 years, and he took, as a wife, Judith the daughter of Beeri the Hittite, and Basemath the daughter of Elon the Hittite" (Gen 26:34); "Joseph was a son of 17 years, and he became a shepherd with his brothers among the flock" (Gen 37:2); "And Joseph was a son of 30 years when he stood before Pharaoh the king of Egypt" (Gen 41:46); "And Moses was a son of 80 years and Aaron was a son of 83 years when they spoke to Pharaoh" (Exod 7:7).

600th year (Gen 7:6). In R's chronology, the flood begins in the 600th year of Noah's life (Gen 7:11) and ends in his 601st year (Gen 8:13–14). An additional datum concerns the time that the ark finally lands on the mountains (Gen 8:4–5).

Sometimes the characters themselves establish dates by naming their ages at a notable event. The date of the settlement of Jacob and his family in Egypt is presented in such a way:

> And Joseph brought in his father Jacob and stood him before Pharaoh, and Jacob blessed Pharaoh. And Pharaoh said to Jacob, "How many are the days of the years of your life?" And Jacob said to Pharaoh, "The days of the years of my residences are 130 years. Few and bad have been the days of the years of my life, and they have not reached the days of the years of my forefathers' lives in the days of their residences" (Gen 47:7–9).

The Deuteronomistic Historian also uses this method. For example, when dating the succession of Joshua and the entry into Canaan according to the life of Moses, the information is presented in the first person:

> And [Moses] said to them, "A son of 120 years I am today. I am not able to go out and come in anymore...." (Deut 31:2).

Similarly, the sending out of the spies, as well as the death of Joshua and the apportionment of the land of Canaan, is dated according to the life of Caleb and stated in the first person:

> [Caleb said:] "A son of 40 years I was when Moses the servant of Yahweh sent me out of Qadesh-barnea to spy out the land.... And now, here Yahweh has kept me alive, just as he gave his word, these 45 years since Yahweh gave this word to Moses when Israel walked in the desert. And now here I am today a son of 85 years" (Josh 14:7, 10).[2]

Although P, R, and to a lesser degree the DH date many events by people's ages, a collection of these references does not constitute a chronology. All of them would be meaningless to the ancient (or modern) reader unless the

---

2. It might be argued that this is a P account, because it seems to be referring to the P passages in Numbers, in which Caleb is sent out of Qadesh with the spies (Num 13:6; 14:6–9). However, the J version in the same chapter of Numbers also features Caleb as one of the spies (Num 13:30–31), and Caleb's mention of the Anakim (giants) here in Joshua (14:12) is a clear reference to the J version (Num 13:22, 33). The Deuteronomistic History draws from J frequently, but not from P. "Anakim" appears to be a Deuteronomic equivalent to J's "Nephilim."

3. GENEALOGICAL CHRONOLOGIES

lives of the various ancestors were associated with known dates. If I know that event X occurs in year Y of individual Z, I still do not know when event X took place unless I know when individual Z was born. In other words, these dates are dependent on other information. For P, this information takes the form of a genealogy containing chronological data. The genealogy provides a framework for the history of the world, by which events in that history may be dated.

3.2. Genealogical Lists Containing Chronological Information

3.2.1. Description

P's chronological framework, which anchors its dates to an absolute chronology, is found throughout Genesis but is concentrated in chapters 5 and 11, where we can see its basic form. In those chapters we find a list of ante- and post-diluvian ancestors recounted, along with the age of each ancestor at the birth of a significant son, the age of each ancestor at death, and the length of time between these two events. This scheme forms the basis of a lengthy chronology based on a family line running from Adam, through Seth, Noah, Shem, and then Abraham, Isaac, and Jacob. In the latter sections of Genesis, the data tend to be dispersed throughout the narrative, but the nature of the data remains the same.

The basic form of the presentation of the chronology is as follows:

> And PN1 came to be # years old, and he sired PN2; and PN1 lived, after his siring PN2, # years, and he sired sons and daughters. [And all the days of PN1 came to be # years, and he died.]

The final phrase (in brackets) is omitted in the list of Gen 11.[3] A striking feature of the list is the abnormally long life spans of the individuals listed. We should note, however, that the ages of the ancestors at their deaths have no bearing whatsoever on the chronology, which is set only by their ages at the births of their sons.

3.2.2. List Making in the Ancient World

In order to understand the genealogical lists, it would be advantageous to consider the importance of lists in ancient scribal tradition. From our modern perspective, we might have trouble understanding an interest in the dry and

---

3. The Samaritan Pentateuch, however, includes it.

repetitive recitation of seemingly pointless pieces of information, but the ability to memorize and recite lists, especially those that required counting and measuring, was, in the ancient world, an evidence of knowledge and wisdom, "a powerful medium for creating, organising, and disseminating knowledge of the past."[4] In ancient Mesopotamia, for example, lists were attempts to understand the universe by classifying and organizing its contents. Names were considered *substances,* inseparable emanations from the object named and an expression of divine will.[5]

In Greece the practice of reciting lists to articulate segments of time and space is evident in Homer's Catalogue of Ships in Book 2 of the *Iliad* and in Hesiod's *Theogony* (eighth century B.C.E.). These lists are likely to predate the works in which they are now found. In other words, they stand out as literary forms different from the narratives in which they are embedded and which they serve to enhance. Homer's Catalogue of Ships is a survey of the Achaean and Trojan armed forces at the time of the Trojan War (*Il.* 2:494–759, 816–877). When Homer begins to recite the ship catalogue, he makes a point of drawing attention to the difficulty of such a task, even invoking the Muses before he does so (2:484–493). He is able to divide up the armies into constituent parts, bringing clarity to the list through the use of names and numbers. That he can successfully recite the list demonstrates his skill as a cataloguer. Hesiod uses genealogies to explain the origins of the gods and as a way of introducing separate mythical episodes. He has memorized many lists of names, often giving the number of names in a list.[6] The P genealogy, containing names and specific figures, is just the sort of catalogue a priest might recite, or record, to demonstrate his grasp of complex data.

From time to time, when reciting these lists, the ancient poets highlight outstanding elements, perhaps, as in Homer, making note of the most able leader, or the most handsome soldier, or the best or most numerous troops, or the best horses, or, in Hesiod, the most beautiful, or the oldest, of the gods. These interjections or glosses of the poets evidence their knowledge of the memorized list and ability to size it up.[7] Similarly, the priestly reciter of the biblical genealogy sometimes highlights notable figures, such as Enoch, who "walked with God" (Gen 5:22).

---

4. Jeremy Graeme Taylor, "Framing the Past: The Roots of Greek Chronography" (Ph.D. diss., University of Michigan, 2000), 107.

5. Jean Bottéro, *Mesopotamia: Writing, Reasoning, and the Gods* (Chicago: University of Chicago Press, 1992), 29–31, 97–102.

6. See the discussion of both Homer and Hesiod in Taylor, "Framing the Past," 107–39.

7. Taylor, "Framing the Past," 118–19.

When lists were committed to writing, the scribes not only had opportunity to sort and classify material within each list, but also to compare and juxtapose lists with one another. When documents covering the same subject matter were collected, lists incorporating information from more than one document would be created.[8] This was true of lists of a chronological nature as well. The ancient chronographers viewed time as a constant, universal principle, and it was very important to their worldview that lists cohered with one another. They spent much time and energy dating significant events and individuals, and it was important for their chronologies to adhere to their historiographies. Often contradictions between two documents were found; since it was important for the documents to be consistent with one another, adjustments would need to be made, either to the original lists or to the diachronic list prepared from them, to calibrate the data. It is apparent that lists were not static in nature, but dynamic, constantly changing and being adapted. An analysis of the genealogical chronology of P reveals that it was affected by the same phenomena.

3.2.3. Textual Variants of Genesis 5 and 11 and Their History

3.2.3.1. Genesis 5

There are three main textual witnesses that we may consult for Gen 5 and 11: the Masoretic Text (MT), the Samaritan Pentateuch (SP), and the Greek Septuagint (LXX). The Masoretic Text is a medieval text tradition in Hebrew, for a long time accepted as the authoritative text in Judaism, but which represents only one biblical textual tradition out of many that existed in ancient times. The Samaritan Pentateuch is another Hebrew text preserved by the Samaritan community that includes just the Torah and is written in what appears to be an early Hebrew script. Though our oldest representative of SP is likewise from the Middle Ages and contains some late Samaritan revisions, we believe the basic text can be traced back to ancient times. The Septuagint is a text tradition having its origins in the first translation made of the Hebrew biblical texts into a foreign language, that is, Greek. The translation was begun by the Jewish community in Alexandria, Egypt, some time in the third century B.C.E. Although it is not in Hebrew, it probably derives from a Hebrew text, no longer extant, which predates the translation. It therefore may be used as a witness to another ancient text tradition of the Bible. A comparison of these

---

8. Taylor, "Framing the Past," 164–74.

three witnesses reveals a significant number of differences with respect to the figures found in Gen 5 and 11, the core of P's genealogical chronology.

A natural question would be to ask *why* such discrepancies exist. Clearly the variations are the result of scribal editing, but what was the motivation for such editing? If the biblical chronographers operated in much the same way as other ancient chronographers, we would expect there to be two chief motivations: 1) to bring the chronology into harmony with the chronologies of respected outside historical sources, and 2) to "correct" inconsistencies in the text that they inherited. Although we lack, for comparison, an actual hard copy of the presumed parent text of these three manuscript families, an examination of the variants contained in them supports the above conclusion. Moreover, the verification that there were indeed inconsistencies in the archetypal or parent text, which the scribes saw the need to "correct," would suggest that the genealogical chronology therein logically could not itself be, or be drawn from, a homogeneous document. Rather, it would have to be an imperfect synthesis of more than one chronographic source.

Before this last conclusion can be demonstrated, however, it is necessary to show how an inconsistent archetypal text and a desire to harmonize the chronology with other histories are the most intellectually satisfying explanations for the variant readings in the texts we possess. We will turn first to Gen 5 (see table 3.1 on pp. 70–71).

Several recent textual studies of Gen 5 have advanced our understanding of the formation of the variants.[9] A general observation of the different readings reveals that MT and SP agree on all entries except for those of Jared, Methuselah, and Lamech. LXX differs from MT and SP in that one hundred years are added to the age of begetting and one hundred years are subtracted from the remaining years of life in every entry, except for Jared, Methuselah, and Lamech. The scribes seem to have found the data regarding these three patriarchs problematic. The studies of Ralph W. Klein, Jeremy Hughes, Donald V. Etz, and Ronald S. Hendel together have built a strong case that, in the earliest manuscripts, three of the antediluvian patriarchs (Jared, Methuselah, and Lamech) were given life spans in the genealogical chronology that placed their deaths after the flood (i.e., after Noah's six hundreth year). However, according to the generally accepted understanding of the flood as universal in scope, their survival of the flood would be an impossibility (Gen

---

9. Ralph W. Klein, "Archaic Chronologies and the Textual History of the Old Testament," *HTR* 67 (1974): 255–63; Hughes, *Secrets of the Times*, 5–53; Donald V. Etz, "The Numbers of Genesis V 3–31: A Suggested Conversion and its Implications," *VT* 43 (1993): 171–89; Ronald S. Hendel, *The Text of Genesis 1–11: Textual Studies and Critical Edition* (New York: Oxford University Press, 1998), 61–80.

7:23). Therein lies the inconsistency. *The date for the flood (the 600th year of Noah) was in conflict with the basic genealogical chronology found in Gen 5.* The problem apparently went unnoticed by the original editor, but scribes from different manuscript traditions attempted to alleviate the difficulties in their own ways, and their activity explains the variations in the manuscripts we now possess.

Thus we find that, in the Samaritan tradition, the life spans of the three problem ancestors were shortened, so that they would not extend beyond the flood. The artificiality of their ages is apparent, when one notices that all three now die in the exact year of the flood. The scribes took off only as many years as was absolutely necessary.

In the MT tradition, an early scribe or scribes made the decision to remove the lives of Jared, Methuselah, and Lamech further from the flood by adding years to the ages of each of them at the birth of his son, and subtracting the same number from the years remaining in the life of the father, thereby retaining the original reading of the father's age at death. To Jared's age at the birth of Enoch 100 years were added, and this was sufficient to correct the problem. In the case of Methuselah, 100 years was not quite enough, so an even 120 years was added to his age at the birth of Lamech. This put Methuselah's death in the year of the flood. There is disagreement among Klein, Hughes, Etz, and Hendel regarding what MT did with Lamech. We should expect that a similar adjustment would have been made, that is, an addition to Lamech's age at the birth of Noah. However, we will need to take a closer look at all the versions before confirming this conclusion.

In general, the case that the previously cited studies make to explain the reason for the revisions in SP and MT is very strong. The reasons for the adjustments in LXX, however, need to be examined again. According to the theory advanced by Hendel, the motivations for the changes made in the LXX tradition were the same as in the others: three men survived the flood. So a similar strategy was employed as in MT (adding 100 years to the age of each father at the birth of his son, and subtracting 100 years from the years remaining in his life, thereby retaining the original reading of the father's age at death).[10] However, instead of merely correcting the years for Jared, Methuselah, and Lamech, as MT did, LXX apparently decided to make the same adjustment to *all* the fathers in the list. By pushing the ancestors backward in time, it was assumed that none of the three problematic ancestors would then have survived the flood. Unfortunately, perhaps because of an

---

10. Hendel, *The Text of Genesis 1–11*, 64.

TABLE 3.1. VARIANT READINGS OF THE NUMBERS IN GENESIS 5

Citation	Ancestor	Proposed Archetype	SP	MT	LXX
Gen 5:3	Adam	130 + 800 = 930 (−1177 + 800 = −377)	130 + 800 = 930 (−1177 + 800 = −377)	130 + 800 = 930 (−1526 + 800 = −726)	230 + 700 = 930 (−2012 + 700 = −1312)
Gen 5:6	Seth	105 + 807 = 912 (−1072 + 807 = −265)	105 + 807 = 912 (−1072 + 807 = −265)	105 + 807 = 912 (−1421 + 807 = −614)	205 + 707 = 912 (−1807 + 707 = −1100)
Gen 5:9	Enosh	90 + 815 = 905 (−982 + 815 = −167)	90 + 815 = 905 (−982 + 815 = −167)	90 + 815 = 905 (−1331 + 815 = −516)	190 + 715 = 905 (−1617 + 715 = −902)
Gen 5:12	Kenan	70 + 840 = 910 (−912 + 840 = −72)	70 + 840 = 910 (−912 + 840 = −72)	70 + 840 = 910 (−1261 + 840 = −421)	170 + 740 = 910 (−1447 + 740 = −707)
Gen 5:15	Mahalalel	65 + 830 = 895 (−847 + 830 = −17)	65 + 830 = 895 (−847 + 830 = −17)	65 + 830 = 895 (−1196 + 830 = −366)	165 + 730 = 895 (−1282 + 730 = −552)
Gen 5:18	Jared	62 + 800 = 962 (−785 + 800 = 15)	62 + 785 = 847 (−785 + 785 = 0)	162 + 800 = 962 (−1034 + 800 = −234)	162 + 800 = 962 (−1120 + 800 = −320)

3. GENEALOGICAL CHRONOLOGIES

Gen 5:21	Enoch	65 + 300 = 365 (−720 + 300 = −420)	65 + 300 = 365 (−720 + 300 = −420)	65 + 300 = 365 (−969 + 300 = −669)	165 + 200 = 365 (−955 + 200 = −755)
Gen 5:25	Methuselah	67 + 902 = 969 (−653 + 902 = 249)	67 + 653 = 720 (−653 + 653 = 0)	187 + 782 = 969 (−782 + 782 = 0)	167 + 802 = 969 (−788 + 802 = 14)
Gen 5:28	Lamech	53 + 724 = 777 (−600 + 724 = 124)	53 + 600 = 653 (−600 + 600 = 0)	182 + 595 = 777 (−600 + 595 = −5)	188 + 565 = 753 (−600 + 565 = −35)
Gen 5:32	Noah	500 (−100)	500 (−100)	500 (−100)	500 (−100)
Gen 7:6; 9:28	Noah's age at flood	600 + 350 = 950 (0 + 350 = 350)	600 + 350 = 950 (0 + 350 = 350)	600 + 350 = 950 (0 + 350 = 350)	600 + 350 = 950 (0 + 350 = 350)

First # = age at becoming father; second # = remaining years of life; third # = total life span
Numbers in parentheses represent years before the flood

oversight, Methuselah still survived the flood. Indeed, in LXX Methuselah still lives fourteen years beyond the flood date.

Considering, however, that LXX's changes to the figures for every one of the fathers were insufficient to alleviate the problem of the flood date, I do not think it likely that they have anything to do with the flood date, or with Jared, Methuselah, and Lamech. Let us consider: is it not strange that LXX's systematic revisions, which consisted of adding one hundred years to the ages of *all* the fathers at the births of their sons, while retaining their total ages, did not ensure that all three of the problematic characters (Jared, Methuselah, and Lamech) died before the flood? If the date of their deaths was such a concern, how could Methuseleh remain uncorrected? Why go through all that trouble only to fail to achieve the intended goal? The adjustments in SP are confined to the life spans of the three problematic characters. The adjustments in MT are confined to the ages of the three problematic characters at the births of their sons. If that is all that was necessary, there was no need for the LXX scribes to change the ages of *all* the ancestors. Nevertheless, that is precisely what they did. They must have had another reason for making the revisions. What was that reason? Hendel's language, namely that the increase in the figures "serves to delay the onset of the flood," obscures the nature of the changes. From the point of view of the editors, none of the adjustments in *any* of the manuscripts delays the onset of the flood, because the flood's date is fixed by the chronology that comes after it. The flood happened a fixed number of years before the present. (All chronographers measure time back from their present. After all, this is the whole purpose of chronology.) What the increase in LXX's figures actually does is push the ancestors further away from their own time, as well as push back the date of creation. In the archetypal text, the date of creation would have been 1,307 years before the flood. As other chronological documents became available and were compared with this chronology, some might have seen that the date of creation was far too recent and needed to be pushed back. This was more likely the motivation of the 100-year increases in LXX.[11]

The Greek Septuagint was born in a period when Hellenistic Jews were becoming increasingly interested in biblical chronology. Just before the translation first appeared, Berossus' *History of Babylonia* (ca. 290 B.C.E.) and Manetho's *History of Egypt* (mid-third century B.C.E.) were published. Both of these works greatly influenced Jewish understanding of history, and attempts were made to harmonize the findings of these works with biblical

---

11. Cf. Gerhard Larsson, "The Chronology of the Pentateuch: A Comparison of the MT and LXX," *JBL* 102 (1983): 401–9.

chronology.[12] While we may never be able to know precisely how the LXX translators interpreted Berossus and Manetho, nor even know what version of the manuscripts they possessed, it is probable that the histories of Berossus and Manetho stretched further back into the past than the biblical history.[13] The Septuagint translation was being prepared for a Hellenistic audience, and the Bible's history needed to be palatable to that audience. We

---

12. See the illuminating discussion by Ben Zion Wacholder, "Biblical Chronology in the Hellenistic World Chronicles," *HTR* 61 (1968): 451–81.

13. We might find an explanation for the variants by considering some of the following observations about Berossus and Manetho: Berossus begins his history of Babylonia 432,000 years before the flood (he was influenced by the Sumerian King List), which is irreconcilable with biblical chronology. See Alden A. Mosshammer, ed., *Georgii Syncelli: Ecloga Chronographica* (Leipzig: Teubner, 1984), §53. The Jews and early Christians, however, did not lack ingenuity. The medieval chronographer George Syncellus (ninth century C.E.), who names two Egyptian monks from ca. 400 C.E. as his sources, tells us in his *Chronological Excerpts* that it was common among Jews and Christians to interpret Berossus's years as days in this section of his history (Mosshammer, ed., *Georgii Syncelli: Ecloga Chronographica*, §30–33). The equation of years with days and vice versa was sometimes done for chronological purposes in the Hellenistic period (cf. Dan 9:24–27). Since 432,000 days is equal to 1,183½ solar years, with this understanding the beginning of Babylonian history would have commenced about 1,184 years before the flood. It is quite possible that such an interpretation, or a similar one, was held by the Hellenistic Jews who translated the Septuagint. In the original chronology of Gen 5 (column 1 in table 3.1), Berossus's date for the beginning of Mesopotamian history would have fallen in the time of Adam before the birth of his son Seth. A synchronism would be impossible. The biblical chronology could be harmonized with Berossus only by extending the length of the period from Adam to Noah, and this is precisely what LXX does. As for Manetho, he does not mention a flood, but there is some evidence to suggest that some Jews and Christians considered the first eight dynasties that ruled from Memphis as antediluvian. John Malalas (sixth century C.E.) in his *Chronicle* preserves a tradition that makes Sesostris of Dynasty XII the first Egyptian king of the line of Ham, the son of Noah (Ioannis Malalae, *Chronographia; ex recensione Ludovici Dindorfii* [Bonnae: Weber, 1831], 21). This suggests that the flood was understood by some to have occurred not long before Sesostris. Three dynasties of Herakleopolian kings immediately precede Sesostris, and the first of these (Dynasty 9) sits right at a major transition point in Egyptian history—the end of the reigns of the original kings of Memphis and the beginning of a new period (Gerald P. Verbrugghe and John M. Wickersham, *Berossus and Manetho, Introduced and Translated* [Ann Arbor: University of Michigan Press, 1996], 137). This would have been an ideal location for Jewish chronographers to have placed the flood. Most significantly, such a view explains quite well the changes we find in LXX. Apart from the mythological reigns of the gods, Manetho's Dynasties 1–8 cover approximately 1,600 years (Mosshammer, ed., *Georgii Syncelli: Ecloga Chronographica*, §§99–145). In the biblical chronology, 1,600 years before the flood was well prior to the creation of humankind. LXX, by extending the period in the chronology of Gen 5, makes the two chronologies appear compatible.

should look at the LXX antediluvian chronology in this context.[14] It is possible that the alterations adopted by the Septuagint were a product of the system of the Jewish chronographer Demetrius, who was the first to make a defense of LXX's chronology.

So far we have seen evidence that the LXX readings were affected by incompatibility with outside historical sources. However, there are other tamperings in LXX that seem to have been motivated by a desire for internal chronological harmony. Special attention needs to be given to the entry for Lamech in order to get closer to an explanation for the anomalous readings. The issue is somewhat complicated and requires explication. Hendel, in agreement with Klein, argues that none of the three manuscript traditions retains the archetypal reading of the age of Lamech at the birth of Noah, and that the readings of MT and SP are the result of scribal errors.[15] Although mechanical errors are always possible, it is somewhat suspicious that nowhere else in the list of Gen 5 do MT and SP have such errors, but they both happen to make mistakes in the same entry for the same person, one of the problematic ancestors, probably the most problematic of them all. Moreover, the scribal errors are said to be the result of the influence of readings several lines away and on the other side of the closest figure (two verses previously in MT and three verses later in SP). Most detrimental to their theory is the fact that the Samaritan Pentateuch clearly has no error in its reading, because, if it did and the original reading for the age of Lamech at Noah's birth was eighty-eight (as Klein and Hendel suggest), then Lamech's death presently would be set thirty-five years after the flood. But in fact, as was mentioned above, the date for the flood and for Lamech's death in SP coincide exactly. If a scribal error were made, there would be no such correspondence between the man's death and the flood date. The perfect alignment demonstrates that the readings in SP are precisely as the scribes intended them to be.

I would argue, instead, that the archetype for Lamech's age at the birth of his son is in the Samaritan Pentateuch (53), in agreement with Hughes, and that none of the figures for Lamech in the three traditions are mistakes, but all are by design. We must keep in mind that nowhere else in SP is the figure for the age of the father at the birth of his son adjusted. In all cases it is the age at death that is altered. In MT and LXX, on the other hand, the usual recourse is to adjust the age of the father at the birth of his son. It is therefore more

---

14. Directly below, in the discussion of Gen 11, we shall encounter further evidence of SP and LXX lengthening the chronology.

15. Hendel, *The Text of Genesis 1–11*, 66–67.

likely that their figures for Lamech's age at the birth of Noah are adjusted than that SP's are.

In regard to the age of Lamech at his *death*, SP's reading, in light of the above considerations, is unlikely to be original. SP is more inclined to adjust the death age. We had best look to MT and LXX for the archetypal reading. However, MT and LXX differ in their readings, so which one are we to prefer? Klein argues that MT's figure of 777 is an artificial revision aimed at mimicking the 77-fold vengeance of the other Lamech from Cain's family line (4:24).[16] Hughes similarly suggests that the "obviously symbolic" figure is unlikely to be original.[17] Hendel posits a scribal error influenced by a "reminiscence" of 4:24.[18] It is unclear to me why a symbolic number necessarily must be ruled out as the archetype. Are we to assume that the archetypal readings are actual ages, and that no symbolism is to be expected in any of them? We need only to point to the age for Enoch at his death (365), often remarked to be based on the number of days in a solar year, to demonstrate that some of the archetypal numbers employed here may be symbolic. Even if the number 777 is based on the J genealogy of Gen 4, this does not necessarily mean that it is not the archetype of the P text or of the redacted Torah, both of which are aware of J.

There is stronger evidence that LXX's figure for the age of Lamech at his death (753) is adjusted. One is immediately struck by its similarity to SP's figures (53 and 653). If, as has been established, SP's reading of 53 is the archetype for the age of Lamech at the birth of Noah, then we should expect that LXX would have adjusted this figure to 153, in keeping with its usual practice (153 + 600 = 753). If so, then it is interesting that its reading for the age of Lamech at his death (753) would put Lamech's death exactly in the year of the flood. This suggests that the number 753 is a revision (and reduction), just as SP's figure of 653 is a revision (and reduction). I think, therefore, that we should prefer MT's higher reading of 777 for the archetype of Lamech's death age.

At this point it is possible to reconstruct an editorial history of the Lamech entry in the genealogy. The original reading was 53 for the age of Lamech at the birth of Noah, and 777 for the age of Lamech at his death (53 + 724 = 777). However, according to such a reading, Lamech would have died after the flood. To correct this problem, SP followed its usual practice and

---

16. Klein, "Archaic Chronologies and the Textual History of the Old Testament," 261.
17. Hughes, *Secrets of the Times*, 15.
18. Hendel, *The Text of Genesis 1–11*, 66.

reduced Lamech's death age to 653, putting his death date in the year of the flood.

In MT, the adjustment was to add 129 years to the age of the father at the birth of the son, and to subtract 129 from the remaining years of his life. Technically, only 124 years needed to be added to the figure to make Lamech 177 when Noah was born, but the scribes apparently decided to add five more years, so as to put a decent gap between Lamech's death and the flood. Why did they do this? It may have to do with God's statement to Noah that Noah, his wife, his sons, and his sons' wives are the only righteous people alive (Gen 7:1; cf. also 6:5–8). Lamech's prophecy in Gen 5:29 clearly places him on the side of the righteous, so if he had lived up until the flood, we would expect that he too would have been singled out as one deserving of special mention. To solve this problem, MT chose to end his life five years ahead of the flood, thus preserving the image of Lamech as an upright man.

In LXX, Lamech's entry reflects three stages of revision:

(1) In order to push back the date of creation, one hundred years were added to all of the fathers' ages at the birth of their sons, and Lamech was no exception. This change may have been made during the preparation of the original translation into Greek, as Demetrius (third century B.C.E.) assumes this long chronology (though not exactly) and lived during the time the translation was made.

(2) However, after adding one hundred years to the age of each father at the birth of his son, both Methuselah and Lamech still survived the flood, Methuselah by fourteen years and Lamech by twenty-four years. A later scribe noticed that Lamech lived beyond the flood (he did not notice Methuselah), so he decided to reduce the figure of 777 to 753, putting Lamech's death in the year of the flood.

(3) That problem was solved, and the reading sat like this (153 + 600 = 753) for a time, but a further adjustment was then made. The figure of 153 was increased by 35 to 188 (and the figure of 600 was reduced by 35 in order to retain the life span), which had the effect of placing Lamech's death a full generation (35 years) before the flood. The intention may have been the same as for MT: to avoid any implication that Lamech was among the wicked generation mentioned in Gen 6:5–8 and 7:1. The scribe in the LXX tradition felt the gap between Lamech's death and the flood should be larger than what the scribe who made the similar decision in the MT tradition felt.

3.2.3.2. Genesis 11

In the second major section of the genealogy (Gen 11:10–32), Klein and Hendel attribute most of the variations to a motivation to correct perceived internal inconsistencies. Although I find evidence of one alteration made for this reason, the rest seem to me to have been motivated by a desire to calibrate the chronology with outside historical sources (see table 3.2).

We see some of the same patterns in this portion of the list as we saw in Gen 5. In this case, however, MT, rather than SP, has the shortest chronology, and SP follows the pattern that LXX displayed in Gen 5. Apart from the last two entries, the ages for the fathers at the births of their sons in SP are one hundred years greater than in MT, and one hundred years fewer for the remaining years in the father's life. Thus the life spans in SP and MT are the same (except for Eber, whom we will consider below). LXX is also one hundred years greater than MT in the ages of the fathers at the birth of their sons, but the remaining years in the father's life are exactly the same as in MT, and this results in total life span that are one hundred years greater than they are in MT and SP (except for Arpachshad and Shelah, whom we will discuss below).

Another interesting feature is that SP is the only text that actually records the life spans. The life spans in the other two are present only by implication (the reader must do the math). It would seem SP added the life span totals to make the pattern conform to the one in Gen 5. The reason for the absence of the life span totals in the archetype of Gen 11 will be discussed in section 3.3.3 below.

From what we have considered in Gen 5, we may reconstruct the basic textual history of the variants in Gen 11 with some confidence.

(1) The short chronology of MT is likely to represent the earliest form of the text.

(2) SP has added one hundred years to the ages of the fathers at the births of their sons (except for Nahor, to which only fifty years were added), and subtracted the same number of years from the remaining time in the father's life, so as to retain the original life spans.

(3) LXX has also added one hundred years to the ages of the fathers at the births of their sons (except for Nahor, to which only fifty years were added), but apparently was not concerned about altering the total life spans of the fathers (after all, the life spans are not provided in LXX as they are in SP), so the remaining years in the father's life went untouched, and the lifespans were increased as a result.

In regard to this list, Hendel argues, in agreement with Klein, that the adjustments in SP and LXX were made to prevent so great an overlap of generations in the archetypal text.[19] Apparently, the early scribes would have seen a

---

19. Hendel, *The Text of Genesis 1–11*, 62–63.

TABLE 3.2: Variant Readings of the Numbers in Genesis 11

Citation	Ancestor	Proposed Archetype	SP	MT	LXX
Gen 11:10	adjustment to flood date	+2 (−1112)	+2 (−1762)	+2 (−1112)	+2 (−1677)
Gen 11:10	Shem	100 + 500 [= 600] (−1110 + 500 = −610)	100 + 500 = 600 (−1760 + 500 = −1260)	100 + 500 [= 600] (−1110 + 500 = −610)	100 + 500 [= 600] (−1675 + 500 = −1175)
Gen 11:12	Arpach-shad	35 + 403 [= 438] (−1010 + 403 = −607)	135 + 303 = 438 (−1660 + 303 = −1357)	35 + 403 [= 438] (−1010 + 403 =− 607)	135 + 430 [= 565] (−1575 + 430 = −1145)
Gen 11:13	Kenan				130 + 330 [= 460] (−1440 + 330 = −1110)
Gen 11:14	Shelah	30 + 403 [= 433] (−975 + 403 = −572)	130 + 303 = 433 (−1525 + 303 = −1222)	30 + 403 [= 433] (−975 + 403 = −572)	130 + 330 [= 460] (−1310 + 330 = −980)
Gen 11:16	Eber	34 + 370 [= 404] (−945 + 430 = −515)	134 + 270 = 404 (−1395 + 270 = −1125)	34 + 430 [= 464] (−945 + 430 = −515)	134 + 370 [= 504] (−1180 + 370 = −810)
Gen 11:18	Peleg	30 + 209 [= 239] (−911 + 209 = −702)	130 + 109 = 239 (−1261 + 109 = −1152)	30 + 209 [= 239] (−911 + 209 = −702)	130 + 209 [= 339] (−1046 + 209 = −837)
Gen 11:20	Reu	32 + 207 [= 239] (−881 + 207 = −674)	132 + 107 = 239 (−1131 + 107 = −1024)	32 + 207 [= 239] (−881 + 207 =− 674)	132 + 207 [= 339] (−916 + 207 = −709)

3. GENEALOGICAL CHRONOLOGIES

Gen 11:22	Serug	30 + 200 [= 230] (−849 + 200 = −649)	130 + 100 = 230 (−999 + 100 = −899)	30 + 200 [= 230] (−849 + 200 = −649)	130 + 200 [= 330] (−784 + 200 = −584)
Gen 11:24	Nahor	29 + 119 [= 148] (−819 + 119 = −700)	79 + 69 = 148 (−869 + 69 = −800)	29 + 119 [= 148] (−819 + 119 = −700)	79 + 129 [= 208] (−654 + 129 = −525)
Gen 11:26, 32	Terah	70 [+ 135] = 205 (−790 + 135 = −655)	70 [+ 75] = 145 (−790 + 75 = −715)	70 [+ 135] = 205 (−790 + 135 = −655)	70 [+ 135] = 205 (−575 + 135 = −440)

First # = age at becoming father; second # = remaining years of life; third # = total life span
Numbers in brackets are implied, but not written
Numbers in parentheses represent years before the exodus*

---

* From the birth of Abraham to the birth of Isaac we count 100 years, to the birth of Jacob 60 years, to Jacob's entry into Egypt 130 years, to the exodus 430 years. The LXX counts differently: from the birth of Abraham to his entry into Canaan 75 years (Gen 12:4–5), to the exodus 430 years (Exod 12:40). (Note that the period from Abraham's arrival in Canaan to Jacob's arrival in Egypt, in all three manuscript traditions, is 215 years, exactly half of 430 years. LXX, therefore, effectively cuts the oppression period in half.)

problem with the fact that many of the ancestors were alive in Abraham's lifetime. I think more is being made out of this situation than need be. There is nothing in the narrative to militate against such an overlap. In the case of Gen 5, it is understandable that adjustments would need to be made for some of the fathers to die before the flood. According to the narrative, their survival would be *impossible*. On the other hand, no impossibilities or anachronisms are created by an overlap of generations in Gen 11. Would alterations really be called for? The nature of the revisions in Gen 11 also weaken the argument. We find that LXX has, as it did in Gen 5, added one hundred years to the ages of the fathers at the births of their sons, but this time no effort is made to preserve the original life spans of these fathers. This tells us that the motivation for the changes must have nothing to do with making sure the ancestors die by a certain time, because the changes merely increase the ages of the men at their deaths. SP repeats what it did in Gen 5 (reducing a life span) only in 11:32, and this suggests that only in this single instance is the change motivated by a desire to ensure the death of one of the fathers before a certain year. MT makes no adjustments to the chronology whatsoever, so at least in this tradition, the overlap of generations was not of sufficient concern to the scribes for them to make changes.

We must presume that LXX's revisions in Gen 11 (including the addition of another ancestor, a second Kenan beside the one in 5:12) serve the same purpose they do in Gen 5: to move the generations further back in time. Indeed the addition of a full generation between Arpachshad and Shelah can serve no other function.[20] LXX's chronology pushes the flood date back a further 565 years (cf. Gen 5 in LXX above). SP probably has similar motivations. Its flood date has been pushed back 650 years. As in the case of Gen 5, it seems likely that knowledge of other chronologies outside of the Bible, which placed the flood further back in time, prompted these revisions. Josephus's famous passage from *Against Apion* (1.14), which equates the Israelite oppression in Egypt with the rule of the Hyksos ("shepherd kings") is based on Manetho's *History of Egypt*. Josephus's version of Manetho assigns Dynasties 16 and 17 to the rule of the shepherd kings; Africanus's version equates

---

20. Jeremy Northcote, "The Schematic Development of Old Testament Chronography: Towards an Integrated Model," *JSOT* 29 (2004): 9–11, proposes that the extra generation was added to the chronology *prior* to the publication of LXX. The age of Shelah at the birth of this extra Kenan, however, is 130, and this number is clearly reflective of the LXX system, in which all of the ages have been expanded by 100 years. In order for Northcote's theory to be correct, we would have to assume, first that a generation of anomalous length was inserted into the earlier chronology, and second that the LXX translators added 100 years to all the generations except that one. This seems to me highly improbable.

3. GENEALOGICAL CHRONOLOGIES 81

them with Dynasties 15, 16 and 17, while Eusebius's version only gives them Dynasty 17. In all cases, the reign of the shepherds concludes with Dynasty 17. Manetho assigns a lengthy period for Egyptian dynasties 9–17 (3,072 years according to Africanus and 1,300 according to Eusebius).[21] It would not have been possible to harmonize the original chronology of Gen 11 (counting 1,014 years from the flood to the exodus) with Manetho (whether according to Africanus or Eusebius). However, SP's and LXX's figures are compatible with Eusebius's readings. If the scribes of SP and the translators of LXX had a version of Manetho like Eusebius's, the adjustments to the biblical text may be the result of attempts to harmonize the two chronologies.[22]

The one anomalous reading that seems to have been motivated by a perceived internal inconsistency is SP's total age for Terah (145 instead of 205). The life of this patriarch is shortened by 60 years. We should expect a similar rationale as that for SP's shortened life spans in Gen 5: a desire to make sure the person dies by a certain time (in this case, Terah). In Gen 11:32 Terah dies, and the implication is that he does so before Abram's departure from Haran in 12:4–5. If Terah lived until 205, he would have survived Abram's departure by 60 years. SP solves this apparent contradiction by subtracting 60 years from Terah's life span, thus ensuring that Terah dies before Abram leaves (but as late as possible and thus in the exact year of Abram's departure). SP's method for alleviating the difficulty is the same as its method in Gen 5. MT also was concerned about this problem, but solved it a different way: by removing the word בחרן ("in Haran") from the phrase "And the days of Terah *in Haran* were 205 years" in Gen 11:32 (cf. LXX).

This analysis I believe best explains the variant readings in MT, SP, and LXX.[23] We therefore should be relatively confident that a source text common to all three manuscript traditions contained the following figures:

---

21. Verbrugghe and Wickersham, *Berossus and Manetho*, 131–39.

22. If the translators of LXX had before them a version of Manetho similar to that of Eusebius, the period of oppression in Egypt would likely have been thought to coincide with Dynasty 17, which in Eusebius's version amounts only to 103 years. They most certainly would have been uncomfortable with the 430 years given for the oppression period in the biblical text they inherited. The Greek reading of Exod 12:40 ("And the dwelling of the Israelites that they dwelt in the land of *Egypt and in the land of Canaan*: 430 years") may reflect their attempt to overcome the chronological problem by cutting this period in half without changing the number by a slick alteration of the text.

23. There are a few anomalous readings probably attributable to scribal error. With the knowledge that LXX added 100 years to the ages of the fathers at the births of their sons, we should expect that LXX's readings for Arpachshad and Shelah would be 135 + 403 and 130 + 403 respectively. Instead we get 135 + 430 and 130 + 330. In both cases, we have a change for the remaining years in the father's life. Klein is probably correct in

Gen 5:3	Adam	130 + 800 = 930
Gen 5:6	Seth	105 + 807 = 912
Gen 5:9	Enosh	90 + 815 = 905
Gen 5:12	Kenan	70 + 840 = 910
Gen 5:15	Mahalalel	65 + 830 = 895
Gen 5:18	Jared	62 + 800 = 962
Gen 5:21	Enoch	65 + 300 = 365
Gen 5:25	Methuselah	67 + 902 = 969
Gen 5:28	Lamech	53 + 724 = 777
Gen 5:32	Noah	500
Gen 7:6; 9:28	Noah's age at flood	600 + 350 = 950
Gen 11:10	Shem	100 + 500 [= 600]
Gen 11:10	adjustment	+2
Gen 11:12	Arpachshad	35 + 403 [= 438]
Gen 11:14	Shelah	30 + 403 [= 433]
Gen 11:16	Eber	34 + 370 [= 404]
Gen 11:18	Peleg	30 + 209 [= 239]
Gen 11:20	Reu	32 + 207 [= 239]

attributing this discrepancy to scribal error. In the first case, a scribe would have confused שלש for שלשים. In the second, there would be the same mistake, plus a more serious error of writing שלש again instead of (רב). MT also contains an error of the same sort in the entry for Eber. We should expect a reading of 34 + 270 (the latter number preserved correctly in SP), but we get 34 + 430 instead. This error is more difficult to account for, but Hendel is probably right to attribute it to an accidental copying of Shelah's remaining years of life, plus another misreading of שלש for שלשים. Another possibility is that the change was deliberate in order to make the sum of all the lifespans from Adam to Moses equal 12,600 [See Jeremy Northcote, "The Lifespans of the Patriarchs: Schematic Orderings in the Chrono-genealogy," *VT* 57 (2007): 244–49]. With regard to Nahor in LXX (Gen 11:25), a misreading of תשע עשרה (19) as תשע עשרים (29) (the תשע עשרים in the preceding verse may have assisted in the confusion) resulted in a 10-year difference.

3. GENEALOGICAL CHRONOLOGIES

Gen 11:22	Serug	30 + 200 [= 230]
Gen 11:24	Nahor	29 + 119 [= 148]
Gen 11:26, 32	Terah	70 [+ 135] = 205

This, or something close to it, was the genealogical chronology of the redacted Primary History (pre-third century B.C.E.).[24]

3.3. Sources of the Priestly Genealogical Chronology

3.3.1. Preliminary Considerations

We may now work back from this archetypal chronology in order to determine its provenance. The evidence suggests that it has been adapted from more than one earlier chronographic source. Already it is generally held that, whoever included the material now in Gen 5 and 11, either the author of P or the redactor, he gathered his chronological information from at least one written source and incorporated the data into the narrative, perhaps even reproducing the source word-for-word. Many view the statement in Gen 5:1 זה ספר תולדת אדם ("This is the scroll of the generations of Adam") as a citation of the source, or perhaps its own heading.[25] Considering that a similar statement occurs in LXX in Gen 2:4 ("This is the scroll of the generations of the heavens and the earth") and that the phrase "these are the generations" is used frequently throughout Genesis, it is best to assume a consistent use of זה and אלה and see them as referring to the text that follows, rather than as pointers to a source. Our observation that the variations in the manuscripts of Gen 5 and 11 were caused by the conflation of two partially conflicting chronologies (a chronology for the flood and a genealogical chronology) has sufficiently discredited the assumption that the genealogy of Jacob had already been fully harmonized into one unified system, chronology included, before the version we see before us was even composed. These chronologies were *not* fully harmonized before they came into our text. While it is probable that R composed the *toledot* headings, because they have knowledge of

---

24. The ages at begetting correspond to the reconstruction of Alfred Jepsen, "Zur Chronologie des Priesterkodex," *ZAW* 47 (1929): 252–55, who notes that according to this chronology, Abraham was born exactly 1600 years from the creation of Adam (assuming one year for the flood). I suggest that the redactor of the Torah added the two-year adjustment in Gen 11:10 deliberately to achieve this result.

25. See, for example, Friedman, *The Bible with Sources Revealed*, 40.

and organize all of the main Pentateuchal sources,[26] the genealogy of Gen 5 and 11, for reasons I will show below, is most likely from P. If so, the heading cannot be a source citation, because there is no reason to believe that P was known as ספר תולדת אדם ("the scroll of the generations of Adam").

My reason for attributing the genealogy to P comes from the following considerations. First, the date of the flood appears twice. A precise date occurs in Gen 7:11: "In the 600th year of Noah's life, in the 2nd month, on the 17th day of the month, on this day, all the springs of the great deep were burst, and the gates of the skies were opened." This datum we have already established as redactorial (see §1.3.2 above). A more general date occurs in Gen 7:6: "And Noah was a son of 600 years, and the flood came—waters on the earth." Although this statement could also be from the hand of the composer of 7:11, it seems rather unnecessary for him to have provided *both* a general date and a more specific one. More likely is that the text has undergone expansion. The logical direction of growth would be from less specific to more specific information, so it is probable that the original datum is in Gen 7:6, and that it was composed (or inserted) by the author of P. The redactor was unsatisfied with the general time reference, and so added the specific year, month, and day to pinpoint the precise timing of the event. However, always respectful of his sources, and not willing to cut them, he left in the words of Gen 7:6. The same can be said about the wilderness trek. P states that the Israelites were in the wilderness for forty years (Num 14:34). However, R's wilderness chronology adds precision to the general chronology of P, dating events down to the actual month and day in a given year.

Second, at the conclusion of the Noah pericope, we find this statement:

> And Noah lived, after the flood, 350 years. And all the days of Noah were 950 years, and he died. (Gen 9:28–29)

Now according to R, who seems intent on making the flood endure a complete year,[27] Noah was 600 years old when the flood began (Gen 7:11) and 601 when it ended (Gen 8:13). This harmonizes with P's datum, which also makes Noah 600 when the flood occurs (Gen 7:6). However, the year-long duration of the flood creates a conflict with the datum in Gen 9:28–29, which allows Noah a life of only 350 years after the flood, making his total life span 950

---

26. See Cross, *Canaanite Myth and Hebrew Epic*, 301–5; David Miano, "The Twelve Sepharim of the Torah," *Biblical Historian* 1 (2004): 10–19.

27. See note 24 above.

years.²⁸ In R's scheme, Noah's life would add up to 951 years. So R overshoots the total by a year.²⁹ This was not a problem for P, who simply put the entire flood in a single year (when Noah was 600). Thus Gen 9:28–29 is in harmony with Gen 7:6, which belongs to P, and not with Gen 7:11 and 8:13, which belong to R.

Third, the phrasing of Gen 9:28–29 mimics the phrasing found repeated so often in the genealogical list of Gen 5:

> And PN1 lived, after his siring PN2, # years, and he sired sons and daughters. And all the days of PN1 came to be # years, and he died.

The similarity between the statement of Gen 9:28–29 and the statements at the end of each entry in the genealogy of Gen 5 suggests common authorship, particularly because we should expect a concluding rubric for Noah in the genealogy, and the one in Gen 9:28–29 is the only one that exists. In short, the author of P is responsible (either as author or editor) for Gen 5:3–32, Gen 9:28–29, and Gen 11:10b–26, and R is not.

What is interesting is that, while the chronological calculations in Gen 5 are based on the years that fathers beget sons, the chronological calculation of Gen 9:28–29 is based on the year of an event, namely, the flood. We would expect that Noah's death age would be calculated from his age at the birth of his sons Shem, Ham, and Japheth, but such is not the case; it is based on the flood date. Why is this fact significant? Recall that the variants in the manuscripts have suggested to us that earlier in the tradition *the flood date was in conflict with other data in the genealogical chronology.* We concluded that the flood date (the 600th year of Noah) is not likely to have been taken from the same source as the genealogical data. Yet the flood date and the genealogy are interwoven in the present text and are mathematically dependent on one another. If the flood date (the 600th year of Noah) is crucial to the phrase "And Noah lived, after the flood, 350 years" and is not from the same source as the genealogical chronology, then logically *the statements of the same pat-*

---

28. When counting, I am understanding the phrase "after the flood" in the same sense as the phrase "after his fathering PN" in Gen 5 and 11. It could be argued that the 350 years is to be counted from the end of the downpour, rather than the end of the period that the waters overwhelmed the earth, which coincides with J's understanding of the word "flood" (Gen 7:17). However, P explicitly defines the flood as the period that the waters were on the earth (Gen 7:6).

29. The fact that these numbers are inclusively counted makes no difference. Remember that when adding up two or more periods of time, even though the individual units in each block are counted inclusively, the second period begins on the unit *after* the previous period ends (see §2.1).

tern in Gen 5 ("And PN1 lived, after his siring PN2, # years") *also* cannot derive from the source that provided the genealogical chronology. That being the case, while two of the three numbers given in each entry in the genealogy (that is, the age of a father at the birth of his son and the father's total life span) could have come from a written source or sources that the editor possessed, it is doubtful that the middle figure (the years between the birth of a son and the death of his father) did. The intervening years between the event and the death of a patriarch *must be calculations of the editor.* In other words, if that phrase (and PN lived after [event] # years) incorporates numbers from two sources, it itself cannot come from either of those sources. The inference is that the author/editor of P was working with two chronologies and attempting to fit them together. This would mean all the data in P's genealogical chronology do not come from a single source, but probably from two.

In regard to the two written sources from which the priestly author/editor theoretically drew (which most likely go unnamed), although it seems clear that the editor did not reproduce them verbatim, I believe it is possible to identify which information derives from which and to reconstruct most of their chronological data with relative confidence. As we shall see, the first would have contained a generational chronology providing the age of each father at the birth of his son, and the other, which contained a date for the flood (the 600th year of Noah), was part of a different chronology that provided also the long life spans of the patriarchs.

3.3.2. Pedigrees

3.3.2.1. Ancient Linear Genealogies in General

Pedigrees are genealogies that list the male members of a family in a vertical father/son sequence. They may move forward or backward in time. Their linear nature distinguishes them from "branching" genealogies, which spread out horizontally as well as vertically (cf. Gen 10 [branching] with Gen 11 [linear]).[30]

Ancient Mesopotamian pedigrees of a greater depth than three or four generations are most often found in king lists, which list dynasties of rulers, father to son, providing their years of reign. In this group are the Sumerian King List (ca. twenty-first to seventeenth century B.C.E.), the Royal Chronicle

---

30. Alternate terms are "linear genealogy" and "segmented genealogy." See Robert R. Wilson, *Genealogy and History in the Biblical World* (New Haven: Yale University Press, 1977), 9.

3. GENEALOGICAL CHRONOLOGIES 87

of Lagaš (ca. eighteenth century B.C.E.), the Babylonian King List (ca. eighteenth century B.C.E.), and the Assyrian King List (copies range from the eleventh to the eighth century B.C.E.).[31] The last is the best example in that it explicitly and more consistently refers to the genealogical relationship of a king to his predecessor. The beginning of the Assyrian King List contains some etiological genealogies that combine Amorite oral and Sumero-Akkadian written traditions about the ancient ancestors. They are called kings, but this attribution is likely secondary.

Early Greek pedigrees that might be comparable to those found in the Bible include Hecataeus' *Genealogies* and *Circuit of the Earth* (late sixth/early fifth century B.C.E.), both of which are no longer extant, but which are commented on by others. Herodotus recounts an incident where Hecataeus claimed he could recite his ancestry back to the gods (sixteen generations).[32] On a tombstone is inscribed the pedigree of a man named Heropythos, who counts back fourteen generations. The tombstone is generally dated to the first quarter of the fifth century.[33] The pedigree of Miltiades the Elder, consisting of fourteen names, appears in Marcellinus' *Life of Thucydides* (fifth century C.E.), who cites a certain Didymus as his source (probably Didymus Chalcenterus of the first century B.C.E.).[34] Didymus is likely to have obtained the information from a work entitled *Genealogies*, no longer extant, by the famous genealogist Pherecydes of Athens (ca. fifth century B.C.E.).[35] We might also include two Spartan pedigrees of twenty-one generations, reproduced in Herodotus.[36] Technically these are king lists, but like the Assyrian King List from Mesopotamia, they are presented in pedigree form and explicitly mention the genealogical relationship of a king to his predecessor. It would appear that persons are included who never ruled, and Spartan kings who are not in the straight line of descent are omitted. The noble familes of Greece are likely to have kept track of their genealogies.[37] Pedigrees clearly show an interest in connecting the historical period of the present with the age of gods and heroes, and all the major families would have seen the need to provide some

---

31. Texts and translations in Glassner, *Mesopotamian Chronicles*. Full discussion in Wilson, *Genealogy and History in the Biblical World*, 72–114.

32. *Histories* 2.143.1–144.2.

33. E. Schwyzer, ed., *Dialectorum Graecarum Exempla Epigraphica Potiora* (Hildescheim: Olms, 1960), 690.

34. Marcellinus, *Vit. Thuc.* 2–4.

35. Taylor, "Framing the Past," 25.

36. *Hist.* 7.204 and 8.131.2.

37. Alden A. Mosshammer, *The Chronicle of Eusebius and Greek Chronographic Tradition* (Lewisburg, Pa.: Bucknell University Press, 1979), 101.

evidence of their connection to the past.[38] We see evidence of this desire on the part of the postexilic Jewish community in the first several chapters of Chronicles, in which we find examples of living persons tracing their ancestry into the semi-mythic past. The Torah's genealogies do not extend all the way to the time of the writers, but the lists may be preserved portions of longer genealogies.

3.3.2.2. The Life Spans of the Forefathers

When we gather all of the data in the Torah concerned only with the ages of persons at their deaths,[39] we find the life spans of the patriarchs running from Adam to Joshua, and they generally diminish the further down the list we go.

Kenan	910	(Gen 5:14)
Mahalalel	895	(Gen 5:17)
Jared	962	(Gen 5:20)
Enoch	365	(Gen 5:23)
Methuselah	969	(Gen 5:27)
Lamech	777	(Gen 5:31)
Noah	950	(Gen 9:29)
Shem	600	(Gen 11:10–11)
Arpachshad	438	(Gen 11:12–13)
Shelah	433	(Gen 11:14–15)
Eber	404	(Gen 11:16–17)
Peleg	239	(Gen 11:18–19)
Reu	239	(Gen 11:20–21)
Serug	230	(Gen 11:22–23)
Nahor	148	(Gen 11:24–25)
Terah	205	(Gen 11:32)
Abraham	175	(Gen 25:7)
Sarah	127	(Gen 23:1)
Isaac	180	(Gen 35:28–29)
Jacob	147	(Gen 47:28)
Joseph	110	(Gen 50:23, 26)
Levi	137	(Exod 6:16)

---

38. For a discussion of early Greek pedigrees, see Taylor, "Framing the Past," 20–30.
39. The data from Gen 5 and 11 are from our presumed archetypal text.

Kohath	133	(Exod 6:18)
Amram	137	(Exod 6:20)
Aaron	123	(Num 33:39)
Moses	120	(Deut 34:7)
Joshua	110	(Josh 24:29)

The first question to ask is whether all of these data derive from the same source. We have established, already, the likelihood that the data in Gen 5 were composed or copied into the text by P. On the other end of the list of life spans, we are less certain who included them. Let us look at the precise wording of the entries for each person:

"And all the days of Adam, which he lived, were 930 years. And he died."
"And all the days of Seth were 912 years. And he died."
"And all the days of Enosh were 905 years. And he died."
"And all the days of Kenan were 910 years. And he died."
"And all the days of Mahalalel were 895 years. And he died."
"And all the days of Jared were 962 years. And he died."
"And all the days of Enoch were 365 years…. And he was no more, because God took him."
"And all the days of Methuselah were 969 years. And he died."
"And all the days of Lamech were 777 years. And he died."
"And all the days of Noah were 950 years. And he died."
"And the days of Terah were 205 years. And Terah died in Haran."
"And the life of Sarah was 127 years. And Sarah died in Kiriath-arba."
"These are the days of the years of the life of Abraham, which he lived: 175 years. And he expired and died, old and satisfied, and he was gathered to his people."
"And the days of Isaac were 180 years. And he expired and died, old and satisfied with days."
"And the days of Jacob, the years of his life, came to be 147 years…. And he expired and was gathered to his people."
"And Joseph lived 110 years."
"And Joseph died a son of 110 years."
"And the years of the life of Levi were 137 years."
"And the years of the life of Kohath were 133 years."
"And the years of the life of Amram were 137 years."
"And Aaron was a son of 123 years when he died."
"And Moses was a son of 120 years when he died."
"And Joshua the servant of Yahweh died a son of 110 years."

The statements I have bolded are to be set apart from the rest. We know that the entry concerning Aaron is not from P but from R, since it is set directly in a document added by R (Num 33). We know also that the entries for Levi, Kohath, and Amram are from R, since they also are set directly in a pericope added by R (Exod 6:14–27).[40] Since the entry for Moses is worded exactly the same as the one for Aaron and is unlike any other, it can also confidently be assigned to R. The entry on Joshua stands apart, because, first of all, Joshua is not a descendant of anyone on the list, and second, because the entry is found in the book of Joshua (outside the Pentateuch). Of the two authors, only R had anything to do with the book of Joshua, so we should also probably assign the entry to him. We could entertain the idea that the datum is from a Deuteronomic source, but, if so, it would be the only datum of this type from that source, an anomaly. So R is still the best suggestion. The entry on Joseph matches the one on Joshua and is unlike any other, so it too is most likely from R.

We can already see an interesting phenomenon. All the entries so far ascribed to R are at the conclusion of the list, running from Joseph to the end. Moreover, none of the entries by R contain the word ימי ("the days of"), which is a stock phrase of P's genealogy of Gen 5, whereas all of the non-R entries do. The only exception is the entry for Sarah. Is it possible that this entry is from R as well? Without Sarah, P's ages would run a straight male line from Adam to Jacob without any digressions and would therefore form a full and tidy paternal pedigree. Significantly, in contrast to all of the P entries, R's contributions, including Sarah, have no anchor whatsoever to P's genealogical chronology. In other words, it is impossible to date the deaths of the first five persons, and the dating of the deaths of the final three is possible only because of their (coincidental?) connection to the exodus/conquest chronology.

My argument is that one of the lists used by the author of P was a pedigree of the patriarchs from Adam to Jacob, which listed the life durations of each man. As I will go on to demonstrate, it appears this list also gave Noah's age at the time of the flood, namely, six hundred. Suffice it to say for now that the great age of Noah at this event coincides with the extreme ages of the persons on this list.

One might wonder why a list containing the total ages of the patriarchs would ever have been composed. Certainly the list would serve no chronological purpose, since death ages are irrelevant to chronology (unless one wishes to date a death) and cannot be used to create a timeline. (In other words, the years of the list cannot be added up to measure an era, because a son did not begin to live in the year his father died.) We are left with no other conclusion but that the record of life spans serves another, probably ideological, purpose.

---

40. See Friedman, *The Bible with Sources Revealed*, 128–29.

When Hesiod recounts the cycle of ages, he draws attention to the long life spans of those who lived in days past as an evidence of their superiority, and notes how the life spans diminish with each successive age.[41] Similarly, a list showing the great ages of the ancestors of Israel probably emphasizes the strength and greatness of the world's forefathers as a counterexample to the degenerate state of humankind in later times. As in Hesiod, there is a correspondence between the life durations of the patriarchs and the time period in which they live. Thus, those who live prior to the flood (with the exception of Enoch, who is said to have died young) live between seven hundred and one thousand years, those who live from the flood to Abraham (with the exception of Nahor, who is said to have died young) live between two hundred and six hundred years of age, and those who live from Abraham to Moses live between one hundred and two hundred years of age—might we say, an age of gold, an age of silver, and an age of bronze? The ability to recount specific numbers gives evidence of the superior knowledge of the scribe.

3.3.2.3. A Generational Pedigree in Genesis 5 and 11

The second source P used for his genealogical pedigree would have been a list of generations, with a figure indicating the length of each generation. The word דור is not found in P's pedigree, but is a fitting descriptor for the length of time measured in the pedigree.

Although both the life span pedigree and the generational pedigree provided by P run all the way to Jacob and end there, indications are that the two lists originally were of different lengths and that the author of P had to add to the shorter one to make them equal. For the most part, the figures for the ages of the fathers at the births of their sons in P's genealogy are within the parameters of biological possibility, with the notable exception of Noah, and perhaps also Adam, Seth, Shem, and Abraham. When we examine the ages that are given for the fathers when they sire their sons, one notices that there is a descending pattern in the ages, with two notable exceptions in the middle, and three at the end:

130 (Adam begot Seth)
105 (Seth begot Enosh)
90 (Enosh begot Kenan)
70 (Kenan begot Mahalalel)
65 (Mahalalel begot Jared)
62 (Jared begot Enoch)

---

41. *Op.* 109–201.

65 (Enoch begot Methuselah)
67 (Methuselah begot Lamech)
53 (Lamech begot Noah)
500 (Noah begot Shem)
100 (Shem begot Arpachshad)
35 (Arpachshad begot Shelah)
30 (Shelah begot Eber)
34 (Eber begot Peleg)
30 (Peleg begot Reu)
32 (Reu begot Serug)
30 (Serug begot Nahor)
29 (Nahor begot Terah)
70 (Terah begot Abraham)
100 (Abraham begot Isaac)
60 (Isaac begot Jacob)

The entries for Noah and Shem in the middle, and Terah, Abraham and Isaac at the end, containing large, round numbers, are rather conspicuous anomalies in the list. Why might that be? For the middle entries I would suggest that other chronological data in the text are forcing the numbers to be higher. In the cases of Noah and Shem, the important flood chronology is affecting the data. We have very specific information elsewhere that Noah was 600 years old at the time the flood came (Gen 7:6). We also have information that Shem was 600 years old when he died (Gen 11:10–11). As was argued, these data probably come from the life span pedigree. If Noah's age at the birth of Shem was only around 50, as the overall pattern in the above list suggests he would be, and Shem's age was about 45 when he fathered Arpachshad, then we have a problem. Shem would have been 550 years old when the flood occurred, and Arpachshad would have been 505. Actually, several more generations would have been alive at the flood, including the whole family line up to Abraham, Isaac, Jacob and Joseph! None of these persons could have been born before the flood, not even Arpachshad, because the flood story makes it clear that only Noah, his wife, his three sons, and his sons' wives were on the ark. There weren't any grandchildren until afterward. It thus seems that the editor/author of P had to make some adjustments. He could have increased Shem's age to 551 or so at the time of his siring Arpachshad, but it would have been tougher for a reader to swallow the idea that Shem was so old when he accompanied his father on the ark and when he fathered a son. By making Noah (a very special man) 500 years old at the birth of his sons, and Shem 100 at the birth of his son, the story is a bit more believable and the difficulty is alleviated. We therefore have reason to doubt that these readings were in P's source text.

For the entries at the end of the list, the anomalous numbers suggest that the original list did not stretch all the way to Isaac and had to be supplemented. In Terah's case, a motivation for the higher age does not seem to be chronological. We have information from the life span pedigree that he died when he was 205 (Gen 11:32). We also have information that Abraham was 175 years old when he died (Gen 25:7). If Terah were only about 30 years old, as the pattern in the present list suggests he would be, then Terah would have lived just long enough to see the death of his son. However, this observation would not have been sufficient motivation for the priestly editor to alter Terah's age, as is evidenced by the fact that several of Abraham's ancestors live well into his lifetime, and some beyond. The overlap of generations simply was not an issue. To be sure, the text implies that Terah was already dead when Abraham left for Canaan (cf. 11:32a [Terah's death notice] and 12:4b–5 [Abraham's departure], both of which are P texts), and this may have been cause for concern, particularly because the text originally read that Terah lived 205 years *in Haran* (see above), but an increase in Terah's age at Abraham's birth from 30 to 70 would not have resolved that problem. Thus no motivation for an alteration in the case of Terah is apparent, and yet since the reading does not fit the pattern of the pedigree, we are still wise to consider it alien. A reasonable explanation is that the original pedigree concluded with the birth of Terah, and since there was no figure for Terah's age at the birth of his son, or Abraham's at the birth of his, or Isaac's at the birth of his, the priestly editor had to create one. Still, why did he make the numbers so high? There certainly is a case for making Abraham's high, as he is supposed to be an old man at the birth of Isaac (cf. Gen 17:17), and in Isaac's case his wife is said to have been barren for some time (Gen 25:20–21). Yet there is nothing in the narrative that would demand that Abraham be as old as 100 or Isaac as old as 60 when their children are born. The priestly editor most likely was trying to extend the period from the flood to the Israelites' entry into Egypt. Increasing the ages of Terah, Abraham, and Isaac allowed him to add another 100 years or more to the chronology.[42]

The normal length of a generation in P's source can be seen in the more recent entries, that is, Arpachshad through Nahor, and would have fallen between 29 and 35 years. As we go back in time through the list, the generations grow longer.

---

42. Cf. the similar motivations of LXX in Gen 5 and both LXX and SP in Genesis 11 (see §3.2.3 above).

Arpachshad to Nahor = generation range 29–35
Lamech to Shem = generation range x 1.5 (44–53)
Kenan to Methuselah = generation range x 2 (58–70)
Seth to Enosh = generation range x 3 (87–105)
Adam = generation range x 4 (116–140)

While there are five divisions between each section of the generational chronology, each with its own generational norm, the life spans are consistent between Adam and Noah (700–1000 years) and then also between Shem and Abraham (200–600 years). In other words, there is no consistency between the life span norm and the generational norm. We thus have further evidence that the two lists were originally unrelated.[43]

Although it is unusual to find a pedigree with a chronology built in, it is not unusual for pedigrees to be used for chronological purposes. Greek genealogies, for example, although they do not contain chronological data, were sometimes fitted into chronologies. Ever since the study of Eduard Meyer, it has been argued that Greek chronology was often *based* on their pedigrees.[44] Assuming a certain length of time for one generation, the ancient historians would calculate how far back certain persons would have lived. However, it may be more accurate to say that chronologies were created independently and then were harmonized with the genealogies. Greek historians played with generation lengths and imposed them on preexisting genealogies in order to fit famous persons of the past properly into an accepted timeline. No single generational "norm" figure was in use across the board. In fact, even a single chronographer might use more than one figure.[45] P appears to be doing the same thing, and its generational norm is likewise inconsistent.[46]

---

43. Another example of unresolved inconsistency is that Moses, Aaron, and Joshua are in the era of extended life spans, but the curse of 40 years in the wilderness (Num 14:32–34) implies a realistic life span.

44. Eduard Meyer, "Herodots Chronologie der griechischen Sagengeschichte," in *Forschungen zur alten Geschichte* (Halle: Niemeyer, 1892), 151–88. See also Donald Wilson Prakken, *Studies in Greek Genealogical Chronology* (Lancaster, Pa.: Lancaster, 1943).

45. Thus, for example, Herodotus appears to construct chronologies based on several different generation lengths, including 23, 26, 33, 34, 39, and 40 years. See discussion in Mosshammer, *Chronicle of Eusebius*, 105–12. Cf. also John Forsdyke, *Greece before Homer: Ancient Chronology and Mythology* (New York: Norton, 1964), 28–43; Samuel, *Greek and Roman Chronology*, 241–45.

46. As in Greece, Israelite genealogies originally were not created for historical purposes. Only later were they adopted to suit the needs of chronographers. See Wilson, *Genealogy and History in the Biblical World*, 199–200. That the genealogy of Gen 5 once

3.3.3. Conclusions

From what we have seen, the genealogical list that begins in Gen 5 appears to be a conflation of at least two different catalogues. One was a pedigree listing the ages of the fathers at the births of their sons. The numbers tended to be low. The other was a pedigree with the total ages of the patriarchs. The numbers tended to be high, and the flood date was late in the life of Noah (600 years). With their combination, accommodations had to be made: Noah's and Shem's birthdates had to be changed. Moreover, there apparently were no birthdates for Abraham, Isaac, and Jacob, so these were supplied in accordance with the P author's conception of the length of time spanning Terah's and Joseph's lives.

TABLE 3.3. SOURCES OF THE AGES IN THE PRIESTLY GENEALOGY

Genesis Verse	Name	Catalogue 1	Catalogue 2	Editor
5:3	Adam	130 (begot Seth)	930 (died)	
5:6	Seth	105 (begot Enosh)	912 (died)	
5:9	Enosh	90 (begot Kenan)	905 (died)	
5:12	Kenan	70 (begot Mahalalel)	910 (died)	
5:15	Mahalalel	65 (begot Jared)	895 (died)	
5:18	Jared	62 (begot Enoch)	962 (died)	
5:21	Enoch	65 (begot Methuselah)	365 (died)	
5:25	Methuselah	67 (begot Lamech)	969 (died)	
5:28	Lamech	53 (begot Noah)	777 (died)	
5:32	Noah	[50] (begot Shem)		500 (begot 3 sons)
7:6	Noah		600 (flood)	
9:29	Noah		950 (died)	

---

existed without the chronology is evident in that it appears, without the chronology and in an alternate form, in Gen 4. For a comparison of the two genealogies, see ibid., 161.

11:10–11	Shem	[45] (begot Arpachshad)	600 (died)	100 (begot Arpach.)
11:12–13	Arpach-shad	35 (begot Shelah)	438 (died)	
11:14–15	Shelah	30 (begot Eber)	433 (died)	
11:16–17	Eber	34 (begot Peleg)	404 (died)	
11:18–19	Peleg	30 (begot Reu)	239 (died)	
11:20–21	Reu	32 (begot Serug)	239 (died)	
11:22–23	Serug	30 (begot Nahor)	230 (died)	
11:24–25	Nahor	29 (begot Terah)	148 (died)	
11:26, 32	Terah		205 (died)	70 (begot 3 sons)
16:16	Abraham			86 (begot Ishmael)
21:5	Abraham			100 (begot Isaac)
25:7	Abraham		175 (died)	
25:26	Isaac			60 (begot Jacob)
35:28	Isaac		180 (died)	
47:28	Jacob		147 (died)	

When the priestly author/editor composed the lists in Gen 5 and 11, he took the age of the father at the birth of his son from Source 1, calculated the interval between that age and the age of the man's death, as recorded in Source 2, and included the figure for the interval in the list (a number that did not appear in either source). In Gen 11, he appears not to even have bothered to include the total age of the individual from Source 2; he merely gave the figure for the intervening years. The reason for this difference is unclear but may be simply because, while desiring to preserve the lengthy life spans to emphasize the greatness of the ancestors, the priestly author/editor was not entirely comfortable with the chronological implications (the overlap of generations) and did not wish to make them obvious.

4
Rulership Chronologies[1]

4.1. Chronological Sources of the Deuteronomic History

4.1.1. Time as Seen by the Deuteronomistic Historians and their Audiences

The chronology used in the Deuteronomic History is, for the most part, concerned with the exploits of the rulers of Israel and Judah and derived from administrative records or earlier historiographic works.[2] These sources, from which many of the chronological data are derived, need to be distinguished, sorted and compared. Also of interest are the artificial periods of time that the author and later reviser of the DH created to fill in gaps left by the sources. Moreover, we would do well to consider the Historian's and his editor's personal manners of reckoning time, according to the customs of their own day, which they sometimes employ in the DH in addition to the data derived from their sources. What will become apparent is that the original version of the History (DH[1]) contained a limited amount of chronological information and that the second edition (DH[2]) added much more to the History and systematized its chronology.

The chronological orientation of the exilic reviser of the DH is the easiest to apprehend, a great deal more so than that of the original composer/compiler of the History. We find an underlying assumption of a year beginning in the spring. Indeed, Babylonian chronology pervades the closing chapter of the DH (2 Kgs 25). The first edition of the DH, no doubt written in preexilic

---

1. I use the term "rulership chronologies" to refer to those chronologies based upon the periods of time during which leaders of various kinds held sway over a community.

2. The historian cites a number of these sources (see below). Textual analysis has shown dependence on unnamed sources as well. See Mordechai Cogan, *1 Kings: A New Translation with Introduction and Commentary* (AB 10; New York: Doubleday, 2001), 88–95.

times during the reign of Josiah, does not appear to reflect a spring-based calendar (see ch. 1). A theory could be entertained that DH² was produced among the Jewish community in Egypt (cf. 2 Kgs 25:26), but then we should expect an Egyptian calendar to be reflected in the text. Because the calendrical system to which the audience seems to be accustomed is in keeping with that used in Babylon, it probably is best to see the second edition of the DH as a product of the Babylonian community of Jews or of Jews elsewhere under Babylonian dominion.

Because there is clearly a connection between the DH and many of the prose sections of the book of Jeremiah,[3] it would be wise to examine Jeremiah to see what light it can shed on the method of reckoning that might have been employed in calculations related to the rulers of Israel by both the Deuteronomistic Historian and the later editor of the DH.

4.1.2. CHRONOLOGICAL SOURCES FOR THE BOOK OF JEREMIAH

It is important to note that *all* of the chronological material in Jeremiah has to do with events from Jehoiakim's reign forward. There are no data from the reign of Josiah apart from the superscription, which mentions only the thirteenth year of that king (627 B.C.E.), the year of Jeremiah's call. Thus, while there may be a connection between the authorship of the book of Jeremiah and the Deuteronomic History, there is no evidence in the book of Jeremiah of an interest in chronology by Jeremiah himself, or by whatever scribe he employed, at the time the DH was first published.

In the fourth year of King Jehoiakim (605 B.C.E.), some years after the initial publication of the DH and many years before its exilic revision, the scribe Baruch ben Neriah was asked to write a scroll for Jeremiah, which appears to have included both earlier material from the reign of Josiah and new oracles pertaining to the current situation in Judah and the then reigning king Jehoiakim (Jer 36:1–32).[4] The scroll was destroyed, but a new one was composed shortly afterward (ca. 604), and some have argued that the contents of this rewritten scroll corresponded roughly to the first twenty chapters

---

3. See Jack R. Lundbom, "Jeremiah, Book of," *ABD* 3:706–21; Richard Elliott Friedman, "The Deuteronomistic School," in *Fortunate the Eyes that See: Essays in Honor of David Noel Freedman in Celebration of his Seventieth Birthday* (ed. Astrid B. Beck et al.; Grand Rapids: Eerdmans, 1995), 70–80.

4. Jack R. Lundbom, *Jeremiah 1–20: A New Translation with Introduction and Commentary* (AB 21A; New York: Doubleday, 1999), 92–93. The date for the composition of this scroll is arrived at by counting twenty-three years (Jer 25:1–3) from the thirteenth year of Josiah (Jer 1:2), i.e., 627 B.C.E.

4. RULERSHIP CHRONOLOGIES 99

of the present book.⁵ Most of the material is poetry, although small sections of prose are scattered throughout. Little of the writing bears resemblance to the prose of the Deuteronomic History. If Baruch wrote this section in 604, it involved little free composition. It appears to be simply a compilation of Jeremiah's early and current prophecies. Notable is that there are no chronological references anywhere in the poetry or the prose.

From 604 to the end of Jeremiah's career sometime in the exile, a great deal more material was added to the collection by Baruch, and perhaps others. There is a significant amount of prose in these later additions, an indication that Baruch was permitted to compose with greater freedom in relating the experiences of the prophet, and for the first time we are able to glimpse the scribe's literary talent and style. The narrative sections are similar to the prose of the DH and reveal a greater interest in dates, although not as much as we might suppose. There are differences between the chronological notices in Jeremiah and the DH, some of which are governed by the subject matter, as in the case of the common phrase "the word of Yahweh came to Jeremiah," which we naturally would not expect to find in the DH, but which is a common feature of the Jeremianic chronological notices. Another common feature of the Jeremianic notices is the phrase PN ראשית ממלכת ("in the beginning of the reign of PN"), which has sometimes been associated mistakenly with the Akkadian expression *reš šarruti* ("beginning of reign"), a technical term referring to a king's accession year. However, unlike the term שנת מלכ[ת]ו ("in the year of his becoming king"),⁶ which is a closer semantic equivalent of *reš šarruti*, ראשית ממלכת is a nontechnical term used to refer to a general time and does not mean "accession year."⁷ The use of this general expression in the book of Jeremiah suggests that the phrase does not come from a chronological source text, but is rather a creation of the scribe himself, who may be writing from memory. The phrase most often occurs by itself (26:1; 27:1; 49:34). It does, in one case, appear along with more precise data (28:1).

Jeremiah 28:1 makes an excellent case study of the formation of the chronological references in the book. The superscription to the narrative reads as follows:

---

5. Jack R. Lundbom, *Jeremiah: A Study in Ancient Hebrew Rhetoric* (Winona Lake, Ind.: Eisenbrauns, 1997), 42–44; Lundbom, *Jeremiah 1–20*, 93–95. This grouping of chapters is held together by an inclusio, Jeremiah's comment in 20:18 referring back to his call and commission (1:5).

6. As in, e.g., 2 Kgs 25:27.

7. See Mordechai Cogan, "Chronology, Hebrew Bible," *ABD* 1:1006.

ויהי בשנה ההיא בראשית ממלכת צדקיה מלך יהודה בשנת הרבעית
בחדש החמישי

And it happened in that year, in the beginning of the reign of Zedekiah the king of Judah, in the fourth year in the fifth month

The expression בשנה ההיא ("in that year") refers back to the events of the previous narrative (which is mistakenly attributed in MT's reading of 27:1 to the reign of Jehoiakim, but is correctly stated as Zedekiah in a few manuscripts). Of interest is the double time reference that follows. Both "the beginning of the reign of Zedekiah" and "the fourth year in the fifth month" appear. It was hardly necessary for both references to be included by the original writer, and although the more general reference does not mean "accession year," there still is a certain amount of tension between the two dates, so the text has most likely undergone expansion.[8] The logical direction of growth would be from less specific to more specific information, so it is probable that the original reading contained only mention of the beginning of Zedekiah's reign. What this tells us is that a later editor was unsatisfied with the original composer's general time reference, and so he added the specific year and month reference. Interestingly, the phrase "in the fourth year in the fifth month," because it dates an event both to a year and a month, resembles only the chronological notices in the final chapter of the DH (2 Kgs 25), an exilic addition. Revisions like these suggest that the earlier authors of the book of Jeremiah and the Deuteronomic History had less interest in chronological specificity than those who revised the works. We will examine this phenomenon in the Deuteronomic History in more detail below and see how it has a bearing on the chronology itself.

4.1.3. Chronological Sources Relating to the Judges

The earliest chronological data in the DH relating to the leaders of Israel is found in the book of Judges. The introduction to the book (2:6–23) provides a framework for its stories, which contain the following elements:

(1) The Israelites do what is bad in the sight of Yahweh.
(2) Yahweh gives Israel into the power of an oppressor, whom they serve for a specific term of years.
(3) The Israelites cry out to Yahweh.
(4) Yahweh raises up a savior.

---

8. See Jack R. Lundbom, *Jeremiah 21–36: A New Translation with Introduction and Commentary* (AB 21B; New York: Doubleday, 2004), 329.

(5) The savior delivers Israel.
(6) The foe is subdued.
(7) The land is quiet for a specified term of years.

An analysis of the chronological presentation in the book of Judges suggests that this cycle began as a creation of the original composer/compiler of the Deuteronomic History, but was schematized further by the reviser of the History, who wrote the introduction to the Judges narratives.[9] The elements of most interest to us are #2 and #7, each of which provides a chronological datum. The first covers a period of time during which Israel is understood not to have had a leader to govern it. The second apparently represents a period of time that passed between the victory of a judge (#6) and the beginning of the next oppression (#1).

Considering the periods of peace first (item #7), we may make some interesting observations. The term is always given as 40 years, except in one instance, where a term of 80 years is given (3:30). However, the higher figure in this latter instance may be intended to cover the judgeships of both Ehud and Shamgar (3:31), in which case we would have to conclude that the chronological notice of 3:30 presupposes the existence of 3:31. In other words, the 80-year period of peace assumes the existence of both Ehud and Shamgar, so the brief comment concerning Shamgar is unlikely to be a late addition.[10] One might wonder why the author did not simply put a 40-year period of peace after Ehud and then another after Shamgar (separately). The explanation most likely has to do with the fact that the Philistine oppression does not end until the time of Saul. It would therefore be impossible to claim a 40-year calm after the victory of Shamgar over the Philistines. The Philistines are understood to be a thorn in Israel's side for some time afterwards. At the same time, the editor wanted to account for the judgeship of Shamgar. The

---

9. For a discussion of the evidence that suggests that the composer of Judg 2:11–19 was not the same as the composer of the cycle of stories that follow, see Baruch Halpern, *The First Historians: The Hebrew Bible and History* (San Francisco: Harper & Row, 1988), 121–40.

10. It is often argued that the note about Shamgar is a late interpolation that ruins the narrative flow from 3:30 to 4:1 (see, e.g., Soggin, *Judges*, 57–59). Yet verse 30 is incomplete in MT and should have ended with the phrase "And Ehud judged them until he died," as is evidenced by LXX. (The loss is attributable to haplography due to homoeoarcton.) The note that "Ehud had died" in 4:1 only seems necessary if the text had diverged from its context and required a resumptive repetition to bring the audience back to the main storyline. In parallel verses (3:12; 6:1; 10:6; 13:1), we see no such repetition.

simplest way to maintain the pattern was to create a double period of peace after Ehud.

The figures given for the periods of oppression (item 2 on the list above) may or may not exhibit a pattern, but the scale tips slightly in favor of the former.

(1) Judg 3:8	Mesopotamian oppression	8 years
(2) Judg 3:14	Moabite oppression	18 years
(3) Judg 4:3	Canaanite oppression	20 years
(4) Judg 6:1	Midianite oppression	7 years
(5) Judg 10:8	Ammonite oppression	18 years
(6) Judg 13:1	Philistine oppression	40 years

As has been noted by Hughes, there seems to be a form of schematic parallelism between the period of the first three oppressions and the period of the second three.[11] To make the parallel even closer, Hughes suggests that the text concerning the Mesopotamian oppression originally read 7 years. No extant manuscript contains such a reading, however. To support his view, Hughes points out that the figure of 300 years for the period from the settlement to the beginning of the Ammonite oppression given at Judges 11:26 would exactly match the total of the 45 years mentioned at Joshua 14:10 and the first four figures here, plus the 3 years of Abimelech (Judg 9:22), if it were reduced by one year. As tempting as it would be to assume an original reading of "7" in Judges 3:8, the evidence of Judges 11:26 is simply not enough to justify this position. Until a manuscript shows up with this reading, it is best to retain the figure "8." On the other hand, the figures given in this list do seem somewhat artificial. There is an ascending pattern in each group of three numbers, the first two numbers in the sequence are almost identical in each group, and the final number in the second group is exactly double the final number in the first group. This suggests that they did not come from a primary document or inscription and are the creation of an editor, just as the figures for the periods of rest are.

I wish to discuss another set of chronological figures in the book of Judges, which may bear on our understanding of the other periods. These are the terms of office for six of the judges (Tola, Jair, Jephthah, Ibzan, Elon, and Abdon). The chronology associated with these judges has a very different character from the periods of rest and periods of oppression. These judges' terms appear to derive from a source document that was incorporated into

---

11. Hughes, *Secrets of the Times*, 73.

the History at the time of its initial composition.[12] The document is in the form of a list, which recounts a succession of judges in annalistic fashion, many of whom do not have significant narratives about them in Judges, and includes the durations of their hegemonies over Israel. Each entry contains a picturesque description of the judge's kinsmen, which appears to be there as a memory aid, and provides the location of his burial. The document is split in half, the first part appearing in 10:1–5 and the second part in 12:7–15. Similarity in language seems to indicate that fragments also appear in 8:30, 32. The entire extant text (with minor reconstructions) reads as follows:

> [And after him Gideon son of Joash rose up to deliver Israel. And he judged Israel ? years.] And Gideon had seventy sons that issued from his member, for he had many wives. Then Gideon the son of Joash died at a good old age, and he was buried in the tomb of his father Joash at Ophrah of the Abiezrites.
>
> And after [him],[13] Tola the son of Puah the son of Dodo, a man of Issachar, rose up to deliver Israel, and he was a resident in Shamir in the hill country of Ephraim. And he judged Israel twenty-three years. Then he died, and he was buried in Shamir.
>
> And after him, Jair the Gileadite rose up. And he judged Israel twenty-two years. And he had thirty sons who rode on thirty donkeys; and they had thirty towns,[14] which are in the land of the Gilead. Then Jair died, and he was buried in Qamon.
>
> [And after him, Jephthah the Gileadite rose up.][15] And Jephthah judged Israel six years. Then Jephthah the Gileadite died, and he was buried in his town in Gilead.[16]

---

12. Soggin, *Judges*, 195–200.

13. The text reads: "after Abimelech," but Abimelech does not feature in the list, and in all other instances, the list uses the expression: "after him."

14. Reading ערים, as in LXX, instead of MT עירים (see Robert G. Boling, "Some Conflate Readings in Joshua-Judges," *VT* 16 [1966]: 295–96). The following sentence, "Them they call the Villages of Jair to this day," is an addition by the Deuteronomistic Historian, as is evidenced by his typical expression "until this day" (see Jeffrey C. Geoghegan, "Until Whose Day? A Study of the Phrase 'Until This Day' in the Deuteronomistic History" [Ph.D. diss., University of California, San Diego, 1999]).

15. These words are missing in the biblical text, because they had to be removed in order for the narrative as it stands to make sense.

16. MT reads, "in the towns of Gilead," which could only be true if Jephthah's body parts were buried in separate places. LXX's reading ("in his town in Gilead") is preferable.

And after him, Ibzan from Bethlehem judged Israel. And he had thirty sons; and thirty daughters he sent to the outside, and thirty daughters he brought in for his sons from the outside. And he judged Israel seven years. Then Ibzan died, and he was buried in Bethlehem.

And after him, Elon the Zebulunite judged Israel. And he judged Israel ten years. Then Elon the Zebulunite died, and he was buried at Aijalon in the land of Zebulun.

And after him, Abdon the son of Hillel the Pirathonite judged Israel. And he had forty sons and thirty grandsons, who rode on seventy donkeys. And he judged Israel eight years. Then Abdon son of Hillel the Pirathonite died, and he was buried in Pirathon in the land of Ephraim, in the hill country of the Amalekites.

One of the first observations we can make about this document is that the beginning is missing. In all probability, the document was incomplete when the Deuteronomistic Historian put it into the History. If the number of years for Gideon's term was known, the historian would have preferred to retain that figure rather than providing a general 40-year period to cover his time. We know this, because when he incorporated the Jephthah traditions into the work, he retained the six-year figure from this source document, rather than sticking in his usual 40-year figure. There are no instances where the History gives a specific term length for a judge *and* a 40-year period of rest, and this suggests that one set of figures is dependent on the other.

The judges' terms of office as given in this source document do not display any patterns that might suggest that the numbers are artificial. In this they differ greatly from the periods of rest and the periods of oppression. Whether we may trust them as historically reliable is another question, but since they are incomplete and there is no way to anchor any part of this short chronology to a known historical date, they are not likely to be useful for any historical chronological calculations.

Closer examination of the book of Judges seems to indicate that the numbers associated with the periods of oppression were not created by the same editor/author as the one who devised the figures for the 40-year periods of peace. It is usually understood that the calm that sets over the land ("the land had no disturbance") refers to a time that extends from an Israelite victory over one oppressor until the beginning of the next oppression (and this is certainly what the creator of the oppression chronology has in mind). However, the original intention seems to have been to indicate that the 40-years is a *period between wars*. The Deuteronomistic Historian, in a similar description of a period of calm, explicitly says this: "the land had no disturbance *from war*" (Joshua 11:23). In other words, when the 40 years are over, a war should break out. The editor who created the periods of oppression, on the other hand, understands only a period of servitude to follow the 40 years, and not a war. Sometimes the oppressors make raids on Israel, but no real battles take place until a judge rises up. In the original edition of the History, the 40-year periods are more or less equivalent to the terms of the judges. This appears to be confirmed by Judges 4:1, which tells us that Ehud's death, which marked the end of his judgeship, also marked the end of 40 years (see also 3:11 and 8:48). Use of the 40-year gaps was a convenient substitution for a term of office and a way for the Deuteronomistic Historian to move the stories forward in time one generation.

An additional piece of evidence that suggests that the oppression chronology is secondary is in Judges 10:8, where the figure for the period of Ammonite oppression interrupts the flow of the sentence in which it is embedded:

> And they shattered and oppressed the Israelites in that year—18 years—, all the Israelites that were on the side of the Jordan in the land of the Amorites that was in Gilead.

Moreover, the mention of an oppression of both Ammonites *and* Philistines in the previous verse (part of the original DH narrative) sets the stage for the exploits not only of Jephthah, who fought the Ammonites, but of Samson and Samuel, who fought the Philistines, making the notice of a 40-year Philistine oppression in Judges 13:1 superfluous. A final piece of evidence is that, without the oppression periods, the total time of the period from the entry into Canaan to the rise of Jephthah equals 290 years plus the length of the reign of Abimelech (unstated in the first edition), a total that coincides with the 300-year figure mentioned by Jephthah in Judges 11:26.[17]

The purpose of the expanded chronology that included the periods of oppression (and the note about the 3-year kingship of Abimelech in Judges 9:22) is to create a chronological period for the time of the judges that equals 479 years, so that the construction of the temple could be placed in the 480th year after the exodus.[18] Before the additions, the History accounted for only

---

17. Five years for the Conquest (Josh 14:10), 40 years for the passing of one generation (Judg 2:10), 40 years each for Othniel, Ehud, Shamgar, Deborah, and Gideon (200 years total), 23 years for Tola (Judg 10:2), and 22 years for Jair (Judg 10:3). It would seem that the Historian estimated 10 years for Abimelech, although he never states so.

18. The figure is created by the multiplication of two significant numbers, 12 (the number of months in a year) and 40 (the number of years in a generation).

424 (inclusive) years of this period[19] and contained no figure for the reign of Abimelech or a figure covering the interval between the judgeship of Samson and the reign of Saul. Thus the exilic editor saw a need to fill it out and beef it up.[20] The original editor was not as concerned about constructing such a definitive chronology. He had source documents with chronological information that he saw fit to share with his audience, but his inconsistent use of them and his use of round numbers to cover periods between events, and his apparent lack of interest in accounting for every time period, demonstrates that he was not motivated to specificity.

4.1.4. CHRONOLOGICAL SOURCES RELATING TO THE KINGS

4.1.4.1. Preliminary Considerations

Many historians and biblical scholars have attempted to make sense of the chronological data found in the books of the Kings. Some have been more successful than others, but all who have tackled the problem have had significant difficulties in understanding the systems employed. The failure of scholars to comprehend the data is surprising, considering that the chronological notices in the final edition of the Deuteronomic History are presented so systematically. For each king, the length of reign is provided along with a synchronic note tying his accession to a specific year of a contemporary king. For the kings of Judah, their age at accession and their mother's name are also given. Nevertheless, the numbers do not (always) add up. The usual recourse is to invent an elaborate and complicated theory to make the numbers conform to one another and, if necessary to ensure the proper outcome, to make significant emendations to the text under the assumption the data have some-

---

19. Forty-five years for the wilderness wanderings and conquest (Josh 14:10), 40 years for the passing of one generation, 40 years each for Othniel, Ehud, Shamgar, Deborah, and Gideon (200 years total), 76 years from the fragmentary Judges list, 20 years for Samson (Judg 16:31), 40 years for David (1 Kgs 2:11), and 3 years for Solomon (1 Kgs 6:1). Although this total is 424 years, the reviser of the DH believed it accounted for only 384, because while the Josianic historian saw a gap between the death of Joshua and the judgeship of Othniel, the reviser apparently saw Othniel as an immediate successor to Joshua.

20. The gap was filled simply by creating a Philistine oppression period of forty years (Judg 13:1). The note at Judges 15:20, which states a term of twenty years for Samson (and is based on Judges 16:31), places that term "in the days of the Philistines" and thus assumes the period of Philistine oppression mentioned in 13:1 and must be included in the forty years. The note that Samson was active during the days of the Philistines therefore was added by the reviser of the History. The Philistine oppression continues through the judgeship of Samuel. See §2.2.

how been corrupted by miscopying.[21] It is the opinion of the present author that the usual approach is suspect. Instead of considering the chronological systems of each of the Deuteronomistic Historian's sources separately, scholars collect all of the chronological data from all of the sources and treat them homogeneously, hoping to find consistency among them. One must either assume that a system exists that will harmonize all data or abandon all hope of comprehending the data. The problem has only been exacerbated since the discovery of chronological material from kingdoms contemporary with Israel and Judah, in particular Assyria. These data are thrown into the pot as well, and the resulting discord further removes us from a decent understanding of the chronology. This faulty approach to the material is no doubt motivated by a desire to determine the reality behind the numbers in as few steps as possible. However, we can never ascertain the reliability of the biblical data until we first understand each source as an independent unit. Only then can we make comparisons with extrabiblical data and make a judgment.

To be sure, several or all of the Deuteronomistic Historian's sources may contain accurate chronological data that derive ultimately from the king lists of each kingdom or from royal chronicles, and it is also possible that the synchronisms between the two kingdoms might come originally from a document very much like the Synchronistic Chronicle from Assyria.[22] Indeed, if the data come from primary texts that contained historically reliable information, some might argue that there is no need to separate sources, since the data ultimately derive from the same source and should jibe. However, there is no such con-

---

21. Almost every book that has been written on the subject assumes this posture. The most well-known is Thiele, *Mysterious Numbers of the Hebrew Kings*. In his preface, he writes, "For more than two thousand years Hebrew chronology has been a serious problem for Old Testament scholars. Every effort to weave the chronological data of the kings of Israel and Judah into some sort of harmonious scheme seemed doomed to failure. The numbers for the one kingdom could not, it seemed, be made to agree with the numbers in the other.... The problem is one with which I wrestled long before vague outlines of a solution began to crystallize in my mind." In a more recent work, Christine Tetley states: "On the assumption that the compiler of 1–2 Kings wrote a synchronistic record using preexisting annals of Judah and Israel, one expects that the original regnal years and accession synchronisms were internally consistent and coherent. If, through centuries of transmission, an error occurred in a number, the alteration would affect the congruency of an otherwise consistent system" (M. Christine Tetley, *The Reconstructed Chronology of the Divided Kingdom* [Winona Lake, Ind.: Eisenbrauns, 2005], 93).

22. This Babylonian document provides a concise history of relations between Babylonia and Assyria from the reign of Puzur-Ashur III (1503–1479) to Adad-nirari III (811–783). It exists in fragmentary form in seventh-century copies found at Nineveh. Text and translation in Glassner, *Mesopotamian Chronicles*, 176–83.

gruity, neither can a trace to a common source be made; and the author makes no mention of official king lists or a synchronistic chronicle. The works to which he refers at the close of the presentation of each reign and which no doubt provided him with his information are secondary sources, and we do not know their exact relation to the archival data. Moreover, we do not know whether the systems used for calculating regnal years are the same in all the documents. Therefore, unless we know how each system works and that no historical errors have crept into the data, either by accident or by design, we cannot assume a single system of measurement, and then, in an effort to make the numbers conform to reality, restore a presumed original by "correcting" the figures. I, therefore, have decided to organize the data according to source and analyze each system on its own terms.

The historian has provided us with the names of a number of his sources, and three are the most likely to have provided him with chronological data: The Scroll of the Affairs of the Days for the Kings of Judah, The Scroll of the Affairs of the Days for the Kings of Israel, and The Scroll of the Affairs of Solomon. He makes reference to these works in the formulas that close a narrative about a particular king. The first source is cited fifteen times (1 Kgs 14:29; 15:7, 23; 22:45; 2 Kgs 8:23; 12:20 [19]; 14:18; 15:6, 36; 16:19; 20:20; 21:17; 21:25; 23:28; 24:5), the second eighteen times (1 Kgs 14:19; 15:31; 16:5, 14, 20, 27; 22:39; 2 Kgs 1:18; 10:34; 13:8, 12; 14:15, 28; 15:11, 15, 21, 26, 31), and the third once (1 Kgs 11:41). It would seem that these scrolls had a reputation in the author's intended audience and were held to be authoritative. Besides chronological information, it would appear they contained records of wars, public works and other royal projects, tribute payments, conspiracies against the crown, and cultic violations.

The manner in which the chronological data are presented aids us in identifying the source. For example, dated events containing a month reference are rare and occur in only three sections of the Deuteronomic History: in the account of Solomon's building projects (1 Kgs 6, 8), in the story of Jeroboam's new shrine dedication (1 Kgs 12:31–33), and in the history's denouement, which includes the accounts of the final siege of Jerusalem by King Nebuchadnezzar of Babylon, the brief governorship of Gedaliah, and the fate of Jehoiachin (2 Kgs 25). Since the monthly data connected with Solomon's building projects are restricted to a small section of the History, they probably derive from one of the historian's less-used sources, perhaps The Scroll of the Affairs of Solomon (1 Kgs 11:41), which is not referred to elsewhere in the DH. The data for Nebuchadnezzar's siege of Jerusalem come from an unnamed source, but the month references extend from the siege of Jerusalem (588) to the thirty-seventh year of the exile of Jehoiachin (560). All the events could easily have occurred in the lifetime of the reviser of the

4. RULERSHIP CHRONOLOGIES

Deuteronomic History and reflect a Babylonian system of reckoning, and may even come from a Babylonian source, or the dates could have been calculated and recorded by the reviser himself as the events occurred. Either way, the month references in 2 Kgs 25 are from an exilic perspective, and it is unlikely that The Scroll of the Affairs of the Days for the Kings of Judah (hereafter referred to as the Judahite Royal Chronicle) provided any of this information. Dates containing a month reference are conspicuously absent in the history of the period from Rehoboam to Jehoaichin. In Jeremiah, dates containing a month occur for the reigns of two kings of Judah, Jehoiakim and Zedekiah, and of the governorship of Gedaliah, all of which are found in the second half of the book and for which no source is cited. As was discussed above, it is not certain that these dates were originally in a preexilic edition of the book of Jeremiah. Even if some of them were, all the dated events occurred in the lifetimes of Jeremiah and his scribe Baruch, so they may not have been taken from a written source at all. Rather, they simply would be dates that the author recorded personally.

4.1.4.2. King Lists

The framework for the presentation of the chronological data in the books of Kings is very distinctive and easily recognizable. One formula repeated throughout the history of the kingdoms is that of the Judahite accessions, which comes in two patterns:

(1) בשנת # (שנה) ל-PN (בן-PN) (מלך ישראל) PN מלך (בן-PN)
(מלך יהודה) (על־יהודה)
בן-# שנה היה במלכו
ו# שנים מלך בירושלם
ושם אמו PN (בת-PN) (מGN)

In the [#] (year) of PN (the son of PN), (the king of Israel), PN (the son of PN), (the king of Judah), became king (over Judah).
He was [#] years old at his accession,
and [#] years he reigned in Jerusalem,
and the name of his mother was PN (the daughter of PN) (from GN).

(2) בן-# שנה היה במלכו
ו# שנים מלך בירושלם
ושם אמו PN (בת-PN) (מGN)

PN was [#] years old at his accession,
and [#] years he reigned in Jerusalem,
and the name of his mother was PN (the daughter of PN) (from GN).

Elements in parentheses may or may not appear but often do. Pattern 1 appears in the formulas from Rehoboam to Hezekiah and is notable in that it opens with a long chronological datum tying the accession to the specific regnal year of an Israelite king. Pattern 2 appears in the formulas from Manasseh to Zedekiah and omits the synchronism with the kingdom of Israel (for the obvious reason that the Israelite monarchy no longer existed).

It could be argued that the synchronisms do not derive from an actual source but are a creation of the Deuteronomistic Historian, who used the lengths of the reigns of the kings, which *were* derived from an actual source, to calculate the time for the accession of each king in relation to the reign of a king from the sister kingdom. Weighing against this proposition is the fact that there are several synchronisms that could not have been calculated this way (1 Kgs 14:25; 2 Kgs 12:7; 18:9–10, 13); these synchronisms are placed in the midst of king's reigns, rather than at the beginning, and therefore must have been either completely invented or derived from a source used by the Historian. It seems best to assume that the Historian, rather than inventing the synchronisms, had access to a synchronistic source (or sources). Sources of this nature are known from ancient Babylon and are represented by such documents as the Chronicle of the Kings from Nabonassar to Šamaš-šuma-ukin, the Chronicle of the Kings from Nabonassar to Esarhaddon, the Chronicle of Esarhaddon, the Chronicle of Nabopolassar Concerning the Fall of the Assyrian Empire, the Chronicle of the Death of Nabopolassar and the First Years of Nebuchadnezzar, and the Chronicle of Nabonidus, to name just a few. All are from the Neo-Babylonian period (ca. sixth century B.C.E.).[23] A common formula begins each unit in these chronicles: "In the Xth year of PN, such and such happened." Assyrian sources are similar, but date events according to a year *name,* rather than a year *number* that is associated with the reign of a king. The Eponym Chronicles (one from the eighteenth century and one from the seventh century B.C.E.) are the best examples. All of the Mesopotamian documents of this kind are written in prose, give priority to dates, and provide only brief summaries of the events that occurred on those dates.[24]

---

23. Texts, translations, and commentary on all of these are in Glassner, *Mesopotamian Chronicles.*

24. A fragment of a monumental inscription from eighth-century B.C.E. Jerusalem suggests that Judah may have dated events according to numbered years as well. The expression "in the seventh" occurs in the second line and may refer to the seventh year of Hezekiah. The condition of the text, however, is too poor for us to draw any definite conclusions. See Cross, "A Fragment of a Monumental Inscription from the City of David," 44–47.

4. RULERSHIP CHRONOLOGIES

If the synchronisms in the Bible are derived from a similar document (or documents) used by the author of the DH, what is the origin of the document(s)? Several past studies of the chronology of the kings have assumed that the date for the accession of a Judahite king, which mentions a specific regnal year of an Israelite king, came from a Judahite source.[25] For example, the phrase, "In the eighteenth year of King Jeroboam the son of Nebat, Abijam became king over Judah" (1 Kgs 15:1), is said to come from the annals of the kings of Judah because it records the accession of a Judahite king, and because the remainder of the information in the formula (age at accession, length of reign, and mother's name) is undoubtedly Judahite. I find this assumption odd, considering the manner in which this dating formula is used in other places in the history. For example, does the datum, "And it was in the fifth year of Rehoboam that Shishak the king of Egypt came up against Jerusalem" (1 Kgs 14:25), derive from the annals of Shishak? Surely the information about Rehoboam's fifth year does not come from an Egyptian source, but a Judahite one. Or when it is stated, "And it was in the fourth year of King Hezekiah, that is, the seventh year of Hoshea the son of Elah, the king of Israel, that Shalmaneser, the king of Assyria, came up against Samaria," is not the usual interpretation that the datum about Hezekiah came from a Judahite source and that of Hoshea came from an Israelite one? Appealing to an argument for consistency, I find it unlikely that the synchronism ("In the [#] year of PN, PN became king") derives from the same source as that which lists the new king's age, length of reign, and mother. In other words, there are two different sources behind the accession formulas. The composer/compiler combined the information about an accession, which he gleaned from a native source, with a synchronism he obtained from the opposite kingdom. Now it is possible that he had access to a synchronistic chronicle of some kind, although he never mentions such a source among those he cites. However, even if he did, the composer of the synchronistic chronicle would have obtained this information from the same place that the Deuteronomistic compiler would have—an Israelite chronicle. In Abijam's case, it is more likely that the annals of the *North* would have mentioned Abijam's accession in the events of Jeroboam's eighteenth year than that the annals of the *South* would have gone out of their way to mention that Abijam's accession took place in Jeroboam's eighteenth year. For these reasons, we should see Pattern 2 of the accession notices displayed above (that is, the one without the synchronism)

---

25. For example, Thiele, *The Mysterious Numbers of the Hebrew Kings*, 25; John H. Hayes and Paul K. Hooker, *A New Chronology for the Kings of Israel and Judah and Its Implications for Biblical History and Literature* (Atlanta: John Knox Press, 1988), 14.

as the one that most likely reflects the contents of the Judahite source from which the author draws. The mere existence of the second pattern indicates that the Judahite source neither desired nor needed the synchronism with Israel to provide a suitable chronological marker for the accession of its kings.

When the synchronistic notices in the accession formulas are put aside,[26] all differences between Pattern 1 and Pattern 2 are gone, and the information coming from the Judahite source is consistent for all the kings:

> [Rehoboam] was 41 years old at his accession, and he reigned 17 years in Jerusalem…, and his mother's name was Naamah the Ammonitess (1 Kgs 14:21).
>
> [Abijam] reigned 3 years in Jerusalem, and his mother's name was Maacah the daughter of Abishalom (1 Kgs 15:1–2).
>
> [Asa] reigned 41 years in Jerusalem, and his mother's name was Maacah the daughter of Abishalom (1 Kgs 15:9–10).
>
> Jehoshaphat was 35 years old at his accession, and he reigned 25 years in Jerusalem, and his mother's name was Azubah the daughter of Shilhi (1 Kgs 22:41–42).
>
> [Jehoram] was 32 years old at his accession, and he reigned 8 years in Jerusalem (2 Kgs 8:16–17).
>
> Ahaziah was 22 years old at his accession, and he reigned 1 year in Jerusalem, and his mother's name was Athaliah, the daughter of Omri the king of Israel (2 Kgs 8:25–26).
>
> Jehoash was 7 years old at his accession…, and he reigned 40 years in Jerusalem, and his mother's name was Zibiah from Beersheba (2 Kgs 11:21–12:1).
>
> [Amaziah] was 25 years old at his accession, and he reigned 29 years in Jerusalem, and his mother's name was Jehoaddin of Jerusalem (2 Kgs 14:1–2).
>
> [Azariah] was 16 years old at his accession, and he reigned 52 years in Jerusalem, and his mother's name was Jecoliah of Jerusalem (2 Kgs 15:1–2).
>
> [Jotham] was 25 years old at his accession, and he reigned 16 years in Jerusalem, and his mother's name was Jerusha the daughter of Zadok (2 Kgs 15:32–33).

---

26. They will be picked up again in our discussion of Royal Chronicles below.

4. RULERSHIP CHRONOLOGIES 113

[Ahaz] was 20 years old at his accession, and he reigned 16 years in Jerusalem (2 Kgs 16:1–2).

[Hezekiah] was 25 years old at his accession, and he reigned 29 years in Jerusalem, and his mother's name was Abi, the daughter of Zechariah (2 Kgs 18:1–2).

Manasseh was 12 years old at his accession, and he reigned 55 years in Jerusalem, and his mother's name was Hephzibah (2 Kgs 21:1).

Amon was 22 years old at his accession, and he reigned 2 years in Jerusalem, and his mother's name was Meshullemeth, the daughter of Haruz from Jotbah (2 Kgs 21:19).

Josiah was 8 years old at his accession, and he reigned 31 years in Jerusalem, and his mother's name was Jedidah, the daughter of Adaiah from Bozkath (2 Kgs 22:1).

Jehoahaz was 23 years old at his accession, and he reigned 3 months in Jerusalem, and his mother's name was Hamutal, the daughter of Jeremiah from Libnah (2 Kgs 23:31).

Jehoiakim was 25 years old at his accession, and he reigned 11 years in Jerusalem, and his mother's name was Zebidah, the daughter of Pedaiah from Rumah (2 Kgs 23:36).

Jehoiachin was 18 years old at his accession, and he reigned 3 months in Jerusalem, and his mother's name was Nehushta, the daughter of Elnathan of Jerusalem (2 Kgs 24:8).

Zedekiah was 21 years old at his accession, and he reigned 11 years in Jerusalem, and his mother's name was Hamutal, the daughter of Jeremiah from Libnah (2 Kgs 24:18).

The evidence indicates that one of the historians possessed a Judahite document containing specific information, and, it would seem, the document was in the form of a list, rather than a chronicle containing narratives of the exploits of the kings.[27] The information we have preserved from it may represent its entire contents. Evidence for this conclusion is seen in an apparent

---

27. Earlier studies that argue for the existence of a Judahite and an Israelite king list that underlie the DH are: Shoshana R. Bin-Nun, "Formulas from Royal Records of Israel and of Judah," *VT* 18 (1968): 414–32, and William Hamilton Barnes, *Studies in the Chronology of the Divided Monarchy of Israel* (HSM 48; Atlanta: Scholars Press, 1991), 137–49.

textual error in the formula recounting the accession of Asa (1 Kgs 15:9–10). The clause concerning his mother's name is precisely the same as the one appearing in the previous entry concerning Abijam (1 Kgs 15:1–2). It is doubtful that both Abijam and his son Asa had the same mother. More probable is that the historian or a previous copyist, when he was writing down the Abijam formula, accidentally let his eye slip down to the following entry and copied that one instead. For this to have occurred, however, the two entries must have been in close proximity. The most likely scenario is that the accession formulas were listed one right after another with little or no intervening material. The mistake could have existed already in the source document; otherwise it would have been made by whoever copied the information from the list into the text of the DH (either the Deuteronomistic Historian or the reviser of the DH).

The nineteen Judahite accession formulas appear among the stereotypical comments the historian makes to open and close the accounts of the kings' reigns. In addition to the accession formulas, the introductory rubrics contain a verdict about the behavior of the said king in light of his adherence or lack of adherence to the Torah of Moses. The concluding rubrics contain a source citation, notice of death and burial, and the name of the successor. In a systematic study of these regnal formulations, Richard D. Nelson has remarked on the difference between those used for the kings up to and including Josiah, which show evidence of free variation in composition, and those who succeed Josiah, which show almost no variation.[28] The variation seen in the earlier formulations, Nelson attributes not only to variations in the historian's sources, but to "the natural result of the historian writing his own prose freely, using stock phrases from his everyday theological vocabulary, and developing and modifying his structural arrangement as he went along."[29] Nelson concludes, probably correctly, that a different author composed the formulations for the latter kings. However, Nelson's argument relies heavily on analysis of the DH's evaluations of the kings.[30] These evaluations are not likely to be part of the author's source citations and for our purposes should be set aside. What is interesting is that, taken on their own (without the synchronisms and evaluations), the accession formulas, which include the age of the king at his accession, the number of years of his rule, and the name of his mother, exhibit a different pattern. An examination reveals "free and random variation" within the structural arrangement for the entries from

---

28. Nelson, *Double Redaction of the Deuteronomistic History*, 29–42.
29. Nelson, *Double Redaction of the Deuteronomistic History*, 35–36.
30. Nelson, *Double Redaction of the Deuteronomistic History*, 36.

Rehoboam to Manasseh and strict uniformity from Amon to Zedekiah. The first set of entries never lists in a single entry both the mother's hometown and her father's name, while the last set always does. While we could posit that the final entries are fuller simply because there was more information available for the later kings, the absence of any variation whatsoever in the last entries is striking and suggests that they constitute an addition to the original list by a single writer. Strangely, the cut-off point is after Manasseh, not Josiah. The fact that the accession notices change their pattern in a different place (Manasseh) than where the remainder of the material in the opening and closing formulas changes its pattern (Josiah) strongly favors the supposition that the accession notices are from an independent source.

The original version of this king list (without the final six entries) is easy to date. Since it has knowledge of the length of the reign of Manasseh, it must be dated after his death. However, since the list does not include an entry for Amon, it must be dated before Amon's death. Thus the list must have been composed sometime within the two-year reign of Amon.[31] The uniformity in the final six entries suggests a single author for the additions,

---

31. We might at this point recall that the author of Chronicles includes similar information in his own history and employs similar wording. However, he probably did not use this king list as a source, but rather the DH itself. This is evident in the entry for Rehoboam (1 Kgs 14:21; 2 Chr 12:13), which is reproduced in Chronicles verbatim from the DH, including the phrase, "the city that Yahweh had chosen out of all the tribes of Israel to put his name there," which is a Deuteronomic phrase (cf. 1 Kgs 8:16; 11:32) and therefore comes from the hand of the Deuteronomistic editor of the king list and not from the king list itself. It can also be seen in the fact that some of the Chronicler's accession formulas include a synchronism as well (e.g., 2 Chr 13:1–2), and we know that the synchronisms were combined with the information from the king lists by the Deuteronomistic editor. Some have argued that, because the names of the queen mothers disappear in Chronicles after Hezekiah, the Chronicler must have used a Hezekian version of the Deuteronomistic History as a source (see, e.g., Baruch Halpern and David S. Vanderhooft, "The Editions of Kings in the 7th–6th Centuries B.C.E.," *HUCA* 62 [1991]: 197–99). However, because the Chronicler's entry for Hezekiah includes the total number of years he reigned (2 Chr 29:1), the DH that the Chronicler used could not have been Hezekian, as the length of his reign would not have been known until he died. It must have been at least Manassean. Yet we know of no Mannassean edition of the Deuteronomic History, and the evidence here presented suggests that the king list's information was lacking even in the Josianic edition. Therefore we must conclude that the Chronicler used the exilic edition of the DH and that the differences in Chronicles are not reflective of its source. The Chronicler must have omitted (consciously or unconsciously) the names of the mothers of all of the kings after Hezekiah, even though his source contained them. (That he omitted many synchronisms and Asa's accession formula entirely suggests that he was not averse to cutting out some of the information.)

one who possessed information about the final king of Judah and who therefore would have composed all six entries after the destruction of Jerusalem in 586 B.C.E.

That this king list was incorporated into the first edition of the Deuteronomic History is unlikely. If that were the case, to be consistent the Historian would have written entries for the last two kings, Amon and Josiah, that included their ages at accession, their mother's names, and, for Amon, his length of reign. Both of these kings ruled during the Historian's lifetime, and the information would have been easy to obtain, even though the king list did not have it (as the evidence indicates that the list was not updated until after the reign of Zedekiah). However, he did not include the information for these two kings. Alternatively, if the first edition of the DH was written in the reign of Hezekiah, as some have suggested,[32] then this list could not have been in such an edition either, because it had not yet been written. These factors indicate that the Josianic Deuteronomistic Historian did not possess this Judahite king list in either its long or short form, and that the accession formulas were not put into the DH until the second edition.[33] The first edition would have read just as smoothly without them. The typical reading for the accession of kings would have been something like this: "In the # year of PN, the son of PN the king of Israel, PN, the son of PN the king of Judah, became king, and he did what was right in Yahweh's eyes," etc. With regard to the kings after Hezekiah, the transition from king to king would have read something like this: "And PN lay down with his fathers, and PN his son reigned in his stead, and he did what was bad in Yahweh's eyes," etc. (cf. 2 Chr 14:1–2).

One question that arises in connection with these conclusions is, were the final six entries composed specifically for the king list, or were they composed specifically for the Deuteronomic History? In other words, did the reviser of the DH use a king list that had already been updated through Zedekiah, or did he possess the original king list that ended with Manasseh and then add

---

32. E.g., Helga Weippert, "Die 'deuteronomistischen' Beurteilungen der Könige von Israel und Juda und das Problem der Redaktion der Königsbücher," *Bib* 53 (1972): 301–39; Manfred Weippert, "Fragen des israelitischen Geschichtsbewusstseins," *VT* 23 (1973): 415–42; André Lemaire, "Vers l'histoire de la rédaction des livres des Rois," *ZAW* 98 (1986): 221–36; Halpern and Vanderhooft, "The Editions of Kings in the 7th–6th Centuries B.C.E.," 179–244.

33. On the general historical credibility of the information from this list (i.e., the king's accession age, death age, length of reign, and age at the birth of his son), see David Noel Freedman, "Kingly Chronologies: Then and Later," in *ErIsr* 24, *Avraham Malamat Volume* (Jerusalem: Israel Exploration Society, 1993), 41*–65*.

in the final six entries to the DH himself? This question is probably unanswerable and, for my purposes here, does not really matter. However, it is reasonable to suppose that the reviser of the History sought out the information about the final kings from whatever external sources he could find in order to lend historicity to his account. This list (in updated form) may have been one of them.

If we look at the three kings who preceded Rehoboam (Saul, David, and Solomon), we find that the first two kings have accession formulas that fall into the pattern found in the Judahite king list:

> Saul was [...] years old at his accession, and he reigned 2 years over Israel (1 Sam 13:1).

> David was 30 years old at his accession, and he reigned 40 years. He reigned over Judah 7 years in Hebron, and he reigned over all Israel and Judah 33 years in Jerusalem (2 Sam 5:4–5).

It seems probable therefore that the list went as far back as Saul. Problems associated with these early entries, however, suggest that the scroll that contained the king list was damaged at the beginning. Saul's accession age is missing in most manuscripts. David's accession formula is in good shape. It is longer than the rest, but naming the city of rule along with the length of the rule is customary for this list. The second part of David's accession formula is actually related a second time in the DH in his closing formula (2 Kgs 2:11). Solomon's entry, however, is completely missing; no accession formula is present in the DH. In his closing formula there is the statement that he reigned for forty years (1 Kgs 11:42). However, this statement does not conform to the pattern of the other formulas, and an attribution of forty years to Solomon is somewhat suspect, as the number is the round figure usually used to signify a generation (see §§2.3 and 4.1.3). It may be that the king list was damaged where Solomon's formula was written, and the reviser of the DH had to make an educated guess.

Turning to the Israelite accession formulas in the DH, we find far less detail than we do in the Judahite formulas. There are two patterns, spread more or less randomly through the History:

(1) בשנת # (שנה) לPN (מלך יהודה) מלך PN (בן־PN) על־ישראל (בתרצה/בשמרן) # שנים

In the [#](year) of [PN], (the king of Judah), [PN] (the son of PN) became king over Israel (in [Tirzah or Samaria]) for [#] years.

(2) וPN (בן־PN) מלך על־ישראל בשנת # (שנה) לPN מלך יהודה

וימלך (על־ישראל) # שנים
And PN the son of PN became king over Israel in the [#] (year) of PN the king of Judah, and he reigned (over Israel) [#] years.

For the most part, these formulas correspond to the first phrase in the Pattern 1 Judahite accession formula as it appears in the DH. The only notable difference between the two Israelite patterns is the inversion of the first two clauses. Of note also is that the lengths of reign are found at the end of the formulas in all instances. As in the case of the Judahite accession formulas, it is best to understand the synchronisms here to come from the chronicles of the opposite kingdom, and here it would mean those of Judah. The only information, then, to have come from an Israelite source in these formulas is the length of the king's reign (and perhaps the name of the capital city, although this information is not always provided, and the capitals, Tirzah and Samaria, like Jerusalem, were no doubt well known).

Apart from two kings (Jeroboam and Jehu), the reign length for all the kings appears at the end of each accession synchronism. For Jeroboam and Jehu, the reign length appears at the end of their closing formulas (1 Kgs 14:19–20; 2 Kgs 10:34–36). This difference is attributable to the fact that neither of these kings has an accession synchronism to which a reign length could be attached. The reason for the lack of an accession synchronism for these two kings is clear: no synchronism with a Judahite monarch was recorded in the Judahite annals for either king. For Jeroboam, this was no doubt because he was the first king of Israel and the custom had not yet been adopted (and his kingship may not even have been recognized in Judah at the time). For Jehu, a synchronism could not have existed because when he began to rule, he had just slain the king of Judah, and it was unclear who the next king would be. In fact, a legitimate Judahite monarch would not sit on the throne for several years to come. The fact that the reign lengths are included for Jehu and Jeroboam, even though they do not have accession synchronisms, suggests that the reign lengths derive from a different source than the synchronisms. Since the first edition of the DH probably did not include the lengths of the reigns of the monarchs of *Judah*, it would be strange if the lengths of the reigns of the monarchs of *Israel* were included. More probable is that they were likewise absent in the first edition and later added into the second by the reviser of the history to match what he did for Judah.

As in the case of the Judahite kings, the exilic reviser of the history may have had at his disposal a list of the names of the kings of Israel and the total years of their reigns in a separate document. Although it is possible that he calculated the reign lengths himself, simply by tallying the totals he worked out from the synchronisms that were already present in the History, the synchronisms do not actually allow one to narrow down reign totals to within a year's accuracy, and there are contradictions between the synchronisms and the reign totals.[34] Moreover, his knowledge of the precise length of reigns less than a year long (Zechariah, Shallum) makes it improbable that the reign totals were calculated from the synchronisms. The data had to be recorded somewhere, and the reviser gained access to this data. Whatever the case, the supplementary information is as follows:

Jeroboam	22 yrs	(1 Kgs 14:20)
Nadab	2 years	(1 Kgs 15:25)
Baasha	24 yrs	(1 Kgs 15:33)
Elah	2 yrs	(1 Kgs 16:8)
Zimri	7 days	(1 Kgs 16:15)
Omri	12 years	(1 Kgs 16:23)
Ahab	22 years	(1 Kgs 16:29)
Ahaziah	2 years	(1 Kgs 22:52)
Jehoram	12 years	(2 Kgs 3:1)
Jehu	28 years	(2 Kgs 10:36)
Jehoahaz	17 years	(2 Kgs 13:1)
Joash	16 years	(2 Kgs 13:10)
Jeroboam	41 years	(2 Kgs 14:23)
Zechariah	6 mos.	(2 Kgs 15:8)
Shallum	1 mo.	(2 Kgs 15:13)
Menahem	10 years	(2 Kgs 15:17)
Pekahiah	2 years	(2 Kgs 15:23)
Pekah	20 years	(2 Kgs 15:27)
Hoshea	9 years	(2 Kgs 17:1)

4.1.4.3. Royal Chronicles

We have observed that the synchronistic formulations in the DH exhibit a uniform pattern throughout: "In the [#] year of PN, [a certain event happened]." The events include invasions, wars, significant cultic innovations or reforms, and, as mentioned above, accessions of rulers in the sister kingdom. Such a construction demonstrates that the dates are from some sort of chronicle, and since the dates are associated with the kings of both kingdoms, it is best to posit two such chronicles, a Judahite and an Israelite one. These are probably to be equated with The Scroll of the Affairs of the Days for the Kings

---

34. See discussion below.

of Judah and The Scroll of the Affairs of the Days for the Kings of Israel that the historian cites. Moreover, they are clearly an integral part of the first edition of the DH.

In MT, of the thirty-two accession synchronisms in the DH, three set themselves apart (1 Kgs 16:10; 2 Kgs 1:17; 2 Kgs 15:30). These formulas refer to the accessions of Israelite kings. They could not possibly derive from the author's Judahite chronicle, as do the others in the series, for the following reasons: 1) they do not conform to the known patterns of the synchronistic accession formulas; 2) they are doublets of existing synchronistic accession formulas; and, 3) in the case of the latter two, they contradict the data already found in other synchronistic accession formulas. Also of note is that none of these formulas are attested in LXX.

The customary wording we should expect in the description of an Israelite accession is: "In the [#] (year) of [PN], (the king of Judah), [PN] (the son of PN) became king over Israel in [Tirzah or Samaria]," or the inverted pattern, "And PN the son of PN became king over Israel in the [#] (year) of PN the king of Judah." Instead, in these three verses we find the statement, "And PN became king in his stead, in the [x] year of PN, the son of PN (the king of Judah)." (In the case of 1 Kgs 16:10, the wording is inverted.) It is interesting that these three verses are constructed very similarly.

The datum at 2 Kgs 1:17 is a doublet of 2 Kgs 3:1 and directly contradicts the datum found there, which does exhibit the typical pattern for accession formulas.

2 Kgs 3:1	2 Kgs 1:17
And Jehoram the son of Ahab became king over Israel in the 18th year of Jehoshaphat the king of Judah.	And Jehoram became king in his stead, in the 2nd year of Jehoram the son of Jehoshaphat the king of Judah.

Of interest is that, although 2 Kgs 1:17 is absent in LXX, the chronological information it contains is found in the Greek text in a verse not contained in MT (2 Kgs 1:18a). As will be argued below, the datum is an invention of the LXX editors, so it likely reached MT through cross-fertilization.[35]

---

35. In an attempt at harmonization, sometimes the ancient scribes assimilated readings from other manuscript tradtions into their texts. The Greek Kaige and Hexaplaric recensions, for example, were made to conform more closely to MT. See James Donald Shenkel, *Chronology and Recensional Development in the Greek Text of Kings* (Cambridge, Mass.: Harvard University Press, 1968), 11–21.

4. RULERSHIP CHRONOLOGIES 121

The datum at 2 Kgs 15:30 is a doublet of 2 Kgs 17:1 and directly contradicts the datum found there, which does exhibit the typical pattern for accession formulas.

2 Kgs 17:1	2 Kgs 15:30
In the 12th year of Ahaz the king of Judah, Hoshea the son of Elah became king in Samaria over Israel.	And he [Hoshea] became king in his stead, in the 20th year of Jotham the son of Uzziah.

Second Kings 15:30 is absent in LXX.

The datum at 1 Kgs 16:10 does not contradict its doublet (1 Kgs 16:15), but it fits the pattern of the other anomalous notices and not that of the typical accession formulas. The Old Greek version of LXX (the earliest) does not have it. I would suggest that all three of these notices found their way into the text near the end of the fluid period in MT's transmission history (i.e., sometime before the destruction of the Second Temple in 70 C.E.), but long after DH² was published, and were put there to harmonize contradictory figures in the History[36] or to add clarification (as in the case of 1 Kgs 16:10).

By themselves, the synchronisms taken from either the Judahite chronicle or the Israelite chronicle are not sufficient to construct a chronology for the kings of either kingdom. Together, however, they may be of some use. If we can discern how the systems of measurement used in each of the chronicles relate to one another, we can synchronize the dates and arrive at reign lengths for many of the kings. In order to do this, we have to know the answer to one question: Which system of reckoning (postdating or antedating) was employed in the calculations reflected in each source?

In an accession-year system (postdating), the king's first year begins on the first New Year's Day after his accession. His reign may begin several months before that day, but that entire period prior to his first year is counted as the final year of his predecessor. Reign totals based on an accession-year system are equivalent to the actual years of reign, because the first year is not counted. In a non-accession-year system (antedating), the year of a king's accession is counted as his first year, even if he does not reign the entire year. Both he and his predecessor receive credit for that year.[37] Reign totals based

---

36. This will be discussed in more detail below.
37. See Eduard Meyer, "Principien der rechnung nach Königsjahren," in *Forschungen zur alte Geschichte* (Halle: Niemeyer, 1899), 440–53; Jack Finegan, *Handbook of Biblical Chronology: Principles of Time Reckoning in the Ancient World and Problems of Chronology in the Bible* (2nd ed.; Peabody, Mass.: Hendrickson, 1998), 75.

on a non-accession-year system generally are one year greater than the actual years of reign, because the first year is counted.

The Judahite royal chronicle itself leaves us with no clues, but it may be significant that the Judahite king list assumes an accession-year system (postdating). The date for the death of Josiah may be fixed in the year 609 (see below), and if we take the reign totals of his successors (Jehoahaz, 3 months, Jehoiakim, 11 years, Jehoiachin, 3 months, and Zedekiah, 11 years) from the king list and add them up as they are (22 years and 6 months), assuming an accession-year system, we arrive at the date 587 or 586 for the end of the monarchy (which is in keeping with extrabiblical evidence). However, if we assume a non-accession year system, we arrive at the date 589 or 588, which falls short of the date we expect the city to have fallen. In another exercise, if one accepts the argument that Isa 14:28 refers to the death of Assyrian king Tiglath-pileser III in the same year as (or perhaps the year before) the death of King Ahaz, we can put the accession of Hezekiah in 727 or 726. Using the same method of calculation as above and assuming an accession-year system, we can add up the reign totals for Hezekiah through Zedekiah (a total of 139 years and 6 months) and arrive at a date between 588 and 586 for the destruction of Jerusalem. However, if we assume a non-accession year system, we fall short and arrive at a date between 594 and 592 for the destruction of Jerusalem, a date which we cannot accept. The fact that the Judahite king list assumes an accession-year system suggests that, at least in the latter days of the monarchy in Judah, an accession-year system was used. How early this practice was begun is unknown, but since the Judahite royal chronicle used by the Deuteronomistic Historian would have been a late-monarchic document, we should expect that it too assumed an accession-year system.

The Israelite royal chronicle used for the first edition of the DH points to a non-accession year system (antedating). Jehu took the throne of Israel at the same time that Athaliah usurped the throne of Judah (2 Kgs 9:27–28; 11:1). The Historian states that Athaliah ruled Judah for six years (this figure is not from the Judahite king list). The chronicle puts the accession of Jehoash of Judah in the seventh year of Jehu (2 Kgs 12:2). Both of these figures can be correct only if Jehu's seventh year marked six years of Jehu's rulership. Only in a non-accession year system would this be true.

We can corroborate these conclusions if we make a comparison between the reign totals used in the king list from Judah with the one from Israel. Knowing that Rehoboam and Jeroboam began their reigns at approximately the same time, we can use the year of their accession as a point of departure for the two lists. Another date useful to yoke the two lists at a given point would be that for the accession of Jehu, which is to be equated with the date for the deaths of Jehoram of Israel and Ahaziah of Judah. It is interesting that the Judahite king list separates the accession of Rehoboam and the death of Ahaziah by seventy-nine years. However, the Israelite king list separates the accession of Jeroboam and the death of Jehoram by eighty-six years. The two lists do not coincide if we assume accession-year systems in both of the kingdoms. However, if we posit a non-accession year system in Israel, the total years separating the two events would be reduced to seventy-nine years and match the total years given in the Judahite list.[38] This is strong evidence for both an accession-year system in Judah and a non-accession year system in Israel. This is not to say that Judah's use of an accession-year system throughout the entire monarchy was a historical reality, or even that the numbers in the king list are accurate, but only that, by the reckoning used in the exilic king list, an accession-year system is assumed throughout. Similarly, Israel may or may not have used the non-accession year system, but the king list appears to assume it. To be sure, the synchronisms from the chronicles may not reflect the same system as the king lists, but the king lists tell us something about late monarchic practice, and the chronicles are from that period.

With the knowledge that the regnal new year is likely to have begun in the autumn in Judah and in the spring in Israel (see §1.4.2.4 above), and that Judah used an accession-year system and that Israel used a non-accession year system, we can construct a chronology using only the synchronisms and derive regnal totals to compare to those given in the king lists. I will use the data from MT. The readings in MT may be somewhat defective, but at this stage of the study, there is no need to delve into serious textual criticism. The purpose of this exercise is merely to provide a general comparison between the reign lengths assumed by the two sources. The results we achieve from this exercise will not be as precise as we might like them to be. Because the regnal years of the two kingdoms are out of sync (that is, they begin at different times of the year), we can narrow down the reign totals only to within three years. Moreover, since there is no synchronism for Jehu, it is not possible to calculate the length of Joram's reign from the synchronisms alone. Neither is it possible to figure the length of the reign of Ahaziah, the king of Judah. Moreover, no synchronisms exist after the reign of Ahaz. We are thus left with two floating chronologies, one lasting from the accessions of Rehoboam and Jeroboam at the beginning of the divided kingdom to the accession of Ahaziah, and another from the "accessions" of Athaliah and Jehu to the fall of Samaria. The reign of Ahaziah (however many years) would fall between these two chronologies.

---

38. This is noted by Thiele, *The Mysterious Numbers of the Hebrew Kings*, 23–25.

A comparison between the reign lengths assumed in the preexilic chronicles and those provided by the exilic Judahite king list proves interesting.

Royal Chronicles	King List
Rehoboam (16–18 years)	Rehoboam (17 years)
Abijam (1–3 years)	Abijam (3 years)
Asa (40–42 years)	Asa (41 years)
Jehoshaphat (21–23 years)	Jehoshaphat (25 years)
Jehoram (5–7 years)	Jehoram (8 years)
Ahaziah (?)	Ahaziah (1 year)
Jehoash (37–39 years)	Jehoash (40 years)
Amaziah (26–28 years)	Amaziah (29 years)
Azariah (52–54 years)	Azariah (52 years)
Jotham (14–16 years)	Jotham (16 years)
Ahaz (13–15 years)	Ahaz (16 years)

There is some correspondence between the two sources. Although some of the differences are slight, the chronicles' numbers cannot be stretched any further. The reigns of Jehoshaphat, Jehoram, Jehoash, Amaziah, and Jotham all fall at least one year short of the total in the king list. Still, the reign lengths in the chronicles are so very close to the reign lengths in the king list. It is almost as if the chronicles are doing their best to harmonize themselves with the king list, but cannot quite achieve their goal.

Now it is true that the divergences between the two sources can be harmonized if we assume co-regencies or overlaps. In other words, if, for example, Jehoshaphat is understood to have begun ruling within the lifetime of his father Asa and did so for at least two years before he became sole ruler, then we could accept both the figures provided. The chronicles would indicate his kingship as sole ruler, and the king list would provide his total years of rule including the co-regency. Some have argued for the existence of co-regencies in Israel and Judah,[39] citing some indirect evidence that

---

39. E.g., Thiele, *The Mysterious Numbers of the Hebrew Kings*, 32.

4. RULERSHIP CHRONOLOGIES

points to such a practice. For example, the narratives indicate that Solomon was crowned king when his father David was still alive (1 Kgs 1–2); in MT, Jehoshaphat appears to have crowned his son Jehoram in his own lifetime (2 Kgs 8:16); and Azariah's son Jotham seems to have been given executive powers during the lifetime of his father (2 Kgs 15:5). We should not invest too much stock in these examples, however, especially since Solomon and David's situation is portrayed as unusual, the text mentioning Jehoram's coronation in the reign of Jehoshaphat is most likely corrupt,[40] and Azariah is not said to be made king during the reign of his father but is still referred to as "the king's son."[41] It would be a mistake to posit a co-regency simply to harmonize conflicting data between two or more sources. One thing is certain: the king lists and the royal chronicles themselves give no indication of co-regencies.

Here is a comparison of the figures for Israel:

Royal Chronicles	King List
Jeroboam I (24–26 years)	Jeroboam I (21 years)
Nadab (1–2 years)	Nadab (1 year)
Baasha (16–18 years)	Baasha (23 years)
Elah (5–7 years)	Elah (1 year)
Zimri (less than a year)	Zimri (7 days)
Omri (12–14 years)	Omri (11 years)
Ahab (19–21 years)	Ahab (21 years)
Ahaziah (1–2 years)	Ahaziah (1 year)
Joram (?)	Joram (11 years)
Jehu (28–30 years)	Jehu (27 years)
Jehoahaz (13–15 years)	Jehoahaz (16 years)
Joash (16–18 years)	Joash (15 years)
Jeroboam II (63–65 years)	Jeroboam II (41 years)

---

40. The phrase "and Jehoshaphat was king of Judah" is omitted in some manuscripts and many codices of LXX. It is probably a case of dittography.
41. See Hayes and Hooker, *A New Chronology for the Kings of Israel and Judah*, 12; Hughes, *Secrets of the Times*, 99–107.

Zechariah (1–2 years)	Zechariah (6 months)
Shallum (less than a year)	Shallum (1 month)
Menahem (10–12 years)	Menahem (9 years)
Pekahiah (1–3 years)	Pekahiah (1 year)
Pekah (27–29 years)	Pekah (19 years)
Hoshea (8 years)	Hoshea (8 years)

In this chart, one year was subtracted from each of the reign totals provided by the king list with the understanding that Israel used an antedating system. Although the figures from each source tend to be close, there are many more disagreements than we observed for Judah. There is a significant discrepancy with regard to the reign of Jeroboam II, the chronicle assuming a highly improbable reign of sixty-three to sixty-five years. (It is doubtful that Jeroboam served some twenty-two to twenty-four years as coregent.) Another significant difference is seen in the reign of Pekah, the chronicles' figure again being much higher.

In MT the reign lengths for the kings of Judah obtained from the synchronisms correspond so much more closely to the king list than the reign lengths for the kings of Israel. Why is that? All the reign lengths for the kings of both kingdoms have been calculated from the same repository of data, so a difference between Judah and Israel is unexpected. I can see only two possible reasons for this: either because Judah's king list is more reliable than Israel's (which is not likely, since the Israelite king list's figures seem more reasonable than those of the chronicles), or there was a deliberate effort on the part of someone to make sure that the synchronisms of the Judahite kings corresponded to the stated reign lengths, while no such effort was made for Israel. It is my contention that this was, in fact, the case, and that in an earlier version of the text, the data from the chronicles and the king lists diverged even more greatly than they do now. The best explanation of the contradictory data is that the historiographic works containing the synchronisms used and cited in the first edition of the Deuteronomic History presented a much different chronology than that of the king lists, which was added later.

4.1.4.4. Textual Difficulties in Kings

Any attempt at understanding the systems employed in the royal chronicles, or any of the chronological sources, must be based on a reliable text, that is, one containing an accurate set of numbers. By "accurate," I do not necessarily mean *historically* accurate. I mean that we want the synchronisms as they would have appeared in the first edition of the Deuteronomic History, just as we would wish to know the numbers from the king lists as they first would have appeared in the second edition of the History. We also are interested in knowing the data as they appeared in the sources prior to their incorporation into the History (if different). We have in our possession two chief textual witnesses to the royal chronicles, as we do to the king lists, one witness associated with the texts in the Masoretic tradition, and the other with the texts in the Greek tradition. The two text traditions differ very little in their representation of the data from the king lists. With regard to the information from the royal chronicles, however, significant variants in the figures associated with the kings of Israel and Judah occur in the various manuscripts.

The texts of Kings in the MT family are fairly consistent, and so a clear reading of the figures in the MT tradition is possible. However, the recensions of LXX are somewhat varied. Nevertheless, it is possible to determine the earliest forms of the Greek text tradition. The pertinent studies are those of Paul de Lagarde,[42] Dominique Barthélemy,[43] and James D. Shenkel,[44] which understand there to have been a single translation of the books of Samuel and Kings into Greek. All the versions of the Greek text, therefore, are not new translations but simply variant text forms of a single Old Greek translation. This theory has more to commend it than the opposing one, commonly associated with Paul Kahle,[45] that the Septuagint was formed through a process of selective canonization of several different translations.

In this study, references to the data in LXX will be primarily to the Old Greek translation (henceforth OG) of Samuel-Kings, which derives from an Egyptian Hebrew text that existed sometime between the fourth and third centuries B.C.E. Our best witness to the OG is Codex Vaticanus, but only in 1 Samuel, 2 Sam 1:1–9:13, and 1 Kgs 2:12–21:43. For the sections of OG that are wanting in Codex Vaticanus, our recourse is to the Lucianic text (Luc.), which, as has been demonstrated by others, contains an ancient stratum datable to the second or first century B.C.E. that preserves some of OG, although,

---

42. Paul de Lagarde, *Ankündigung einer neuen Ausgabe der griechischen Übersetzung des alten Testaments* (Göttingen, 1882).
43. Dominique Barthélemy, *Les devanciers d'Aquila* (VTSup 10; Leiden: Brill, 1963).
44. Shenkel, *Chronology and Recensional Development in the Greek Text of Kings*.
45. Paul Kahle develops his view principally in the following works: Paul Kahle, "Untersuchungen zur Geschichte des Pentateuchtextes," *TSK* 88 (1915); idem, "Die Septuaginta: Principielle Erwägungen," in *Festschrift Otto Eissfeldt* (Halle: Niemeyer, 1947); idem, *The Cairo Geniza* (2nd ed.; New York: Praeger, 1959).

as we shall see, rather imperfectly. The manuscripts used in this study as witnesses of the Lucianic text are the miniscules b, o, and e_2.[46]

Our conclusion that the first edition of the DH did not contain the reign lengths of the kings assists us in ascertaining the original form of the text that gave rise to both the MT and the OG text traditions. It would appear that the variants arose after the reign totals were added to the History, when later editors noted the contradictions between the chronologies inherent in the synchronisms and the king lists and tried to fix the discrepancies.

The first example of such an adjustment can be seen in a comparison between the figures in MT and LXX with regard to the reign of Jeroboam and his contemporaries. MT has a synchronism for the accession of Asa in the twentieth year of Jeroboam (1 Kgs 15:9–10). LXX places Asa's accession in Jeroboam's twenty-fourth year (1 Kgs 15:8–10). The Israelite king list gives Jeroboam a total reign of twenty-two years. LXX's figure is irreconcilable with the reign total of twenty-two years. It therefore is more likely to be original. The variants arose this way: the original synchronism for Asa's accession was the twenty-fourth year of Jeroboam. The figure of twenty-two years, taken from the king list, was inserted into the DH by its exilic reviser. Later scribes noticed that Jeroboam could not have had a twenty-fourth year if he reigned only twenty-two years. The problem was handled differently in each text tradition. An MT scribe reduced the synchronism to the twentieth year to alleviate the difficulty. An LXX scribe simply removed the reign total of Jeroboam from the text (the datum is absent in LXX; see table 4.1).

One might wonder why the editors of proto-MT reduced the synchronism by four years (twenty-fourth to twentieth) when they only needed to reduce it by two (twenty-fourth to twenty-second). The answer appears to lie in the number of the regnal years attributed to Asa's predecessor, Abijam of Judah, whose reign overlapped with Jeroboam's. Abijam is said, in both traditions, to have taken the throne in the eighteenth year of Jeroboam. Abijam's reign length, according to the synchronisms in LXX, would have to be six to seven years (eighteenth to twenty-fourth year of Jeroboam). According to the synchronisms in MT, Abijam's reign length would be two to three years (eighteenth to twentieth year of Jeroboam). The reign total of Abijam in LXX is six years, and it is three years in MT. If, as argued in the previous paragraph, MT's synchronism for the accession of Asa (twentieth year of Jeroboam) is secondary, then the reign length of Abijam indicated by the

---

46. b = Rome, Chigi, R. vi. 38 (tenth century C.E.) and Rome, Vat. Gr. 330 (fourteenth century C.E.); o = Paris, Bibl. Nat., Coislin Gr. 3 (twelfth–thirteenth century C.E.); e2 = London, B.M. Reg. i. D. 2 (thirteenth century C.E.).

synchronisms is shorter in MT than it once was. They originally would have suggested a six- to seven-year reign for Abijam. If the proto-MT scribes tried to accommodate the king list's reign length for Jeroboam by adjusting a synchronism, they also may have tried to accommodate the king list's figure for Abijam (presumably three years, according to MT). Indeed, the scribes could have accommodated *both* Jeroboam's and Abijam's reign lengths by adjusting only one synchronism. If the synchronism for Asa's accession were reduced from the twenty-fourth year of Jeroboam only to the twenty-second year, then Jeroboam's reign length of twenty-two years would be harmonized with the synchronisms, but the length of Abijam's reign indicated by the synchronisms would be four years, overshooting the king list's total by one year. However, by reducing the synchronism for Asa's accession even further to Jeroboam's twentieth year, the proto-MT editors were able to accommodate both Jeroboam's reign total of twenty-two years *and* Abijam's reign total of three years. The editors of OG handled the discrepancy in another way. They left the synchronisms alone and increased the length of Abijam's reign from three years to six years. (They had already omitted Jeroboam's reign total.)

TABLE 4.1. READINGS FOR ABIJAM, ASA, AND JEROBOAM

	Archetype	LXX	MT
Royal Chronicles	Abijam accedes in 18th of Jeroboam	Abijam accedes in 18th of Jeroboam	Abijam accedes in 18th of Jeroboam
	Asa accedes in 24th of Jeroboam	Asa accedes in 24th of Jeroboam	**Asa accedes in 20th of Jeroboam**
King List	Jeroboam rules 22 years	**[Jeroboam's reign length omitted]**	Jeroboam rules 22 years
	Abijam rules 3 years	**Abijam rules 6 years**	Abijam rules 3 years

The next example of an adjustment made after the reign totals were added to the History is seen in a discrepancy between MT and LXX with regard to the synchronism for the accession of Elah of Israel (1 Kgs 16:8). MT places Elah's accession in the twenty-sixth year of Asa. LXX places the event in the twentieth year of Asa. Both traditions agree that Elah's predecessor Baasha took the throne in Asa's third year. So the reign length for Baasha in MT is somewhere between twenty-three and twenty-five years. In LXX, a reign length of seventeen to nineteen years is assumed. Considering that the reign length given for Baasha is twenty-four years, we should take the Greek synchronism, which contradicts this figure, as original. When an editor of proto-MT saw that the synchronism would not allow Baasha a reign of twenty-four years, he pushed Elah's accession forward to the twenty-sixth year of Asa to accommodate the new information.

TABLE 4.2. READINGS FOR BAASHA AND ELAH

	Archetype	LXX	MT
Royal Chronicles	Baasha accedes in 3rd of Asa	Baasha accedes in 3rd of Asa	Baasha accedes in 3rd of Asa
	Elah accedes in 20th of Asa	Elah accedes in 20th of Asa	**Elah accedes in 26th of Asa**
King List	Baasha rules 24 years	Baasha rules 24 years	Baasha rules 24 years

The twelve years given to Omri by the reviser caused some serious problems, and both text traditions had difficulty in rectifying them (and neither is entirely successful). In the original text (1 Kgs 16:23), the Deuteronomistic Historian placed Omri's succession in the thirty-first year of Asa and mentioned that he had already reigned six years in Tirzah. These six years no doubt coincided with the rule of Omri's rival Tibni (1 Kgs 16:21–22).[47] Counting back six years from the thirty-first of Asa we arrive at the twenty-fifth of Asa for the beginning of the parallel reigns of Omri and Tibni (see table 4.3).

---

47. The six years are counted inclusively, as they are a calculation of the Historian (actual regnal totals were not in the original edition of the DH). Even if this were a regnal total from an Israelite source, the northern kingdom used antedating and therefore counted inclusively. However, keep in mind that, while in reality, Omri's first regnal year would also have been Tibni's final year, this is not so when counting. The custom, when putting together two inclusively counted blocks of time, is not to overlap (see ch. 2).

4. RULERSHIP CHRONOLOGIES

TABLE 4.3. TOTALING THE YEARS OF OMRI

Judah	Israel	Count of years
25th of Asa	Omri and Tibni	1
26th of Asa	Omri and Tibni	2
27th of Asa	Omri and Tibni	3
28th of Asa	Omri and Tibni	4
29th of Asa	Omri and Tibni	5
30th of Asa	Omri and Tibni	6
31st of Asa	1st of Omri	7
32nd of Asa	2nd of Omri	8
33rd of Asa	3rd of Omri	9
34th of Asa	4th of Omri	10
35th of Asa	5th of Omri	11
36th of Asa	6th of Omri	12
37th of Asa	7th of Omri	13
38th of Asa	8th of Omri	14

However, the reign length of twelve years makes no sense in the context of the narrative about Omri. If the twelve years are counted from the beginning of Omri's rule in Tirzah (the twenty-fifth of Asa), the twelve years fall short of the thirty-eighth year of Asa, in which Omri is supposed to have died. If the twelve years are counted from the beginning of Omri's rule in Samaria (the thirty-first year of Asa), the twelve years overextend the thirty-eighth year of Asa. In other words, the archetypal reading did not accommodate the twelve-year reign length.

The MT and LXX traditions handled the matter in different ways. It would appear that *none* of the witnesses preserve the original date for the rise and fall of Zimri, which was the year that Omri began his rule in contest with Tibni. If it began six years prior to the thirty-first year of Asa, as 1 Kgs 16:23 suggests, then the assassination of Zimri would have been placed around the twenty-fifth year of Asa. In the Old Greek text, the synchronism for the rise and fall of Zimri was simply omitted (1 Kgs 16:15). This did not help a great deal, since the lengths of the reigns of Elah and Zimri were still in the text and would indicate that Omri began ruling in Samaria in the twenty-ninth year of Asa.[48] Nevertheless, it made the problem less obvious. Of greater concern was making Omri's rule equal twelve years. The archetypal text put Omri's accession in the thirty-first year of Asa, and so this datum was accepted. To make his total years twelve, the editor counted forward twelve years and saw that Omri's death would have had to occur, not in the thirty-eighth year of Asa, but in the second year of Jehoshaphat. Thus he moved Omri's death forward four years.

The proto-MT editors had to account for an additional problem they created earlier when they moved Elah's accession from Asa's twentieth year to his twenty-sixth year (see above), because the new synchronism would have conflicted with the original date for the fall of Zimri (twenty-fifth year). So first they pushed the accession of Zimri to the twenty-seventh year of Asa, allowing Elah two inclusive years to coincide with the king list. At this point, only some four years separated Omri's assassination of Zimri and his ascendancy to the rule of all Israel in Asa's thirty-first year, but at least the total of Omri's years now equaled twelve. The editors could have changed Omri's accession date to accommodate the six years of co-rule with Tibni, but they chose the path of least adjustment and decided to ignore the problem.

In the Lucianic tradition, the figure of two years for the reign of Elah prompted a later editor to place Zimri's accession two years after Elah's accession, that is, in the 22nd year of Asa. In this text, some nine years separated Omri's assassination of Zimri and his ascendancy to the rule of all Israel (three years more than the six it should have been). However, the matter with Omri and his six years in Tirzah were too difficult to accommodate, so the editor left the rest alone.

TABLE 4.4. COUNTS FOR OMRI ASSUMED IN THE MANUSCRIPTS

Years of Asa	Archetype	MT	OG and Luc
25th of Asa	Omri and Tibni		
26th of Asa	Omri and Tibni	1st of Elah	
27th of Asa	Omri and Tibni	1st Zimri/ 1st Omri	
28th of Asa	Omri and Tibni	2nd of Omri	

---

48. OG attributes two years to Elah and seven years to Zimri (1 Kgs 16:8, 15).

4. RULERSHIP CHRONOLOGIES

29th of Asa	Omri and Tibni	3rd of Omri	
30th of Asa	Omri and Tibni	4th of Omri	
31st of Asa	1st of Omri	5th of Omri	1st of Omri
32nd of Asa	2nd of Omri	6th of Omri	2nd of Omri
33rd of Asa	3rd of Omri	7th of Omri	3rd of Omri
34th of Asa	4th of Omri	8th of Omri	4th of Omri
35th of Asa	5th of Omri	9th of Omri	5th of Omri
36th of Asa	6th of Omri	10th of Omri	6th of Omri
37th of Asa	7th of Omri	11th of Omri	7th of Omri
38th of Asa	8th of Omri	12th of Omri	8th of Omri
39th of Asa			9th of Omri
40th of Asa			10th of Omri
1st of Jehoshaphat			11th of Omri
2nd of Jehoshaphat			12th of Omri

The length of the reign of Omri caused other difficulties. Both MT and LXX decided to forget about the six years in Tirzah and focus on the twelve-year reign length. MT decided that the twelve years should count from the twenty-seventh year of Asa, when Omri was supposed to have assassinated Zimri, and LXX decided that the twelve years should count from the thirty-first year of Asa, when Omri took Samaria. Both of their synchronisms for the accession of Omri's son Ahab reflect these respective understandings. MT places Ahab's accession twelve years after the twenty-seventh year of Asa in the thirty-eighth year of Asa (1 Kgs 16:29). LXX places Ahab's accession twelve years after the thirty-first year of Asa in the 2nd year of Jehoshaphat (1 Kgs 16:29). Which of the synchronisms is correct? Is either? One might be quick to discard MT's reading, since it created the artificial synchronism in the twenty-seventh year of Asa, from which it counts the twelve years. On the other hand, since MT ceases its consistent adjustments to the synchronisms at this point, it is possible that once it arrives at Asa's thirty-eighth year, it has been able to reconcile the figures that were given it and does not need to make any more alterations. The twelve-year reign fits. So far the Greek text has been reluctant to change the synchronisms, but the perfect fit of twelve years between the thirty-first year of Asa and the second year of Jehoshaphat arouses suspicion, and from this point the Greek text does not prove as reliable when it comes to the synchronisms, suggesting that a different method of accommodating the reign totals is at work. Keeping in mind that both MT and LXX place Omri's accession in the thirty-first year of Asa, and LXX is the one whose synchronism makes Omri's reign an even twelve years from that date, I opt for MT's reading for the death of Omri. The most likely scenario is that Omri's official reign in Samaria ran from the thirty-first to the thirty-eighth year of Asa (seven to eight years) and that, after the reviser added in the twelve-year datum, an editor in the Greek tradition moved the latter synchronism forward to the second year of Jehoshaphat to accommodate the new figure (see table 4.5).

TABLE 4.5. READINGS FOR ZIMRI, TIBNI, OMRI AND AHAB

	Archetype	LXX (OG)	MT
Royal Chronicles	Zimri accedes and dies in [25th] of Asa Tibni and Omri reign 6 years Omri accedes in 31st of Asa Ahab accedes in 38th of Asa	**[Zimri synchronism omitted]** Tibni and Omri reign 6 years Omri accedes in 31st of Asa **Ahab accedes in 2nd of Jehoshaphat**	Zimri accedes and dies in 27th of Asa Tibni and Omri reign 6 years Omri accedes in 31st of Asa Ahab accedes in 38th of Asa
King List	Zimri reigns 7 days Omri reigns 12 years	**Zimri reigns 7 years** Omri reigns 12 years	Zimri reigns 7 days Omri reigns 12 years

LXX's adjustment to the date of Ahab's death had repercussions. In MT, Ahab rules from the 38th year of Asa to the seventeenth year of Jehoshaphat (twenty to twenty-two years). In LXX, Ahab rules from the second year to the twenty-fourth year of Jehoshaphat (twenty-one to twenty-three years). The datum added by the reviser of the DH is a twenty-two-year reign for Ahab. The synchronisms in both LXX and MT correspond to Ahab's reign length. However, we should opt for MT's reading, because we have already determined that LXX's synchronism for the beginning of Ahab's reign (second of Jehoshaphat) is not the archetype. The Greek witness shows an attempt to harmonize the data. The synchronism for the end of the reign of Jehoshaphat was extended to the twenty-fourth year in order to give Ahab his needed twenty-two years, and the synchronism for the accession of Jehoshaphat, which would contradict the new synchronism for Ahab's accession, was omitted (see table 4.6).

Table 4.6. Readings for Ahab, Jehoshaphat and Ahaziah

	Archetype	LXX*	MT
Royal Chronicles	Ahab accedes in 38th of Asa Jehoshaphat accedes in 4th of Ahab Ahaziah accedes in 17th of Jehoshaphat	**Ahab accedes in 2nd of Jehoshaphat** [Jehoshaphat synchronism omitted] **Ahaziah accedes in 24th of Jehoshaphat**	Ahab accedes in 38th of Asa Jehoshaphat accedes in 4th of Ahab Ahaziah accedes in 17th of Jehoshaphat
King List	Ahab reigns 22 years	Ahab reigns 22 years	Ahab reigns 22 years

* The accession of Ahab is the last datum we have for OG. The rest of LXX's readings are from Luc (Lucianic text).

As might be expected, this last adjustment created an additional problem for LXX. Ahab's son Joram is said to have begun to reign in the eighteenth year of Jehoshaphat, a synchronism that is impossible if Ahab died in Jehoshaphat's twenty-fourth year. So this synchronism had to be moved forward as well, and LXX put Joram's accession in the second year of Jehoram of Judah (2 Kgs 1:18a). Strangely enough, the datum that puts Jehoram of Judah's accession in the fifth year of Joram of Israel (2 Kgs 8:16–17) was kept as is, even though it is quite impossible with the revised synchronisms. It no doubt was overlooked because of its distance from 2 Kgs 1:18 (see table 4.7).

TABLE 4.7. READINGS FOR AHAZIAH, JORAM AND JEHORAM

	Archetype	LXX	MT
Royal Chronicles	Ahaziah accedes in 17th of Jehoshaphat	**Ahaziah accedes in 24th of Jehoshaphat**	Ahaziah accedes in 17th of Jehoshaphat
	Joram accedes in 18th of Jehoshaphat	**Joram accedes in 2nd of Jehoram**	Joram accedes in 18th of Jehoshaphat
	Jehoram accedes in 5th of Joram	Jehoram accedes in 5th of Joram	Jehoram accedes in 5th of Joram

A further example of an instance where the insertion of the reign totals prompted an adjustment in the synchronisms is in the case of the reign of Jehoram of Judah. Both MT and LXX begin his reign in the fifth year of Joram of Israel (2 Kgs 8:16). MT concludes his reign in Joram's twelfth year, making his reign seven to eight years long, and LXX concludes his reign in Joram's eleventh year, making his reign six to seven years long (2 Kgs 8:25). The reign length in LXX does not coincide with the reign total of eight years provided by the Judahite king list. That of MT does. So again it would seem that in MT the synchronism was pushed forward from Joram's eleventh year to his twelfth year to accommodate the new datum. The formula at 2 Kgs 9:29 in both MT and LXX retain the original synchronism in the eleventh year of Joram. The contradiction between 2 Kgs 9:29 and 2 Kgs 8:25 seems to have gone unnoticed in MT, perhaps because it is uncustomary for a synchronism to be repeated and the datum in 9:29 is not in the typical location for synchronisms (see table 4.8).

TABLE 4.8. READINGS FOR JEHORAM AND AHAZIAH

	Archetype	LXX	MT
Royal Chronicles	Jehoram accedes in 5th of Joram	Jehoram accedes in 5th of Joram	Jehoram accedes in 5th of Joram
	Ahaziah accedes in 11th of Joram	Ahaziah accedes in 11th of Joram	**Ahaziah accedes in 12th of Joram**
King List	Jehoram reigns 8 years	Jehoram reigns 8 years*	Jehoram reigns 8 years
* This reading is in the b manuscript only. Manuscripts o and e_2 read "10 years."			

Despite the numerous alterations that were made, neither the Hebrew nor the Greek textual traditions satisfyingly harmonized the variant data so that all inconsistencies were eliminated. (This much we knew already.) In 1 Kgs 14–16, the OG reading appears to retain the original synchronisms more consistently than MT, while MT retains the original reign lengths. However, in 1 Kgs 16–2 Kgs 3, where the OG is not extant, MT appears to be more reliable than the Lucianic texts when it comes to the synchronisms. In one final case, 2 Kgs 8:25, the Lucianic texts seem to preserve a more original reading than MT in the synchronism for Ahaziah of Judah. From this point in the texts forward, however, both traditions agree in their figures. In regard to 2 Kgs 21–25, this is not surprising, since the section contains no synchronisms (because Israel was destroyed), and therefore no data from the Judahite king list would contradict any existing chronological information. However, the fact that the Greek and Hebrew text traditions are at odds so frequently in 1 Kgs 14–2 Kgs 8 and suddenly agree in all respects in 2 Kgs 9–20 should make us somewhat suspicious. To be sure, the reason for the agreement could be simply that the data for the reigns of the latter monarchs in the king lists and chronicles were already in harmony. A strong possibility exists, however, that the editors of MT continued to harmonize the figures they inherited (as they have done consistently up to this point) and that the Lucianic texts have been adjusted to conform to MT in this section of the text.[49] Neither of these two text traditions have been reliable up to this point, and we have no copy of OG for this portion of the text. There is a good chance that the original readings no longer exist in either tradition. Is there any chance of our recovering the earlier readings? Perhaps. The text does provide us with a few clues that enable reconstruction.

The existence of an anomalous datum, which appears to have escaped the editor's pen, suggests that changes were indeed made. There is reason to believe that an adjustment to a synchronism to accommodate a reign total occurred in 2 Kgs 15:1. According to both MT and LXX, Azariah (Uzziah) acceded to the throne of Judah in the twenty-seventh year of Jeroboam. However, in a datum within a narrative about Azariah's father Amaziah, it is asserted that Amaziah lived fifteen years (inclusive) after the death of King Joash of Israel, and therefore fifteen years from the accession of Jeroboam, who was Joash's son (2 Kgs 14:17). If this datum were true, then Azariah would have succeeded his father Amaziah in the fourteenth, fifteenth, or sixteenth year of Jeroboam,

---

49. It is generally held that portions of Luc were made to conform to the Hexaplaric text, which is well known for its conformity to MT. See Shenkel, *Chronology and Recensional Development in the Greek Text of Kings*, 8, 18–21; Emanuel Tov, *Textual Criticism of the Hebrew Bible* (2nd rev. ed.; Minneapolis: Augsburg Fortress, 2001), 148.

rather than the twenty-seventh (we are unable to narrow it down further). Two traditions are in conflict. Both cannot be correct. In one, Amaziah rules from the second year of Joash until the twenty-seventh year of Jeroboam (a longer reign). In the other, Amaziah rules from the second year of Joash until the fourteenth, fifteenth, or sixteenth year of Jeroboam (a shorter reign). The fact that the contradictory information exists in the same text suggests that there was an editorial alteration, but that one of the two data was overlooked. We should expect a change in a synchronism to have been made in the usual spot (the accession notice), and the synchronism implied by the statement at 2 Kgs 14:17 is found in an obscure passage and thus more likely to have been passed over. It seems best to consider the datum placing Amaziah's death in the fourteenth, fifteenth, or sixteenth year of Jeroboam as more reflective of an original chronology than the one at 2 Kgs 15:1. Josephus appears to have had a manuscript that preserved the older reading; he states that Azariah took the throne of Judah in the fourteenth year of Jeroboam (*Ant.* 9.216, 227). The patterns that have been displayed in the text traditions noted above suggest that the same sort of deliberate harmonization that occurred there occurred here. Second Kings 15:1 originally read the fourteenth year of Jeroboam, but was changed to the twenty-seventh to extend the reign of Amaziah to make it total twenty-nine years, in accordance with the reign total provided by DH². If that were the case, then the reign length of Amaziah indicated by the original synchronism would have been about eleven to thirteen years shorter than the twenty-nine years from the king list and would have equaled about fifteen to seventeen years (see table 4.9).

TABLE 4.9. READINGS FOR AMAZIAH AND AZARIAH

	Archetype	LXX	MT
Royal Chronicles	Amaziah accedes in 2nd of Joash	Amaziah accedes in 2nd of Joash	Amaziah accedes in 2nd of Joash
	Amaziah lives 15 years after death of Joash	Amaziah lives 15 years after death of Joash	Amaziah lives 15 years after death of Joash
	Azariah accedes in 14th of Jeroboam	**Azariah accedes in 27th of Jeroboam**	**Azariah accedes in 27th of Jeroboam**
King List	Amaziah reigns 29 years	Amaziah reigns 29 years	Amaziah reigns 29 years

4. RULERSHIP CHRONOLOGIES   139

Another inference can be drawn from 2 Kgs 14:17. If Amaziah lived fifteen years after the death of Joash until Jeroboam's fourteenth year, then Joash would have died in Amaziah's second year,[50] and his son Jeroboam would have succeeded him then. However, this is in contradiction with the datum provided by 2 Kgs 14:23, which states that Jeroboam took the throne in the fifteenth year of Amaziah. It would appear that another alteration was made to accommodate the king list. The datum in 2 Kgs 14:23 originally put Jeroboam's accession in Amaziah's second year, making the length of Joash's reign four to five years long, but when it was noted that the king list gave Joash sixteen years, about eleven to twelve years were added to the synchronism to accommodate the new figure.

There would have been a major repercussion to this last change that the editors simply could not have ignored, and we cannot either. By moving the synchronism for Jeroboam's accession from the second year of Amaziah to the fifteenth of Amaziah, the reign of Jeroboam would have been shortened by twelve to fourteen years. In order to restore his reign to its proper length, no fewer than five synchronisms, all set in the reign of Azariah of Judah, would have to have been pushed forward twelve to fourteen years. These would be the accession years of Zechariah, Shallum, Menahem, Pekahiah, and Pekah. If this is true, then the current synchronisms for these Israelite kings are twelve to fourteen years too late. Instead of their accessions taking place in the thirty-eighth, thirty-ninth, thirty-ninth, fiftieth, and fifty-second years of Azariah, respectively, the original dates would have been about the twenty-sixth, twenty-seventh, twenty-seventh, thirty-eighth, and fortieth years of Azariah respectively.[51] The chronicles (synchronisms) would have given Azariah a reign of about forty years. The twelve-year adjustment would have had the added benefit (or perhaps this was the primary motivation) of bringing the length of Azariah's reign into harmony with the king list (fifty-two years; consider that his successor Jotham acceded in the second year of Pekah; see table 4.10).

---

50. He could not have died in Amaziah's first year, because this would fall before Jeroboam's first year, and he could not have died in Amaziah's third year, because this would not equal fifteen (inclusive) years.

51. I assume a twelve-year difference on the ground that the editors would have chosen the minimum amount necessary to correct the problem.

TABLE 4.10. READINGS FOR JOTHAM, AHAZ AND HOSHEA

	Archetype	LXX	MT
Royal Chronicles	Jotham accedes in 2nd of Pekah	Jotham accedes in 2nd of Pekah	Jotham accedes in 2nd of Pekah
	Ahaz accedes in [3rd] of Pekah	**Ahaz accedes in 17th of Pekah**	**Ahaz accedes in 17th of Pekah**
	Hoshea accedes in 12th of Ahaz	Hoshea accedes in 12th of Ahaz	Hoshea accedes in 12th of Ahaz
King List	Jotham reigns 16 years	Jotham reigns 16 years	Jotham reigns 16 years

The anomalous datum in 2 Kgs 15:30, which probably is not original, as argued above, nevertheless indicates there was another problem that later editors attempted to rectify. It states that Hoshea came to the throne of Israel in the twentieth year of Jotham of Judah. This is in direct contradiction of 2 Kgs 17:1, which states that Hoshea came to the throne in the twelvth year of Ahaz. We might dismiss 2 Kgs 15:30 out of hand, but its very existence should give us pause. Why was the datum invented? What contradiction was it trying to correct? The lengthening of Jotham's reign would have had the effect of lengthening also the reign of Pekah. This is likely to have been the intention. Since Jotham is stated as taking the throne in the second year of Pekah (16:1), if Hoshea took the throne in the twentieth year of Jotham, then Pekah's reign would come out to be twenty to twenty-one years. It would appear that this was an attempt to make the length of Pekah's reign conform to the reign length provided by the king list (twenty years). Second Kings 15:30 stands apart from MT's and LXX's other chronological data and may be set aside for the time being. Nevertheless, it does indicate that the reign of Pekah, as suggested by the original synchronisms, had been shorter than twenty years, and therefore that at least one of the synchronisms of 2 Kgs 16:1 and 17:1, which taken together give Pekah a reign of twenty-eight years, must be incorrect. Since multiple pieces of evidence affirm that Hoshea was a contemporary of the young King Hezekiah of Judah, we would expect that he would have been crowned somewhere near the end of the reign of Ahaz, and so the synchronism in 17:1 is more likely to be original than the one in 16:1. No doubt an editor, in an attempt to lengthen the reign of Jotham to the sixteen years ascribed to him in the king list, advanced the accession of Ahaz to Pekah's seventeenth year. Unfortunately no existing manuscript of Kings, nor any other unnoticed reading in Kings, gives us a clue as to what the original reading was. Nevertheless, a datum in a Deuteronomic section of Isaiah may be of assistance. It sets the reign of Ahaz sixty-five years (inclusive) before Ephraim is "shattered from being a people" (Isa 7:8). If we knew when this event took place, we might be able to sort this matter out. To do this, we have no choice but to look to extrabiblical evidence. According to Assyrian chronology, after his capture of Sidon in 677, the Assyrian king Esarhaddon deported the population of Samaria (cf. Ezra 4:2), and this appears to be what Isaiah is referring to. Counting back 64 years from 677 or 676 B.C.E. (when this event occurred) brings us to 739 or 740 B.C.E. This should be sometime in Ahaz's reign. If Samaria fell in Hoshea's 9th year (2 Kgs 18:9–10), and this was the year 720 (see below), then 739 or 740 would correspond to Pekah's second or third year. This is about as early as we can make Ahaz's accession, so we will tentatively assume the original reading assigned his accession to Pekah's third year.

To sum up, in the block of material from 2 Kgs 9 to 20, the data preserved in 2 Kgs 14:17 and 15:30 indicate that a total of eight synchronisms may have been tampered with. Fortunately, the original readings can be reconstructed more or less from the textual evidence (with only the last having to appeal to extrabiblical sources). I can find no other evidence within the biblical text to suggest that any other alterations were made between 2 Kgs 9 and 20.

4.1.4.5. Conclusions

Before proceeding, a review of the conclusions that have been reached so far may be worthwhile.

(1) For the time of the kings, the original version of the Deuteronomic History contained chronological data only from the Judahite and Israelite royal chronicles, which placed events in specific regnal years, but did not provide totals for the length of kings' reigns. Neither of the chronicles contained dates that indicated the month and day that an event occurred; only years were recorded. Neither kingdom kept track of the regnal years of the other. However, they would take note of the accession of a new king in the other kingdom.

(2) The total counts for kings' reigns were added to the DH during the exile and derive from king lists that were not directly connected with the royal chronicles.

(3) The chronological notes in MT 1 Kgs 16:10, 2 Kgs 1:17, and 2 Kgs 15:30 do not appear to derive from either the chronicles or the king lists and are probably later additions.

(4) The biblical evidence suggests that Judah counted its kings' regnal years from the autumn. Evidence for a civil calendar beginning in the autumn strengthens this conclusion.

(5) There is sufficient evidence to indicate that Israel counted its kings' regnal years from a different time of year than Judah did, so they probably had a spring-based regnal calendar.

(6) The Judahite king list assumes an accession-year system in Judah. The Judahite royal chronicle used by the Deuteronomistic Historian appears to agree, and this evidence suggests that the kingdom employed this system throughout its history.

(7) The difference in year totals between the Israelite and Judahite king lists suggests that Israel employed the non-accession-year system in its early period.

(8) In their chronicles, neither kingdom noted co-regencies of the other kingdom, so they either ignored them, or there were no co-regencies.

(9) Discrepancies within the Deuteronomic History between reign lengths and synchronisms were variously adjusted in both MT and OG.

4.2. Historical Reconstructions

Now that we know the chronological sources of the Deuteronomic History and can approximate their data, we may examine in more detail the question of historical reliability. Such an exercise may assist in determining how far removed from the reality each of the sources is and perhaps a little about their independent textual history. At this point, we will concern ourselves only with the chronology of the kings. It is very possible that both the chronicles and the king lists will present a chronology that is at variance with the historical reality, or at least with the data that comes from Assyria and Babylon, since chronological data from earlier times may have been inadequately preserved (a statement we could make about the foreign material as well).

The records of kingdoms neighboring Israel and Judah occasionally make reference to interactions with those two countries and sometimes mention kings by name. Rarely, however, is an exact date associated with one of these references. Surprisingly, in the entire history of the Israelite and Judahite kingdoms, only two dated events in extrabiblical sources may be matched with dated events in biblical sources:

(1) *Year 21 of Nabopolassar of Babylon = Year 4 of Jehoiakim of Judah.* Prince Nebuchadnezzar, in the twenty-first year of his father, defeated the Egyptians in the Battle of Carchemish in May/June of 605 B.C.E. (BM 21946). Jeremiah 46:2 places this battle in the fourth year of Jehoiakim. Keep in mind

that the Mesopotamian regnal year began in the spring, and the Judahite regnal year in the autumn.

(2) *Year 17 of Nabopolassar of Babylon = year of the death of Josiah.* The Babylonian Chronicle (BM 21901) informs us that, in the year following Nabopolassar's 16th year, "a large army of Egypt" allied with the king of Assyria invaded the Levant with the intention of taking Harran back from the Babylonians (summer of 609 B.C.E.). This is almost certain to be the force that King Josiah engaged in battle and by whom he was slain (2 Kgs 23:29).[52]

A possible third synchronism, equating Year 4 of Sennacherib of Assyria with Year 14 of Hezekiah of Judah, cannot be maintained (see Appendix B).

Three further synchronisms are provided by Jeremiah's scribe and by the exilic reviser of the Deuteronomic History in the final chapter of Kings and are probably reliable:

(1) *Year 19 of Nebuchadnezzar of Babylon = Year 11 of Zedekiah of Judah and the destruction of Jerusalem* (2 Kgs 25:2, 8).

(2) *Year 18 of Nebuchadnezzar of Babylon = Year 10 of Zedekiah of Judah* (Jer 32:1).

(3) *Year 8 of Nebuchadnezzar of Babylon = the accession of Zedekiah of Judah.* The Babylonian Chronicle (BM 21946, rev., ll. 11–13) provides us with an exact date for Nebuchadnezzar's deposal of Jehoiachin, which corresponds to March 16, 597 B.C.E. in the Julian calendar (the tail end of Nebuchadnezzar's 7th year). The deposal of Jehoiachin by Nebuchadnezzar is mentioned also in the DH (2 Kgs 24:10–11), but a date is not given. Nevertheless, it also tells us that Jehoiachin (who had only reigned three months) was taken to Babylon the following year (24:12), probably a month or two after his deposal. We should keep in mind that Judah is not likely to have accepted the deposal of Jehoiachin (at least not officially) while he was still present in Jerusalem, despite what Nebuchadnezzar may have declared. The fact that the Judahites

---

52. For a discussion of these two synchronisms, see David Noel Freedman, "The Babylonian Chronicle," *BA* 19 (1956): 50–60. An alternate view has been put forth by Paul K. Hooker and John H. Hayes ("The Year of Josiah's Death: 609 or 610 BCE?" in *The Land That I Will Show You: Essays on the History and Archaeology of the Ancient Near East in Honour of J. Maxwell Miller* [ed. John A. Dearman and Matt P. Graham; JSOTSup 343; Sheffield: Sheffield Academic Press, 2001], 96–103) that Josiah was killed by Pharaoh Necho in the previous year (610). While it is true that the Babylonian Chronicle reports that the Egyptians assisted Assyria in their defense of Harran that year (a defense that failed), it seems unlikely that this was the year Josiah was killed, because according to the biblical account, the king of Egypt came down from the region of the Euphrates to meet Josiah at Megiddo. This would indicate that the pharaoh had already been in the north, rather than on his way to the north, as Hooker and Hayes suggest. This must have occurred after the fall of Harran and therefore after Adar (February/March) of 609.

dated the end of the reign of Jehoiachin and the accession of Zedekiah early in Nebuchadnezzar's 8th year confirms this. For the Judahites, Jehoiachin's reign would have ended when, and only when, he had left the country.[53]

There are three other synchronisms we can reconstruct with a reasonable amount of certainty:

(1) *Year 10 of Sargon of Assyria = Year 14 of Hezekiah of Judah*. The year of an Assyrian punitive campaign against the Philistines in 712 B.C.E. also involved the Judahites (Nineveh Prism A, Fragment D). For a full discussion of this synchronism, see Appendix B.

(2) *Year 2 of Sargon of Assyria = Year 6 of Hezekiah of Judah and Year 9 of Hoshea of Israel*. In many of his inscriptions, Sargon claims to have fought against Samaria in his first two years of kingship and conquered it completely by his second year, 720 B.C.E. (II.3, ll. 10–17). The DH provides the Judahite and Israelite synchronisms (2 Kgs 18:10–11).

(3) *Year 5 of Shalmaneser V of Assyria = Year 4 of Hezekiah of Judah and Year 7 of Hoshea of Israel*. The Babylonian Chronicle claims that Shalmaneser ravaged Samaria (most likely referring to the country rather than the city) sometime during his short reign (I, ll. 27–30). The DH confirms this (2 Kgs 18:9). Since Sargon was king the following year, the year of Shalmaneser's campaign against Israel must have been his fifth and last (722 B.C.E.).

Finally, there are several historical events recorded in extrabiblical sources that pertain to kings of Israel or Judah and which, although they cannot be placed in a precise year, assist us generally in ascertaining approximate synchronisms.

(1) *Early in the reign of Ashurbanipal of Assyria = sometime in the reign of Manasseh of Judah*. The Prism C inscription of Ashurbanipal (I, l. 25) includes Manasseh in a list of kings bearing tribute from the coastlands. These vassals are said to have assisted Ashurbanipal in his invasion of Egypt (664–663 B.C.E.).

(2) *Year 4 or 5 of Esarhaddon of Assyria = sometime in the reign of Manasseh of Judah*. An inscription of Esarhaddon refers to Manasseh giving tribute to the Assyrian king (Nineveh prism A, V, l. 55). The precise year of the event is unclear, but Manasseh is listed among twenty-two "seacoast and sea kings" who gave tribute sometime after the fall of Sidon in 677 B.C.E., so

---

53. Considering we know for certain that Jehoiakim's accession year ended in the autumn of 609 and that Jehoiachin ended his three-month reign sometime in or after March 597, there is no way around the fact that Jehoiachin took the throne in Jehoiakim's twelfth year. Jehoiakim's reign length in the Judahite king list (eleven years) is therefore one year short of the reality.

this is likely to have occurred either in Esarhaddon's fourth or fifth year (677 or 676 B.C.E.).

(3) *Year 4 of Sennacherib of Assyria = sometime in the reign of Hezekiah of Judah.* While the synchronism of Sennacherib's fourth year with Hezekiah's 14th can no longer be maintained (see Appendix B), it is certain that Sennacherib did attack Hezekiah in 701 B.C.E., and this is likely to have occurred sometime after Hezekiah's fourteenth year.

(4) *Sometime in the reign of Marduk-apla-iddina II of Babylon = Year 14 of Hezekiah.* The DH refers to a visit of the Babylonian king (Merodachbaladan) to Hezekiah's court (2 Kgs 20:12–19). The trip is prompted by Hezekiah's illness, which is dated to his 14th year (20:6; cf. 18:13 with 20:1). Marduk-apla-iddina reigned from 722 to 710 B.C.E.

(5) *Soon after the death of Tiglath-pileser III of Assyria = accession of Hezekiah.* A prophecy of Isaiah (14:28–32) places the death of Ahaz shortly after "the staff of the one striking [Philistia]" was "broken." This no doubt refers to Tiglath-pileser, who died in 727 B.C.E.. The death of Ahaz probably occurred in that year or the year after.

(6) *Year 15 or 17 of Tiglath-pileser III of Assyria = coronation of Hoshea of Israel.* Tiglath-pileser claims to have replaced Peqah with Hoshea on the throne of Israel (Summary Inscription 4, ll. 15–19; Summary Inscription 9, ll.10–11). The latter text puts Hoshea's accession during Tiglath-pileser's campaign against Sarrabani in Babylonia. Apparently, Hoshea or one of his messengers traveled quite a distance to secure the kingship. Tiglath-pileser's presence in Sarrabani could be associated with the campaign against southern Babylonia that included the siege of Shapiya in 731 B.C.E. (according to the Eponym Chronicle) or the next campaign against southern Babylonia in 729 (according to the Eponym Chronicle). The records are too fragmentary to pinpoint the year exactly.

(7) *Year 11, 12, or 13 of Tiglath-pileser III of Assyria = sometime in the reign of Ahaz of Judah.* Ahaz is mentioned in a list of Levantine tribute-bearing kings (Summary Inscription 7, rev. l. 11). The date of this event is disputed, but it probably occurred somewhere between 735 and 733 B.C.E.

(8) *Sixty-four years before Esarhaddon of Assyria deported the population of Phoenicia-Samaria = sometime in the reign of Ahaz.* After his capture of Sidon in 677, Esarhaddon deported the population of the area (cf. Ezra 4:2). The Deuteronomic narrative in Isa 7 sets the reign of Ahaz sixty-five years (inclusive) before this event, when Isaiah prophesies, "In yet 65 years, Ephraim will be shattered from being a people" (Isa 7:8). Counting sixty-four years back from 677 or 676 brings us to 739 or 740 B.C.E. This should be sometime in Ahaz's reign. (This synchronism was also discussed in §4.1.4.4 above.)

(9) *Sometime in the reign of Tiglath-pileser III of Assyria = sometime in the reign of Menahem of Israel.* The date of Menahem's payment of tribute to Assyria has been hotly debated. Some have argued that the Assyrian records (Iran Stele, IIIA, l. 5; Ann. 13*:10; Ann. 27:2) indicate two different payments. Because of the fragmentary nature of the Assyrian materials, the matter is far from settled, and cases have been made for 743, 740, and 738 B.C.E..[54]

(10) *Sometime in the reign of Adad-nirari III of Assyria = sometime in the reign of Joash of Israel.* Joash is listed among tribute-bearers to Adad-nirari III (Tell al-Rimah inscription, l. 8). The exact year is unknown. Adad-nirari reigned from 811 to 783 B.C.E.

(11) *Year 18 of Shalmaneser III of Asssyria = sometime in the reign of Jehu of Israel.* The bearing of tribute by Jehu is attested in several inscriptions of Shalmaneser (Black Obelisk, relief B; IM 55644; annals of year 20 of the city of Ashur: III, l. 45—IV, l. 15; Kurba'il Statue, 29–30) and can be confidently dated to 841 B.C.E.

(12) *Year 6 of Shalmaneser III of Assyria = sometime in the reign of Ahab of Israel.* Ahab is mentioned in the somewhat unreliable Kurkh Monolith inscription (II: l. 91) in association with the Battle of Qarqar, which took place in 853 B.C.E.

(13) *Sometime in the reign of Shoshenq I of Egypt = Year 5 of Rehoboam of Judah.* Egyptian chronologists, using a combination of archaeological evidence, monumental inscriptions, astronomy, and Egyptian king lists, place Shoshenq's reign ca. 945–925 B.C.E.[55]

Let us first compare the eight precise synchronisms and the thirteen approximate synchronisms with the Judahite king list that fell into the hands of the reviser of the DH. On its own it provides a chronology of the monarchy of Judah from Rehoboam to Zedekiah. Working back from an absolute date of 586 for the end of the kingdom,[56] we arrive at the following dates B.C.E. for the kings of the divided kingdom:

---

54. See discussions in Thiele, *The Mysterious Numbers of the Hebrew Kings*, 139–62; Hayim Tadmor, *The Inscriptions of Tiglath-pileser III, King of Assyria* (Jerusalem: Israel Academy of Sciences and Humanities, 1994), 274–75.

55. For a summary of the evidence, see Kenneth A. Kitchen, "The Historical Chronology of Ancient Egypt, A Current Assessment," in *The Synchronisation of Civilisations in the Eastern Mediterranean in the Second Millennium B.C.* (ed. Manfred Bietak; Wien: Verlag der Österreichischen Akademie der Wissenschaften, 2000), 39–52; A. J. Shortland, "Shishak, King of Egypt: The Challenges of Egyptian Calendrical Chronology," in *The Bible and Radiocarbon Dating* (ed. Thomas E. Levy and Thomas Higham; London: Equinox, 2005), 43–54.

56. For the date 586, see §1.4.1.4. For evidence that Zedekiah took the throne in Nebuchadnezzar's eighth year, see the discussion on extrabiblical synchronisms directly above.

4. RULERSHIP CHRONOLOGIES

Rehoboam (973–956)
Abijam (956–953)
Asa (953–912)
Jehoshaphat (912–887)
Jehoram (887–879)
Ahaziah (879–878)
Jehoash (878–838)
Amaziah (838–809)
Azariah (809–757)
Jotham (757–741)
Ahaz (741–725)
Hezekiah (725–696)
Manasseh (696–641)
Amon (641–639)
Josiah (639–608)
Jehoahaz (608)
Jehoiakim (608–597)
Jehoiachin (597)
Zedekiah (597–586)

It is important to note that the scheme above assumes that the years attributed to each king in the king list represent actual years. In a postdating system (in which the accession year of a king is not counted), the number of regnal years for each king is equal to the number of actual years he reigned. It could be objected that the ancient Israelite who compiled the data counted the totals inclusively. Nevertheless, as was demonstrated above, each block of time would be added exclusively, so an inclusive count would only affect the year of the accession of Rehoboam (making it 972). The rest of the years would remain the same.

Considering that the core of the list was composed in the reign of Amon and was supplemented sometime between the end of the monarchy and the revision of the DH during the exile, there is the possibility that some of the figures, particularly the earlier ones, are inaccurate. Extrabiblical synchronisms fit the king list's chronology in many instances in the later reigns. For example, the conquest of Jerusalem by Nebuchadnezzar of Babylon, in year 7 of his reign (597), and the installation of Zedekiah a few months later match the dates here. Also, the Assyrian king Sennacherib mentions King Hezekiah and an invasion of Judah in the fourth year of his reign (701), which falls within the years attributed to Hezekiah here. In Hezekiah's reign, the king list is close but appears to have lost a year somewhere. It is prior to Ahaz that the dates seem to fall further and further short of what they should be. The reign of Shoshenq I (ca. 945–925) covers a period of years falling well after Rehoboam's reign here. The dates for the reign of Rehoboam are thus far too early.

TABLE 4.11. COMPARISON OF EXTRABIBLICAL DATES WITH JUDAHITE KING LIST DATES

Extrabiblical Synchronisms	King List Dates
Sometime during the reign of Shoshenq I of Egypt (ca. 945–925) = Year 5 of Rehoboam. **No match**	Rehoboam (973–956)
	Abijam (956–953)
	Asa (953–912)
	Jehoshaphat (912–887)
	Jehoram (887–879)
	Ahaziah (879–878)
	Jehoash (878–838)
	Amaziah (838–809)
	Azariah (809–757)
	Jotham (757–741)
64 years before Esarhaddon of Assyria deports the population of Phoenicia-Samaria (740 or 739) = sometime in the reign of Ahaz. **Match**	Ahaz (741–725)
Year 11, 12 or 13 of Tiglath-pileser III of Assyria (735, 734 or 733) = sometime in the reign of Ahaz. **Match**	
Soon after the death of Tiglath-pileser III of Assyria (727 or 726) = accession of Hezekiah. **No match**	Hezekiah (725–696)
Year 5 of Shalmaneser V of Assyria (722) = Year 4 of Hezekiah. **No match**	
Year 2 of Sargon of Assyria (720) = Year 6 of Hezekiah. **No match**	

10 of Sargon of Assyria (712) = Year 14 of Hezekiah of Judah. **No match** →	
sometime in the reign of Marduk-apla-iddina II of Babylon (722–710) = Year 14 of Hezekiah. **Match** →	
Year 4 of Sennacherib of Assyria (701) = sometime in the reign of Hezekiah of Judah. **Match** →	
Year 4 or 5 of Esarhaddon of Assyria (677 or 676) = sometime in the reign of Manasseh of Judah. **Match** →	Manasseh (696–641)
early in the reign of Ashurbanipal of Assyria (664 or 663) = sometime in the reign of Manasseh of Judah. **Match** →	
	Amon (641–639)
	Josiah (639–608)
	Jehoahaz (608)
	Jehoiakim (608–597)
	Jehoiachin (597)
Year 8 of Nebuchadnezzar of Babylon (597) = the accession of Zedekiah of Judah. **Match** →	Zedekiah (597–586)

The king list, therefore, has given us reason not to accept its earlier dates at face value. We do not know what sources the compiler of the king list used, although the information seems ultimately to have its origin in primary documentation. Whatever the historical value of the Judahite king list used by the reviser of the History, we must accept that these are its dates and that it represents the chronology of the person(s) who composed it, whether they had access to reliable information or not. Even if it drew from a common tradition with the other chronological sources used in the DH, it must be understood independently from those sources and from the historical reality as well.

When we add up the lengths of the reigns of the kings of Israel (assuming the figures are antedated years), we arrive at a date ca. 946 B.C.E. for the division of the kingdom. This date falls short of the Judahite total by some seventeen years.

Jeroboam (946–925)
Nadab (925–924)
Baasha (924–901)
Elah (901–900)
Zimri (900)
Omri (900–889)
Ahab (889–868)
Ahaziah (868–867)
Jehoram (867–856)
Jehu (856–829)
Jehoahaz (829–813)
Joash (813–798)
Jeroboam (798–758)
Zechariah (758)
Shallum (757)
Menahem (757–748)
Pekahiah (748–747)
Pekah (747–728)
Hoshea (728–720)

The two lists are incompatible with each other as they stand (further corroborating our conclusion that they come from two different sources).

Because Judah used a postdating system, and Israel used an antedating system, we should expect that the Judahite king list provides us with actual years, and that the Israelite king list provides us with antedated years. This conclusion is justified by our observation of the cases of two kings whose reign lengths are stated explicitly by both a king list and a chronicle. For Israel, we have the example of Hoshea, about whom it is said that he reigned nine years (2 Kgs 17:1) and about whom it is also said that his reign ended in his ninth year (2 Kgs 18:10). The first datum comes from the Israelite king list, the second from the Israelite chronicle. We know that the chronicle uses antedating. Thus the ninth year = eight actual years. Since the king list gives nine years, it must also be antedated. For Judah, we have the example of Zedekiah, about whom it is said that he reigned eleven years (2 Kgs 24:18) and about whom it is also said that his reign ended in his eleventh year (2 Kgs 25:8). The first datum comes from the Judahite king list and the second from the Judahite chronicle. We know that the chronicle uses postdating. Thus the eleventh year = eleven actual years. Since the king list gives eleven years, it is stating actual years.

4. RULERSHIP CHRONOLOGIES

The numbers from the Israelite king list, when compared with the extrabiblical synchronisms listed above, clearly are defective. The reigns of the kings do not coincide with the historical reality very well at all.

TABLE 4.12. COMPARISON OF EXTRABIBLICAL DATES
WITH ISRAELITE KING LIST DATES

Extrabiblical Synchronisms		King List Dates
		Jeroboam (946–925)
		Nadab (925–924)
		Baasha (924–901)
		Elah (901–900)
		Zimri (900)
		Omri (900–889)
Year 6 of Shalmaneser III of Assyria (853) = sometime in the reign of Ahab of Israel. **No match**	→	Ahab (889–868)
		Ahaziah (868–867)
		Jehoram (867–856)
Year 18 of Shalmaneser III of Asssyria (841) = sometime in the reign of Jehu of Israel. **Match**	→	Jehu (856–829)
		Jehoahaz (829–813)
Sometime in the reign of Adad-nirari III of Assyria (811–783) = sometime in the reign of Joash of Israel. **Match**	→	Joash (813–798)
		Jeroboam (798–758)
		Zechariah (758)
Sometime in the reign of Tiglath-pileser III of Assyria (743, 740, or 738) = sometime in the reign of Menahem of Israel. **No match**		Shallum (757)
	→	Menahem (757–748)
		Pekahiah (748–747)
		Pekah (747–728)
Year 15 or 17 of Tiglath-pileser III of Assyria (731 or 729) = coronation of Hoshea of Israel. **No match**	→	Hoshea (728–720)

There is nothing extraordinary about the two extrabiblical synchronisms that are in harmony with the king list. Both cover very broad ground. It may be that only a small number of reign lengths are incorrect and are throwing the rest off, but we cannot put great trust in the figures. Unlike the Davidic dynasty in Judah in which all kings were from a single family, the northern kings often succeeded by usurpation. The constant turnover of government may account for the northern king list's greater inaccuracy.

It is clear, then, that we must get the second opinion offered by the chronicles, which, though incomplete, may nevertheless provide valuable information. Unfortunately, there is also the chance that, for some kings, neither the figure in the king lists nor the one in the chronicles is historically accurate. In cases where the extrabiblical data suggest this, we may have to make some educated guesses about the historical reality. In cases where there is a discrepancy between the king lists and the royal chronicles, and there is no extrabiblical evidence to suggest one or the other or either are correct, we will tentatively take the testimony of the chronicles as the most reliable.

Below is a list of the twenty-four events that are dated by a synchronism with the regnal year of a Judahite monarch and that therefore may be understood as coming from the Judahite royal chronicle used as a source by the Deuteronomistic Historian:

Dates from the Judahite Royal Chronicle

Rehoboam Year 5—Shishak the king of Egypt came up against Jerusalem (1 Kgs 14:25)

Asa Year 2—Nadab the son of Jeroboam became king over Israel (1 Kgs 15:25)

Asa Year 3—Baasha the son of Ahijah became king over Israel in Tirzah (1 Kgs 15:33)

Asa Year 20—Elah the son of Baasha became king over Israel in Tirzah (1 Kgs 16:8)[57]

Asa Year [25]—Zimri became king over Israel in Tirzah (1 Kgs 16:15)[58]

Asa Year 31—Omri became king over Israel (1 Kgs 16:23)

Asa Year 38—Ahab the son of Omri became king over Israel in Samaria (1 Kgs 16:29)[59]

---

57. MT has this as Asa Year 26.

58. MT has this as Asa Year 27; Luc has this as Asa Year 22. DH[1] puts this event six years before Asa Year 31 (1 Kgs 16:23).

59. OG has this as Jehoshaphat Year 2.

4. RULERSHIP CHRONOLOGIES 153

Jehoshaphat Year 17—Ahaziah the son of Ahab became king over Israel in Samaria (1 Kgs 22:52)[60]

Jehoshaphat Year 18—Joram the son of Ahab became king over Israel in Samaria (2 Kgs 3:1)[61]

Jehoash Year 23—Repairs made to the temple (2 Kgs 12:7); Jehoahaz the son of Jehu became king over Israel in Samaria (2 Kgs 13:1)

Jehoash Year 37—Joash the son of Jehoahaz became king over Israel in Samaria (2 Kgs 13:10)

Amaziah Year [2]—Jeroboam the son of Joash became king over Israel in Samaria (2 Kgs 14:23)[62]

Azariah Year [25]—Zechariah the son of Jeroboam became king over Israel for 6 months in Samaria (2 Kgs 15:8)[63]

Azariah Year [26]—Shallum the son of Jabesh became king over Israel for 1 month in Samaria (2 Kgs 15:13); Menahem the son of Gadi became king over Israel in Samaria (2 Kgs 15:17)

Azariah Year [37]—Pekahiah the son of Menahem became king over Israel in Samaria (2 Kgs 15:23)

Azariah Year [39]—Pekah the son of Remaliah became king over Israel in Samaria (2 Kgs 15:27)

Ahaz Year 12—Hoshea the son of Elah became king over Israel in Samaria (2 Kgs 17:1)

Hezekiah Year 4—Shalmaneser the king of Assyria came up against Samaria and laid siege to it (2 Kgs 18:9)

Hezekiah Year 6—Samaria was captured (2 Kgs 18:10)

Hezekiah Year 14—Sennacherib the king of Assyria came up against all the fortified cities of Judah and laid siege to them (2 Kgs 18:13)

Josiah Year 18—The king begins his religious reforms (2 Kgs 22:3); Passover celebrated (2 Kgs 23:23)

It is not certain whether the final date was derived from the chronicle or not, as the event recorded is understood to have occurred in the lifetime of the Historian.

---

60. Luc has this as Jehoshaphat Year 24.
61. Luc has this as Jehoram Year 2.
62. The readings of MT and LXX are rejected in favor of the datum in 2 Kgs 14:17, which states that Amaziah died fifteen years after Joash's death and thus fifteen years after the accession of Jeroboam. A reign length of sixteen or seventeen years is suggested by the change made in 2 Kgs 15:1, an addition of eleven to twelve years from the original number.
63. The restoration of Jeroboam's original accession date (see n. 62) requires an equal restoration of the five dates in Azariah's reign, beginning with Zechariah. See above.

Below is a list of the thirteen events that are dated by a synchronism with the regnal year of an Israelite monarch and which therefore may be understood as coming from the Israelite royal chronicle used as a source by the Deuteronomistic Historian:

DATES FROM THE ISRAELITE ROYAL CHRONICLE

Jeroboam Year 18—Abijam became king over Judah (1 Kgs 15:1)
Jeroboam Year 24—Asa became king of Judah (1 Kgs 15:9)[64]
Ahab Year 4—Jehoshaphat the son of Asa became king over Judah (1 Kgs 22:41)[65]
Joram Year 5—Jehoram the son of Jehoshaphat became king alongside Jehoshaphat (2 Kgs 8:16)
Joram Year 11—Ahaziah the son of Jehoram the king of Judah became king (2 Kgs 8:25; 9:29)[66]
Jehu Year 7—Jehoash became king (2 Kgs 12:2)
Joash Year 2—Amaziah the son of Jehoash the king of Judah became king (2 Kgs 14:1)
Jeroboam Year [14]—Azariah the son of Amaziah the king of Judah became king (2 Kgs 15:1)[67]
Pekah Year 2—Jotham the son of Uzziah the king of Judah became king (2 Kgs 15:32)
Pekah Year [3]—Ahaz the son of Jotham the king of Judah became king (2 Kgs 16:1)[68]
Hoshea Year 3—Hezekiah the son of Ahaz the king of Judah became king (2 Kgs 18:1)
Hoshea Year 7—Shalmaneser the king of Assyria came up against Samaria and laid siege to it (2 Kgs 18:9)
Hoshea Year 9—Samaria was captured (2 Kgs 18:10)

---

64. MT has this as Jeroboam Year 20.
65. OG has this as Omri Year 11.
66. MT has this as Joram Year 12 at 2 Kgs 8:25.
67. The readings of MT and LXX are rejected in favor of the datum in 2 Kgs 14:17, which states that Amaziah died fifteen years after Joash's death and therefore fifteen years after the accession of Jeroboam.
68. The existence of the anomalous datum in 2 Kgs 15:30 suggests that Pekah's reign has been artificially lengthened and therefore that the synchronism of 2 Kgs 16:1 is incorrect. See above.

4. RULERSHIP CHRONOLOGIES 155

TABLE 4.13. CHRONOLOGY OF THE HEBREW KINGS BASED UPON THE SYNCHRONISMS

Judahite Record		Years B.C.E.	Israelite Record	
Autumn Years			Spring Years	
		935		
	REHOBOAM Ac	934		
	1	933	JEROBOAM 1	
	2	932	2	

	3	4	5	6	7
	931	930	929	928	927
	3	4	5	6	7

Shishak attacks 5th of Rehoboam 1 Kgs 14:25

4. RULERSHIP CHRONOLOGIES

8	9	10	11	12

926	925	924	923	922

8	9	10	11	12

					Abijam
13	14	15	16	17	18th of
921	920	919	918	917	
13	14	15	16	17 ABIJAM	Ac

4. RULERSHIP CHRONOLOGIES

Jeroboam
1 Kgs 15:1

18	19	20	21	22
916	915	914	913	912
1	2	3	4	5

	Asa 24th of Jeroboam 1 Kgs 15:9					
23	24	25 NADAB 1	2 BAASHA 1	2		
911	910	909	908	907		
6 ASA Ac	1	2	3	4		

Nadab 2nd of Asa 1 Kgs 15:25   Baasha 3rd of Asa 1 Kgs 15:33

4. RULERSHIP CHRONOLOGIES 161

	3	4	5	6	7	
	906	905	904	903	902	
5	6	7	8	9		

8	9	10	11	12
901	900	899	898	897
10	11	12	13	14

4. RULERSHIP CHRONOLOGIES

13	14	15	16	17	18
896	895	894	893	892	

15	16	17	18	19

164 SHADOW ON THE STEPS

ELAH	1	2	3	4	5
	891	890	889	888	887
	20	21	22	23	24

Elah
20th of Asa
1 Kgs 16:8

4. RULERSHIP CHRONOLOGIES

	TIBNI 1	2	3	4	
6	7 ZIMRI / OMRI 1	2	3	4	
886	885	884	883	882	
25	26	27	28	29	

Zimri & Omri [25th] of Asa
1 Kgs 16:10, 15, 16

SHADOW ON THE STEPS

	Omri 6 yrs in Tirzah 1 Kgs 16:23			
5	6			
5	6	7	8	9
881	880	879	878	877
30	31	32	33	34

Omri
31st of Asa
1 Kgs 16:23

4. RULERSHIP CHRONOLOGIES 167

10	11	12	13 AHAB	1	2
876	875	874	873	872	
35	36	37	38	39	

Ahab
38th of Asa
1 Kgs 16:29

168   SHADOW ON THE STEPS

	Jehoshaphat 4th of Ahab 1 Kgs 22:41			
3	4	5	6	7
871	870	869	868	867
40	41 JEHOSHAPHAT Ac	1	2	3

4. RULERSHIP CHRONOLOGIES 169

8	9	10	11	12
866	865	864	863	862
4	5	6	7	8

13	14	15	16	17
861	860	859	858	857
9	10	11	12	13

4. RULERSHIP CHRONOLOGIES

	18	19	20	21	22 AHAZIAH	1	2
	856	855	854	853	852		
14	15	16	17	18			

Ahaziah
17th of Jehoshaphat
1 Kgs 22:51
Joram
18th of Jehoshaphat

172   SHADOW ON THE STEPS

	JORAM 1	2	3	4	5 Jehoram / 5th of Joram / 2 Kgs 8:16
	851	850	849	848	847
2 Kgs 3:1	19	20	21	22 JEHORAM Ac	1

4. RULERSHIP CHRONOLOGIES

						Ahaziah 11th year
6	7	8	9	10		
846	845	844	843	842		
2	3	4	5	7 AHAZIAH Ac		

	11	12 JEHU 1	2	3	4	of Joram 2 Kgs 8:25
	841	840	839	838	837	
ATHALIAH 1	1	2	3	4	5	Athaliah 6 yrs 2 Kgs 11:1–3

4. RULERSHIP CHRONOLOGIES 175

	Jehoash 7th of Jehu 2 Kgs 12:2				
5	6	7	8	9	
836	835	834	833	832	
	JEHOASH 1	2	3	4	
6					

10	11	12	13	14
831	830	829	828	827
5	6	7	8	9

4. RULERSHIP CHRONOLOGIES

15	16	17	18	19
826	825	824	823	822
10	11	12	13	14

178   SHADOW ON THE STEPS

20	21	22	23	24
821	820	819	818	817
15	16	17	18	19

4. RULERSHIP CHRONOLOGIES 179

25	26	27	28	JEHOAHAZ 1	2
816	815	814	813	812	
20	21	22	23	24	

Jehoahaz
23rd of Jehoash
2 Kgs 13:1

3	4	5	6	7
811	810	809	808	807
25	26	27	28	29

4. RULERSHIP CHRONOLOGIES 181

8	9	10	11	12

806	805	804	803	802

30	31	32	33	34

		Amaziah 2nd of Joash 2 Kgs 14:1			
13	14	15 JOASH	1	2	3
801	800	799	798	797	
35	36	37	38 AMAZIAH Ac	1	
	Joash 37th of Jehoash 2 Kgs 13:10				

4. RULERSHIP CHRONOLOGIES 183

		JEROBOAM				
4	5	1	2	3	4	
796	795	794	793	792		
2	3	4	5	6		

Jeroboam [3rd] of Amaziah 2 Kgs 14:17

5	6	7	8	9
791	790	789	788	787
7	8	9	10	11

4. RULERSHIP CHRONOLOGIES

					Azariah 14th of Jeroboam 2 Kgs 15:1
10	11	12	13	14	
786	785	784	783	782	
12	13	14	15	16	AZARIAH Ac

15	16	17	18	19
781	780	779	778	777
1	2	3	4	5

4. RULERSHIP CHRONOLOGIES 187

20	21	22	23	24
776	775	774	773	772
6	7	8	9	10

25	26	27	28	29
771	770	769	768	767
11	12	13	14	15

4. RULERSHIP CHRONOLOGIES 189

30	31	32	33	34
766	765	764	763	762
16	17	18	19	20

190 SHADOW ON THE STEPS

35	36	37	38	39
761	760	759	758	757
21	22	23	24	25

4. RULERSHIP CHRONOLOGIES 191

		ZECHARIAH	SHALLUM MENAHEM		
40	41	1	1	2	3
756	755	754	753	752	
26	27	28	29	30	

Zechariah [26th] of Azariah 2 Kgs 15:8
Menahem [27th] of Azariah 2 Kgs 15:17

4	5	6	7	8
751	750	749	748	747
31	32	33	34	35

4. RULERSHIP CHRONOLOGIES 193

					Jotham 2nd of Pekah 2 Kgs 15:32
9	10	11	12 PEKAHIAH 1	2 PEKAH 1	
746	745	744	743	742	
36	37	38	39	40 JOTHAM Ac	

Pekahiah [38th] of Azariah 2 Kgs 15:23

Pekah [40th] of

SHADOW ON THE STEPS

	Ahaz [3rd?] of Pekah 2 Kgs 16:1				
2	3	4	5	6	
741	740	739	738	737	
1	2 AHAZ Ac	1	2	3	

Azariah
2 Kgs 15:27

4. RULERSHIP CHRONOLOGIES

	7	8	9	10	11	
	736	735	734	733	732	
	4	5	6	7	8	

							Hezekiah
12	13	14	15	HOSHEA 1	2		
731	730	729	728	727			
9	10	11	12	13			

Hoshea
12th of Ahaz
2 Kgs 17:1

4. RULERSHIP CHRONOLOGIES 197

3rd of Hoshea 2 Kgs 18:1					Shalmaneser attacks Samaria 7th of Hoshea 2 Kgs 18:9
3	4	5	6	7	
726	725	724	723	722	
14 HEZEKIAH Ac	1	2	3	4	
			Shalmaneser attacks Samaria 4th of Hezekiah		

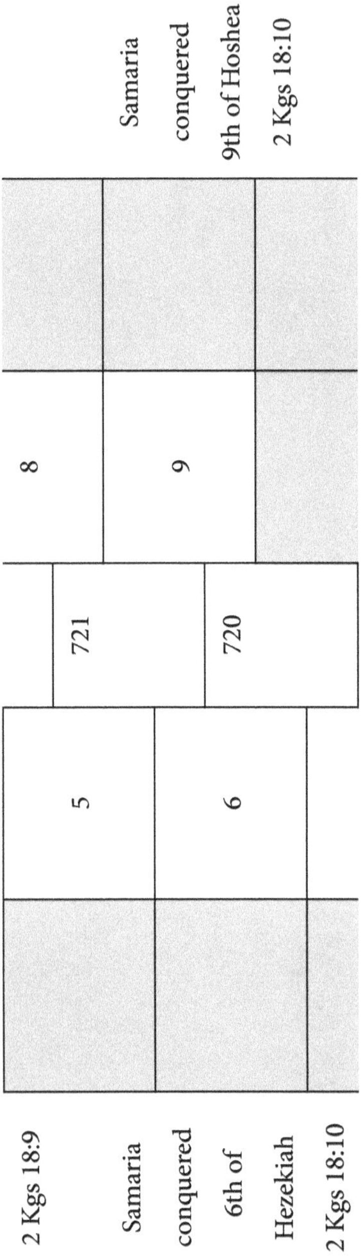
2 Kgs 18:9
Samaria
conquered
6th of
Hezekiah
2 Kgs 18:10
5
6
721
720
8
9
Samaria
conquered
9th of Hoshea
2 Kgs 18:10

4. RULERSHIP CHRONOLOGIES

To summarize the reconstruction of the table, we arrive at the following years for each of the kings:

Judah	Israel
Rehoboam (934–917)	Jeroboam (934–910)
Abijam (917–911)	Nadab (910–909)
Asa (911–870)	Baasha (909–892)
Jehoshaphat (870–848)	Elah (892–886)
Jehoram (848–842)	Zimri (886)
Ahaziah (842–841)[72]	Omri (886–874)
Jotham (742–740)	Ahab (874–853)
Ahaz (740–726)	Ahaziah (853–852)
Ahaz (740–726)	Jehoram (852–841)
Hezekiah (726–)	Jehu (841–814)
	Jehoahaz (814–800)
	Joash (800–796)
	Jeroboam (796–756)
	Zechariah (756)
	Shallum (755)
	Menahem (755–743)
	Pekahiah (743–742)
	Hoshea (729–720)

A comparison of these years with the extrabiblical synchronisms above reveals that there is nothing clearly defective in the chronological material of the chronicles (as reconstructed independently of the extrabiblical evidence). This is not to say that there are no errors in the reconstruction or in the presumed original synchronisms, but only that the data appear to be very close to the historical reality.

---

72. In this one case, I was forced to rely on the reign total from the Judahite king list.

TABLE 4.14. COMPARISON OF EXTRABIBLICAL DATES
WITH CHRONICLE DATES FOR THE KINGS OF JUDAH

Extrabiblical Synchronisms	Chronicle Dates
Sometime during the reign of Shoshenq I of Egypt (ca. 945–925) = Year 5 of Rehoboam. **Match**	Rehoboam (934–917)
	Abijam (917–911)
	Asa (911–870)
	Jehoshaphat (870–848)
	Jehoram (848–842)
	Ahaziah (842–841)
	Jehoash (841–798)
	Amaziah (798–782)
	Azariah (782–742)
	Jotham (742–740)
64 years before Esarhaddon of Assyria deports the population of Phoenicia-Samaria (740 or 739) = sometime in the reign of Ahaz. **Match**	Ahaz (740–726)
Year 11, 12, or 13 of Tiglath-pileser III of Assyria (735, 734, or 733) = sometime in the reign of Ahaz. **Match**	
Soon after the death of Tiglath-pileser III of Assyria (727 or 726) = accession of Hezekiah. **Match**	Hezekiah (726–)
Year 5 of Shalmaneser V of Assyria (722) = Year 4 of Hezekiah. **Match**	
Year 2 of Sargon of Assyria (720) = Year 6 of Hezekiah. **Match**	
10 of Sargon of Assyria (712) = Year 14 of Hezekiah of Judah. **Match**	

sometime in the reign of Marduk-apla-iddina II of Babylon (722–710) = Year 14 of Hezekiah. **Match**	→
Year 4 of Sennacherib of Assyria (701) = sometime in the reign of Hezekiah of Judah. **Match**	→

TABLE 4.15. COMPARISON OF EXTRABIBLICAL DATES WITH CHRONICLE DATES FOR THE KINGS OF ISRAEL

Extrabiblical Synchronisms		Chronicle Dates
		Jeroboam (934–910)
		Nadab (910–909)
		Baasha (909–892)
		Elah (892–886)
		Zimri (886)
		Omri (886–874)
Year 6 of Shalmaneser III of Assyria (853) = sometime in the reign of Ahab of Israel. **Match**	→	Ahab (874–853)
		Ahaziah (853–852)
		Jehoram (852–841)
Year 18 of Shalmaneser III of Asssyria (841) = sometime in the reign of Jehu of Israel. **Match**	→	Jehu (841–814)
		Jehoahaz (814–800)
Sometime in the reign of Adad-nirari III of Assyria (811–783) = sometime in the reign of Joash of Israel. **Match**	→	Joash (800–796)
		Jeroboam (796–756)
		Zechariah (756)
		Shallum (755)
Sometime in the reign of Tiglath-pileser III of Assyria (743, 740, or 738) = sometime in the reign of Menahem of Israel. **Match**	→	Menahem (755–743)

	Pekahiah (743–742)
	Pekah (742–729)
Year 15 or 17 of Tiglath-pileser III of Assyria (731 or 729) = coronation of Hoshea of Israel. **Match**	→ Hoshea (729–720)

It is clear, therefore, that the synchronisms are more reliable historically than the figures in the king lists and should be used first and favored when attempting to put together an accurate chronology.

5
Conclusions and Implications

This study has concentrated on ancient Israelite measurement of natural, cyclical time (in the form of clocks and calendars), as well as the Israelite methods for plotting points in linear time (historical chronology). Never was the aim of this work to find a unitary temporal worldview; different subsets of Israelite culture had distinctive and sometimes unique ways of configuring time. So, for example, a careful reading of all of the sources has revealed the existence of more than one calendar in ancient Israel and Judah. An agricultural calendar divided the year into two main parts. Seedtime began in mid-November and ran to mid-April, while the harvest ran from mid-April to mid-November. The Judahite civil year commenced around the time of the autumnal equinox (mid to late September). The liturgical calendar of the priests began near the vernal equinox (mid to late March). Evidence for a regnal year beginning in the autumn in the latter days of Judah suggests that there was no separate regnal calendar, but that king's reigns were calculated according to the civil year. Although at first the northern Israelites too began their civil year in the autumn (as indicated by the Gezer Calendar), the evidence that the regnal years in Samaria were most likely counted from the spring indicates that its civil year was changed sometime after the North's secession from the Davidic kingdom.

With the possible exception of the agricultural year, the timing of which is tied to the regional cycles of nature, the structure of the other calendars was deeply rooted in the psychological orientation of the community that created or adapted them. Since we must assume some continuity between Late Bronze Age Canaanite society and early Iron Age Israelite society, as well as some cross-cultural interaction between Israel and its neighbors in the Levant and further afield, there no doubt was a degree of influence, particularly of the older and the more populous upon the younger and the less populous. So, for example, we found that sources documenting the construction of Solomon's temple were oriented toward the Phoenician calendar, which was likely the result of Phoenician involvement in the actual building work itself.

We discovered also that the civil calendar as reflected in the portions of the Deuteronomic History written during the exilic period was in keeping with the standard civil calendar of Babylon, and this was no doubt attributable to the reality of Babylonian hegemony over the Judahite people (both in their homeland and in Babylon itself).

It is likely that calendars in Israel and Judah were organized according to local concerns as well, though this is more difficult to ascertain, because we do not know precisely the degree of foreign influence in the choice of autumn as the beginning of the civil and regnal years, nor in the choice of spring as the beginning of the liturgical year (which appears to have preceded the time of both Assyrian and Babylonian domination). The lack of evidence for southern Canaanite custom inhibits our ability to assess these matters. However, the change of the civil calendar from autumn to spring in northern Israel after its secession we may ascribe to a desire to be as separate and distinct as possible from the southern kingdom, just as was the case in the building of alternate holy places.

In antiquity religious concepts played a fundamental role in the shaping of time-measuring systems. Activities needed to be coordinated with the wishes of the gods. Failure to observe these rules at the appointed times, it was believed, could result in a god's disfavor and terrible supernatural consequences. Observance involved not only celebrating the feasts and performing rituals at their proper times, but also avoiding activities on certain days that the gods considered sacred. Thus we find in Israelite culture the custom that every seventh day was to be distinguished from the other secular days; it was a holy day on which no work was to be performed.

Then, too, there were secular motivations for marking certain times. It was a practice throughout the ancient world to adapt agricultural activities to the civil calendar in order to coordinate those activities with governmental oversight and ensure the collection of taxes in the form of agricultural produce. Similarly, the adaptation of the agricultural calendar to the liturgical schedule of rituals and festivals made it possible also for the priests to obtain a portion of the farmer's income. The use of regnal years as the backbone of the DH betrays the influence of contemporary politics upon the Deuteronomistic Historian. This may suggest simply a strong monarchical power in his day, or perhaps even that the state had oversight of his work.

We can see, then, some ways in which the social and political structure of a community had a significant effect on the way that time was measured, divided, or emphasized. Implicit here is that calendars are not "neutral" aspects of a community's life; they do something on a community's behalf. Although we cannot say that time measurement alone explains everything about a society's perceptions of time, it does play a role in the way persons or groups of people legitimize, promote, reconcile, celebrate, and even transform themselves.

Without attempting to reduce the complexity of the different strategies of Israelite chronometry to a holistic view, there are elements of it that appear to have been uniform throughout the country and across various calendars. All of the major sources assume a day that begins and ends at sunrise. The broad agreement suggests that this was a general view for a long period of time. P, however, appears to have a different system of reckoning the day when it comes to rituals of the cult. The liturgical day began at sunset. This may be the result of Mesopotamian influence. Yearly festivals appear to have been universally practiced. Phases of the moon were observed by both priestly and non-priestly organizations. Because seasonal events occurred at the same time each year, we can confidently assume that the lunisolar calendar was standard in both civil and priestly practice, even though their calendars began at different times of the year.

The research herein also addressed what was distinctive about Israelite timekeeping, in comparison with other ancient cultures. The appearance of the month name Abib in several early sources indicates that the Israelites named their months at one time, but there is no evidence for such a month name anywhere else. Perhaps the names of the Israelite months were unique to their culture or region. Similarly, the later Judahite practice of referring to months by the numbers one through twelve also seems to have been unusual in that part of the world.[1] P's ritual calendar appears to be our earliest evidence of preexilic usage of numbered months. It would seem that the parts of the DH that refer to months by number are of exilic provenance. If the narrative of 2 Kgs 20:8–11 (= Isa 38:7–8, 22) refers to a clock, the clock described is comparable to shadow clocks used in ancient Egypt. However the form of the clock would suggest a division of the daytime into twenty units, a scheme unattested in the sources of other ancient cultures. We may have here a uniquely Judahite system for measuring time during the day.

It is always important to remind ourselves of how often our own understanding of time can so often misrepresent the Israelite equivalent. In the measurement of linear time, all individual units of time (day, months, years, etc.) were added inclusively; in other words, the Israelites did not use a zero, so the first unit in a sequence bore the number one. Generations also were counted differently in ancient Israel than they are today. Instead of consider-

---

1. The Egyptians numbered months first, second, third, and fourth in each of their three seasons (Depuydt, "Calendars and Years in Ancient Egypt," 45).

ing parents as the first generation, the Israelites reckoned children as the first generation, grandchildren as the second, and so on.

As users of a time grid (B.C.E./C.E.) upon which to fix the position of events in the stream of time, we in the Western world cannot help but think in terms of "dates" (e.g., 539 B.C.E., 1066 C.E., 2001 C.E., etc.), and these dates manifest themselves as the number of years before and after a single event or reference mark in time, the presumed year of the birth of Jesus. However, the ancients did not think in terms of points along a commonly-accepted number line or devise dates based on how far removed an incident was from one famous person of the distant past. They thought of events primarily as occurring in reference to the lives of contemporaries. In other words, a memorable event would be associated with a memorable contemporary person, or, to be more precise, it would be timed with another event in that person's life. For this reason the ancient timekeepers dealt with a vast host of mini eras. These were often so short that multiple years were not even organized into convenient units of set length, such as decades, centuries, or millenniums. So, for example, P's system of chronology is genealogical in nature; an event (such as the flood or Israel's entry into Egypt) is placed in the life of a famous ancestor and fixed according to the time that has passed since his birth. The DH employs a system in which an event is correlated to the time of the accession of a king. An important war or religious event is marked simply by answering the question: "How long after a king took the throne did this event occur?" Even in our modern society the timing of an event is laden with value, but it is even more so for the ancient person. The reasons for an event are bound up somehow with the person in whose time it occurs. This gives the event special meaning and significance.

A scholar studying ancient historiography once remarked that "the Biblical historian never implied ... that he was the first to rediscover the past or to save it from oblivion. He only gave an authoritative version of what everybody was supposed to know."[2] I would have to agree with the first part of that statement; it seems clear that, by citing earlier authorities, the Deuteronomistic Historian was acknowledging the debt he owed to his predecessors. I am inclined to disagree, however, with the second part of the assertion. The historians examined here give plenty of indications in their works that they are attempting to preserve knowledge of the past. I presented evidence for the existence of earlier chronographic sources, which were used in the writing and editing of both the Priestly History and the Deuteronomic History. The search for witnesses to the timing of various events is part of a fight that the historian wages, a fight against time itself, which is always trying to destroy

---

2. Momigliano, "Time in Ancient Historiography," 20.

5. CONCLUSIONS AND IMPLICATIONS

the memories that people have. The historian tries to record, not what his audience knows already, but what is in danger of being forgotten. He may indeed doctor the various stories he reproduces to suit his ideology and agenda, which could include omitting material thought to be unimportant, inaccurate, or derogatory to his protagonists, interpreting the events in the light of the supernatural, offering value judgments, or relating a legend he has heard, even if he is not certain of its accuracy, but his narrative is intended to represent what he perceives to be authentic events and relationships in the past,[3] and none of his stories can be considered historical unless he establishes firmly their timing. Chronological research is more dependent on written records than simple stories are, because historical chronology must be based on evidence. That evidence comes in the form of sources.

The authors/editors of the DH often support their data by appealing to sources, but specifically to a written tradition, rather than an oral one. This is in keeping with Near Eastern practice, which tended to give preference to written records over oral testimony.[4] Moreover, as we observe in the surviving ancient Near Eastern literature, these sources often go uncited; they are simply reproduced to some extent. In fact, it would seem that most of the written sources incorporated in the History are undesignated. So, for example, our examination of the book of Judges revealed that the Deuteronomistic Historian possessed a source document with chronological information that he saw fit to include, which covered the terms of several judges. It is never cited. Similarly, an analysis of the regnal formulas in Kings has revealed the existence of an uncited source document, a list of the kings of Judah from Rehoboam to Zedekiah containing specific information about each of the kings—most importantly their reign lengths. This king list was put into the DH during the exile and was not cited. As in the case of the Judahite kings, the exilic reviser of the history also may have had at his disposal a list of the names of the kings of northern Israel and the total years of their reigns in a separate document, which he likewise incorporated into the exilic edition of the DH without citing it. In contrast, the synchronistic formulations in

---

3. See Ehud Ben Zvi, "Malleability and Its Limits: Sennacherib's Campaign against Judah as a Case-Study," in *"Like a Bird in a Cage": The Invasion of Sennacherib in 701 BCE* (ed. Lester L. Grabbe; London: Sheffield, 2003), 73–105. Kurt L. Noll cannot fathom how anyone could actually believe that an angel slew 185,000 of the Assyrian army (2 Kgs 19:35) and concludes that, if he did believe it, the author must have been delusional (Kurt L. Noll, "The Evolution of Genre in the Book of Kings: The Story of Sennacherib and Hezekiah as Example," in *The Function of Ancient Historiography in Biblical and Cognate Studies* [ed. Patricia G. Kirkpatrick and Timothy Goltz; LHBOTS 489; New York: T&T Clark, 2008], 30–56). This opinion reflects a lack of understanding of not only the ancient mind, but also the modern one.

4. Glassner, *Mesopotamian Chronicles*, 45.

the DH, which bear the pattern, "In the [#] year of PN, [a certain event happened]," suggest that they come from a royal chronicle, and since the dates are associated with the kings of both kingdoms, it is best to posit two such chronicles, a Judahite and an Israelite one. These probably are The Scroll of the Affairs of the Days for the Kings of Judah and The Scroll of the Affairs of the Days for the Kings of Israel, which the historian actually cites.

With these circumstances in mind, we found an explanation for the discrepant regnal figures in the History. The Josianic version of the Deuteronomic History contained chronological data only from the Judahite and Israelite royal chronicles, which placed events in specific regnal years, but did not provide totals for the length of kings' reigns. The total counts for kings' reigns were added to the DH during the exile and derive from king lists that were not directly connected with the royal chronicles. Textual analysis of the manuscripts of Kings has shown that the royal chronicles that contained the synchronisms must have presented a different chronology than the king lists. The contradictions between the reign lengths and the synchronisms were ignored by the exilic reviser of the Deuteronomic History. It would appear that the variants in MT and LXX arose when later scribes noted the discrepancies and tried to repair them.

The written sources behind the DH, therefore, were incorporated into it either with or without a citation. In both cases the historians make no effort to engage critically with those sources. There is no commentary on their truthfulness or reliability, nor is consideration given to alternate or conflicting accounts. This in itself does not mean that the historians had absolutely no interest in presenting an accurate statement of facts. The narrator's voice is generally absent throughout, so this may be a matter of style. However because we have seen a tendency to incorporate contradictory data from variant sources, it may be safe to say that perfect consistency was not on the agenda, though there clearly was some attempt to minimize contradictions. The chief aim was to combine a wide variety of chronographic sources and integrate them all into the composition with only a moderate amount of discrimination. No one source appears to have been favored over another. In the mind of the historians, the quantity of these sources appears to have been more of an indicator of historicity than their quality.

Some have made the argument, based on observations of the work of Herodotus, that an ancient historian might cite a historical source for no other reason than to bolster the credibility of his account. In such cases, he may not ever really have read the source, and may even have invented it.[5] The question then may be raised: Are we to view the royal chronicles cited by the Deuteronomistic Historian in this light? If these chronicles were indeed the sources for the synchronistic data about the kings, our subsequent analysis shows the answer to the question to be no. The discussion of the calendar in the earlier part of this study, as well as a demonstration of the manner in which years were counted in Israel, aided us in our analysis of the royal synchronisms. Using the knowledge we obtained, we were able to calculate a chronology of the kings based on the synchronisms alone. Then we judged the historical credibility of these synchronisms, as well as the reign lengths from the king lists. A comparison with extrabiblical synchronisms demonstrated that the data from the Israelite king list and the Judahite king list, both of which are uncited sources, are defective; the reigns of the kings do not coincide with the historical reality very well at all, particularly those of the early kings. On the other hand, a similar comparison of the extrabiblical synchronisms with the information obtained from the royal chronicles, which are cited sources, revealed that the chronological material of the chronicles is much closer to the historical reality. This can only mean that the chronicles were fairly trustworthy documents that the Deuteronomistic Historian actually read and from which he retrieved chronological data.

The foregoing analysis makes it probable that the original version of the DH contained a limited amount of chronological information and that the second edition supplemented and systematized the rough timeline of the earlier edition. The identification of two different chronologies in the Deuteronomic History not only enables us to explain the inconsistencies in the present text, but also helps us to understand the way Israelite and Judahite history was perceived by the Josianic Deuteronomistic Historian, on the one hand, and the exilic reviser of the DH, on the other.

The second edition of the History makes an effort to be complete and definitive in its chronology. It incorporates figures from the first edition but often reinterprets them (as in the case of the terms of the Judges) or ignores them in favor of new data (as in the reigns of the kings). A historical timeline of Israel's history from the point of view of the exilic reviser of the DH may be put together without much difficulty (see table 5.1).

The exilic editor's desire for a more comprehensive chronology may have been kindled by a sense of loss. What I mean is that, during the Josianic period, when the first edition was produced, the kingdom of Judah was alive

---

5. Giovanni Garbini, "Le Fonti Citate nel 'Libro dei Re,'" *Henoch* 3 (1981): 26–46; Katherine M. Stott, *Why Did They Write This Way? Reflections on Reference to Written Documents in the Hebrew Bible and Ancient Literature* (London: T&T Clark, 2008), 52–60.

TABLE 5.1. CHRONOLOGY OF DH[2]

Period	Length of Period (modern count)	Years B.C.E.
Moses and Joshua (Josh 14:10)	44 yrs (45 minus 1)	1488–1444
Aramean oppression (Judg 3:8)	8 yrs	1444–1436
Rest (Judg 3:11)	40 yrs	1436–1396
Moabite oppression (Judg 3:14)	18 yrs	1396–1378
Rest (Judg 3:3)	80 yrs	1378–1298
Canaanite oppression (Judg 4:3)	20 yrs	1298–1278
Rest (Judg 5:31)	40 yrs	1278–1238
Midianite oppression (Judg 6:1)	7 yrs	1238–1231
Rest (Judg 8:28)	40 yrs	1231–1191
Abimelech (Judg 9:22)	3 yrs	1191–1188
Tola (Judg 10:2)	23 yrs	1188–1165
Jair (Judg 10:3)	22 yrs	1165–1143
Ammonite oppression (Judg 10:8)	18 yrs	1143–1125
Jephthah (Judg 12:7)	6 yrs	1125–1119
Ibzan (Judg 12:8)	7 yrs	1119–1112
Elon (Judg 12:11)	10 yrs	1112–1102
Abdon (Judg 12:14)	8 yrs	1102–1096
Philistine oppression (Judg 13:1)	40 yrs (20 of which Samson was judge [Judg 15:20], 20 of which Samuel was judge [1 Sam 7:13])	1096–1056
Saul (1 Sam 13:1)	2 yrs	1056–1054

5. CONCLUSIONS AND IMPLICATIONS

David (1 Kgs 2:11)	40 yrs	1052–1012
Solomon until temple (1 Kgs 6:1)	3 yrs	1012–1009
Total from exodus to temple (*1 Kgs 6:1*)	479 yrs	1488–1009
Solomon after temple (1 Kgs 11:42)	36 yrs	1009–973
Rehoboam	17 yrs	973–956
Abijam	3 yrs	956–953
Asa	41 yrs	953–912
Jehoshaphat	25 yrs	912–887
Jehoram	8 yrs	887–879
Ahaziah	1 yr	879–878
Jehoash	40 yrs	878–838
Amaziah	29 yrs	838–809
Azariah	52 yrs	809–757
Jotham	16 yrs	757–741
Ahaz	16 yrs	741–725
Hezekiah	29 yrs	725–696
Manasseh	55 yrs	696–641
Amon	2 yrs	641–639
Josiah	31 yrs	639–608
Jehoahaz	3 mos.	608
Jehoiakim	11 yrs	608–597
Jehoiachin	3 mos.	597
Zedekiah	11 yrs	597–586

and well. For the people there was no question about the historicity of their community, because they had something to show for it; the results of all their past exploits could be seen in material form. After the fall of Jerusalem and the deportation of the exiles to Babylon, there was a danger that the old days would be forgotten. Particularly for the new communites outside of the land, there was nothing to remind them of the great kingdoms that once existed, except for the stories, and stories without a clear chronology resemble myth more than history. In other words, the historicity of an event is determined by one's ability to locate it in time. If one can count back a precise number of years to an event, the degree of that event's reality is greater than in cases in which this is not possible. In contrast, happenings that cannot be synchronized with the present fall into the category of myth. The writings of J and E, which present past events without binding them up with a timescale, may be seen in this light. They bear greater resemblance to oral stories, which by nature flow freely in an undetermined past. Oral tradition does not require exact dating. For the exiles, there may have been a desire to prevent the tales of the kings from descending into myth. The stories in the original edition of the DH did indeed have some connection to a historical time line but in a rather general and loose fashion. So the motivation of the exilic editor may have been simply to make the History more historical.

We can reconstruct the chronology of the original Deuteronomic History as follows:

TABLE 5.2. CHRONOLOGY OF DH[1]

Period	Length of Period (modern count)	Years B.C.E.
Moses and Joshua (Josh 14:10)	44 years (45 minus 1)	1464–1420
One generation (Judg 2:10)	40 yrs	1420–1380
Othniel (Judg 3:11)	40 yrs	1380–1340
Ehud and Shamgar (Judg 3:3)	80 yrs	1340–1260
Deborah (Judg 5:31)	40 yrs	1260–1220
Gideon (Judg 8:28)	40 yrs	1220–1180
Abimelech	[10] yrs	1180–1170
Tola (Judg 10:2)	23 yrs	1170–1147

5. CONCLUSIONS AND IMPLICATIONS

Jair (Judg 10:3)	22 yrs	1147–1125
Total from entry into Canaan to Jephthah (Judg 11:26)	299 yrs (300 minus 1)	1424–1125
Jephthah (Judg 12:7)	6 yrs	1125–1119
Ibzan (Judg 12:8)	7 yrs	1119–1112
Elon (Judg 12:11)	10 years	1112–1102
Abdon (Judg 12:14)	8 yrs	1102–1094
Samson (Judg 16:31)	20 yrs	1094–1074
Samuel	none stated (40 yrs?)	1074–1034
Saul	none stated (20 yrs?)	1034–1014
David (1 Kgs 2:11)	40 yrs	1014–974
Solomon (1 Kgs 11:42)	40 yrs	974–934
Rehoboam	17 yrs	934–917
Abijam	6 yrs	917–911
Asa	41 yrs	911–870
Jehoshaphat	22 yrs	870–848
Jehoram	6 yrs	848–842
Ahaziah	undiscernible (1 yr?)	842–841
Jehoash	38 yrs	841–798
Amaziah	18 yrs	798–782
Azariah	53 yrs	782–742
Jotham	15 yrs	742–740
Ahaz	14 yrs	740–726
Hezekiah	29 yrs	726–697
Manasseh	undiscernible (55 yrs?)	697–642
Amon	undiscernible (2 yrs?)	642–640

Josiah until reform	18 yrs	640–622

As can be seen, the chronology of the first edition of the DH is limited, and apart from the figures incorporated from the sources (four were used: a list of judges with term lengths, a chronicle containing dates associated with Solomon's building projects, a kingly chronicle from Judah, and a kingly chronicle from Israel), the author provides little other chronological data, and when he chooses to do so, the numbers are mere estimates, which he offers unapologetically. In a few instances I was forced to make educated guesses, so it is impossible at this time to reconstruct DH1's chronology with absolute certainty. The Deuteronomistic Historian's chronology runs slightly shorter than does that of the exilic reviser. Historically speaking, the dates in the period of the kings are probably not far off base, but the period of the judges is overextended by quite a bit, a consequence of the Deuteronomistic Historian's attribution of a full generation for each judge (and perhaps for Saul, David, and Solomon too). Apart from the list of the minor judges, he had very little chronological information to go on.

An interesting implication of both Deuteronomic chronologies lies in the fact that they both begin their historical timelines at the exodus; their time charts do not extend any further into the past. A limited amount of available evidence no doubt accounts for the limited extent of historical time, but the fact that they make no attempt to fix the time of the entry into Egypt, or the patriarchs, or anything prior (e.g., see Deut 34:4; Josh 24:2–5), is an indication that these stories for them are in the realm of myth and not history. The exodus can then be seen as their myth/history event horizon, when the age of the great heroes ends and a more qualitatively human period emerges.

P, on the other hand, altogether removes the dividing line between myth and history, maintaining a chronology that stretches back to the beginning of the creation of the cosmos (six days before the appearance of the first man). Our analysis enables us to observe the original timeline of P, prior to adjustments/corrections made by R. It would have run as follows (years are Anno Mundi):

Adam (1–930)
Seth (130–1042)
Enosh (235–1140)
Kenan (325–1235)
Mahalalel (395–1290)
Jared (460–1422)
Enoch (522–887)

5. CONCLUSIONS AND IMPLICATIONS

Methuselah (587–1556)
Lamech (654–1431)
Noah (707–1657)
Shem (1207–1807)
Flood (1307)
Arpachshad (1307–1745)
Shelah (1342–1775)
Eber (1372–1776)
Peleg (1406–1645)
Reu (1436–1675)
Serug (1468–1698)
Nahor (1498–1646)
Terah (1527–1732)
Abraham (1597–1772)
Isaac (1697–1877)
Jacob (1757–1904)
Entry into Egypt (1887)
Exodus (2317)
Wilderness Wanderings (2317–2357)

The need for a time structure imposed upon the period before the exodus was clearly a major concern for the composers of P. What the priests attempted to do is facilitate the mapping-out of history in its totality. By calculating the number of years that have elapsed from the very beginning of creation until Moses, the P authors place the people of Israel in the general framework of the history of the human race. Because the stories of J and E are set outside of history, a fundamental distinction exists for the authors between their own time and the time about which they are writing. In contrast there is no such distinction for P. The earliest ancestors are located firmly in history.

However, as we have seen, the Priestly history was not the first document to extend Israel's historical timeline all the way back to creation. The inference of an analysis of P's genealogical chronology is that the author/editor of P was working with two earlier sources and attempting to harmonize their chronologies, making adjustments as necessary. One of these earlier documents counted the years back to the creation of Adam.

We also have found, from our examination of subsequent textual adjustments made to the genealogical chronology, that some time later, when the independence of the Israelite states was lost and the people began finding themselves more and more to be part of a larger and more powerful world, they felt the need to map themselves into that world more explicitly. So, for example, this is what we happened during the creation of the first translation of the Bible, into Greek, among the Egyptian Jews in the Ptolemaic period.

Their horizons expanded, and their idea of how they fit in challenged their previous conception of historical chronology, and thus they needed to recalibrate themselves in the timeline of Mediterranean and Near Eastern history. This no doubt gave them a sense of belonging, but the fact that they made an effort to preserve their antiquity, placing themselves alongside the oldest and most revered civilizations, tells us that they did not wish to be thought of as a younger, and therefore inferior, people.

These concluding thoughts make it clear that, although I have demonstrated the nuts and bolts of the various chronometric systems that were used in ancient Israel, I have only begun to scratch the surface in explaining why they were devised. I hint that foreign influence at some points may have been a factor; I hint at ideological impulses; I hint at regional differences (north and south); I hint at differences that stem from social position (farmers, versus kings, versus priests). However, to explore fully the reasons and motivations behind the various timekeeping systems I have described, further exposition in a future book will be required.

Appendix A: Chronographic Sources Incorporated into the Deuteronomic History

For handy reference, translations of the known uncited chronographic sources used by the Deuteronomistic Historian and the exilic reviser of the Deuteronomic History are provided below.

1. List of the Minor Judges

[And after him Gideon son of Joash rose up to deliver Israel. And he judged Israel ? years.] And Gideon had seventy sons that issued from his member, for he had many wives. Then Gideon the son of Joash died at a good old age, and he was buried in the tomb of his father Joash at Ophrah of the Abiezrites.

And after [him],[1] Tola the son of Puah the son of Dodo, a man of Issachar, rose up to deliver Israel, and he was a resident in Shamir in the hill country of Ephraim. And he judged Israel twenty-three years. Then he died, and he was buried in Shamir.

And after him, Jair the Gileadite rose up. And he judged Israel twenty-two years. And he had thirty sons who rode on thirty donkeys; and they had thirty towns,[2] which are in the land of the Gilead. Then Jair died, and he was buried in Qamon.

---

1. The text reads "after Abimelech," but Abimelech does not feature in the list, and in all other instances, the list uses the expression "After him."

2. Reading ערים, as in LXX, instead of MT עירים (see Boling, "Some Conflate Readings in Joshua-Judges," 295–96). The following sentence, "Them they call the Villages of Jair until this day," is an addition by the Deuteronomistic Historian, as is evidenced by his typical expression "until this day" (see Geoghegan, "Until Whose Day?").

[And after him, Jephthah the Gileadite rose up.]³ And Jephthah judged Israel six years. Then Jephthah the Gileadite died, and he was buried in his town in Gilead.⁴

And after him, Ibzan from Bethlehem judged Israel. And he had thirty sons; and thirty daughters he sent to the outside, and thirty daughters he brought in for his sons from the outside. And he judged Israel seven years. Then Ibzan died, and he was buried in Bethlehem.

And after him, Elon the Zebulunite judged Israel. And he judged Israel ten years. Then Elon the Zebulunite died, and he was buried at Aijalon in the land of Zebulun.

And after him, Abdon the son of Hillel the Pirathonite judged Israel. And he had forty sons and thirty grandsons, who rode on seventy donkeys. And he judged Israel eight years. Then Abdon son of Hillel the Pirathonite died, and he was buried in Pirathon in the land of Ephraim, in the hill country of the Amalekites.

2. The Judahite King List

Saul was [ ] years old at his accession, and he reigned 2 years over Israel.

David was 30 years old at his accession, and he reigned 40 years. He reigned over Judah 7 years in Hebron, and he reigned over all Israel and Judah 33 years in Jerusalem.

[Solomon was … years old at his accession, and he reigned … years in Jerusalem.]

[Rehoboam] was 41 years old at his accession, and he reigned 17 years in Jerusalem…, and his mother's name was Naamah the Ammonitess.

---

3. These words are missing in the biblical text, because they had to be removed in order for the narrative as it stands to make sense.

4. MT reads, "in the towns of Gilead," which could only be true if Jephthah's body parts were buried in separate places. LXX's reading ("in his town in Gilead") is preferable.

APPENDIX A: CHRONOGRAPHIC SOURCES   219

[Abijam] reigned 3 years in Jerusalem, and his mother's name was Maacah the daughter of Abishalom.[5]

[Asa] reigned 41 years in Jerusalem, and his mother's name was Maacah the daughter of Abishalom.

Jehoshaphat was 35 years old at his accession, and he reigned 25 years in Jerusalem, and his mother's name was Azubah the daughter of Shilhi.

[Jehoram] was 32 years old at his accession, and he reigned 8 years in Jerusalem.

Ahaziah was 22 years old at his accession, and he reigned 1 year in Jerusalem, and his mother's name was Athaliah, the daughter of Omri the king of Israel.

Jehoash was 7 years old at his accession..., and he reigned 40 years in Jerusalem, and his mother's name was Zibiah from Beersheba.

[Amaziah] was 25 years old at his accession, and he reigned 29 years in Jerusalem, and his mother's name was Jehoaddin of Jerusalem.

[Azariah] was 16 years old at his accession, and he reigned 52 years in Jerusalem, and his mother's name was Jecoliah of Jerusalem.

[Jotham] was 25 years old at his accession, and he reigned 16 years in Jerusalem, and his mother's name was Jerusha the daughter of Zadok.

[Ahaz] was 20 years old at his accession, and he reigned 16 years in Jerusalem.

[Hezekiah] was 25 years old at his accession, and he reigned 29 years in Jerusalem, and his mother's name was Abi, the daughter of Zechariah.

Manasseh was 12 years old at his accession, and he reigned 55 years in Jerusalem, and his mother's name was Hephzibah.

---

5. LXX reads "6 years" as the length of reign. For the argument in favor of MT's reading, see above.

Amon was 22 years old at his accession, and he reigned 2 years in Jerusalem, and his mother's name was Meshullemeth, the daughter of Haruz from Jotbah.

Josiah was 8 years old at his accession, and he reigned 31 years in Jerusalem, and his mother's name was Jedidah, the daughter of Adaiah from Bozkath.

Jehoahaz was 23 years old at his accession, and he reigned 3 months in Jerusalem, and his mother's name was Hamutal, the daughter of Jeremiah from Libnah.

Jehoiakim was 25 years old at his accession, and he reigned 11 years in Jerusalem, and his mother's name was Zebidah, the daughter of Pedaiah from Rumah.

Jehoiachin was 18 years old at his accession, and he reigned 3 months in Jerusalem, and his mother's name was Nehushta, the daughter of Elnathan of Jerusalem.

Zedekiah was 21 years old at his accession, and he reigned 11 years in Jerusalem, and his mother's name was Hamutal, the daughter of Jeremiah from Libnah.

APPENDIX B: WHAT HAPPENED IN THE FOURTEENTH
YEAR OF HEZEKIAH? A HISTORICAL ANALYSIS OF
2 KINGS 18–20 IN THE LIGHT OF NEW TEXTUAL
CONSIDERATIONS[1]

1. INTRODUCTION

Second Kings explicitly states that in Hezekiah's fourteenth regnal year the Assyrian king Sennacherib came up against Judah (18:13). Sennacherib's annals likewise record this event, placing it in his own fourth year, for which the commonly accepted date is 701 B.C.E.[2] Seemingly, then, we have a concrete synchronism: the fourteenth year of Hezekiah = the fourth year of Sennacherib. However, 2 Kings also says that only eight years prior to Sennacherib's invasion, in the sixth year of Hezekiah, the kingdom of Samaria fell to the Assyrians (2 Kgs 18:10). The historical records of Assyria, through which a firm year-by-year chronology can be fixed, will not allow for such a short span of time between the two events. Although the *exact* date for the fall of Samaria has been disputed, it definitely occurred between the final year of Shalmaneser V (722 B.C.E.) and the second year of his successor Sargon II (720 B.C.E.). Samaria's overthrow, therefore, is separated from the 4th year of Sennacherib by some twenty years.[3] It is no wonder, then, that historians have

---

1. This essay first appeared in Sarah Malena and David Miano, eds., *Milk and Honey: Essays on Ancient Israel and the Bible in Appreciation of the Judaic Studies Program at the University of California, San Diego* (Winona Lake, Ind.: Eisenbrauns, 2007), 113–32, and is reprinted here, with slight revisions, by permission of the original publisher.
2. Mordechai Cogan and Hayim Tadmor, *II Kings: A New Translation with Introduction and Commentary* (AB 11; Garden City: Doubleday, 1988), 246–51; Alan Millard, *The Eponyms of the Assyrian Empire 910–612 BC* (SAA 2; Helsinki: Neo-Assyrian Text Corpus Project, 1994), 12–14, 60.
3. Epigraphs from the time of Sargon II confirm that the length of his reign was no less than sixteen years.

been wrangling over the discrepancy for over a century.[4] Since there is no way to squeeze the events of twenty well-attested years into a mere eight, most have concluded either that Samaria did not fall in Hezekiah's sixth year or that Sennacherib did not invade Judah in Hezekiah's fourteenth year.[5] Either way, it is assumed that one of the chronological tags in the biblical account is inaccurate.[6]

With so much written on this conundrum, it would appear that every angle has been considered and that all possible solutions have been duly examined. Before we resign ourselves to choosing and rationalizing one of the existing hypotheses, however, let us return to the heart of the issue to see whether we may make any further progress in unraveling the difficulties. Previous observations regarding the pertinent biblical passages will need to be noted, but new textual and historical considerations may aid us in calculating the temporal placement of the events recorded in 2 Kgs 18–20 and in shedding further light on this interesting period in Israelite and Assyrian history.

2. Two Narratives

In the text of Kings, the passage dealing with the Assyrian campaign against Judah begins thus:

> [13]In the fourteenth year of King Hezekiah, Sennacherib the king of Assyria came up against all the fortified cities of Judah and seized them. [14]*Hezekiah, the king of Judah, sent a message to the king of Assyria at Lachish as follows: 'I have transgressed. Withdraw from me [and] whatever you impose upon me, I shall bear.'* [15]*So the king of Assyria required from Hezekiah, the king of Judah, 300 silver talents and 30 gold talents. And Hezekiah gave all the silver that was to be found at the house of Yahweh and in the treasury of the king's palace.* [16]*(At that time Hezekiah stripped the doors of the house of Yahweh*

---

4. For an introduction to the problem, see Brevard S. Childs, *Isaiah and the Assyrian Crisis* (SBT 3; London: SCM, 1967), 11–12.

5. For a survey of the opinions, see Galil, *Chronology of the Kings of Israel and Judah*, 99.

6. An alternative argument has also been offered which attempts to reconcile the biblical data by suggesting that a coregency existed between Hezekiah and his father Ahaz and that the statement at 2 Kgs 18:1 refers to Hezekiah's becoming coregent (e.g., Nadav Na'aman, "Historical and Chronological Notes on the Kingdoms of Israel and Judah in the Eighth Century B.C.," *VT* 36 [1986]: 84–85, 90). But see Galil, *Chronology of the Kings of Israel and Judah*, 99–102, for the problems with this theory.

and the doorposts which Hezekiah, the king of Judah, had plated and delivered them to the king of Assyria.)

¹⁷The king of Assyria sent the viceroy, the chief eunuch, and the chief attendant from Lachish to King Hezekiah with a large military force to Jerusalem. (2 Kgs 18:13-17a)

Others have convincingly argued that the section here italicized (vv. 14–16) is derived from a source separate from the main narrative, verses 14–15 perhaps stemming from the state annals of Judah.[7] The parenthetical statement (v. 16) may come from a temple chronicle.[8] Interpreters have often remarked that there are perceptible differences in style between verses 14–16 and the material that surrounds them. The usual observation is that the information provided in these verses is factual, concise, void of embellishments, and written from a political perspective, just as one might find within a state document.[9] In other words, no attempt is made to color the episode to suit a particular bias, as might be expected if the passage came directly from the hand of the person who composed the main body of narrative.[10] The section that follows, in direct contrast to this, is a theologically-driven dramatic presentation in the usual

---

7. See Leo L. Honor, *Sennacherib's Invasion of Palestine: A Critical Source Study* (COHP 12; New York: Columbia University Press, 1926), 36–37. There is clear evidence that the Books of Kings contain extracts from annals, as they frequently refer to such annals as sources (in this case, see 2 Kgs 20:20). This is not to say that all accept this view. John Hull ("Hezekiah, Saint and Sinner: A Conceptual and Contextual Narrative Analysis of 2 Kings 18–20" [Ph.D. diss., Claremont Graduate School, 1994], 91–92), for example, draws attention to the fact that these citations are usually presented as rhetorical questions and thus cannot be used to prove that the writer drew from the source he mentions. However, the expression הנם כתובים in some of these citations (1 Kgs 14:19; 2 Kgs 15:11, 15, 26, 31) implies that the documents were readily available, and there is every reason to believe that the writer would have made use of them.

8. The existence of a temple chronicle is only hypothetical, but the introductory statement "at that time" may indicate a second excerpt. Still, this excerpt may not necessarily be from a different source, but from a different location in the same source (Childs, *Isaiah and the Assyrian Crisis*, 70–71; F. J. Gonçalves, *L'expédition de Sennachérib en Palestine dans la littérature hébraïque ancienne* [Louvain-la-Neuve: Université catholique de Louvain, Institut orientaliste, 1986], 361–63).

9. Gonçalves, *L'expédition de Sennachérib*, 367–70.

10. The passage might be construed as anti-Hezekiah in view of his disfurnishment of the temple, but no judgments are made about Hezekiah's actions within the excerpt itself. (How the passage is used by the Deuteronomistic historian is another matter.)

style of the book.¹¹ However, making an assessment of source derivation on the basis of style is a precarious undertaking. Of more weight and significance would be linguistic features in verses 14–16 that distinguish these verses from the rest of the text. We see such a difference in the manner in which Hezekiah's name is presented. In the surrounding narrative, the king of Judah's name is regularly spelled חזקיהו. The portion of the text under analysis, however, spells the name חזקיה in every instance.¹² Furthermore, it uses the appellation "Hezekiah, the king of Judah" (חזקיה מלך יהודה), a formal title, rather than "King Hezekiah" (המלך חזקיהו), an epithet of familiarity. The latter appellative is the favored designation for the king of Judah in the material immediately before and after verses 14–16.¹³ I believe the presentation of the names is a key to establishing sources in the text and that, by ascertaining these sources, a solution to the chronological problem will begin to manifest itself.

Since the beginning of verse 13 uses the epithet "King Hezekiah," it may be attributed to a source other than that of verses 14–16 and associated instead with the main body of narrative.¹⁴ There has been some question over the origin of the *second half* of verse 13 ("Sennacherib the king of Assyria came up against all the fortified cities of Judah and seized them"). There are indications that it has a stronger kinship with verses 14–16 than with 13a. For instance, the epithet "Sennacherib, the king of Assyria" (סנחריב מלך אשור) matches the form "Hezekiah, the king of Judah" (חזקיה מלך יהודה) found in verses 14 and 16. Additionally, verses 14–16 cannot stand by themselves. They require an introductory statement, not only to provide a setting for the

---

11. It may also be significant that the parallel account of Sennacherib's invasion in the book of Isaiah, which is almost an exact duplicate of the Kings version, entirely omits the small section equivalent to 2 Kgs 18:14–16 (see Isa 36:1–2), but it is more likely that the passage is missing in Isaiah as a result of haplography (וישלח ∩ וישלח).

12. The only two other occurrences of this spelling are at 2 Kgs 18:1 and 10, whose statements might also come from the same source document.

13. Cogan and Tadmor, *II Kings*, 228, 40–41.

14. It is true that Leningrad codex B 19a reads חזקיה in this location, and this form was adopted in the 3rd edition of BHK and in BHS. However, in all other instances within the Hezekiah narratives, חזקיהו, not חזקיה, follows immediately after המלך, and it is significant that the parallel verse at Isa 36:1 contains the longer form in all extant manuscripts except 4QIsaᵃ. The similar phrase at 2 Kgs 18:9a also encourages acceptance of the longer spelling at 18:13a, which is attested in the first two editions of BHK, in Jacob ben Hayyim's "Bomberg Edition" (1524–5), and in all the Kennicott manuscripts prior to 1200. See S. Norin, "An Important Kennicott Reading in 2 Kings XVIII 13," *VT* 32 (1982): 337–38; also Antti Laato, "Hezekiah and the Assyrian Crisis in 701 B.C.," *SJOT* 2 (1987): 50.

report, but also to explain Hezekiah's capitulation.¹⁵ Verses 13b–16 make a suitable parallel with the passage in Sennacherib's own annals dated to his fourth year. Sennacherib describes the event this way:

> (As for) Hezekiah the Judaean (who had not submitted to my yoke), I surrounded and conquered 46 of his strongly fortified walled cities and countless small towns in their vicinity by stamping down siege ramps, bringing up battering rams, the relentless attacks of footsoldiers, bored holes, breaches, and picks. I brought out of their midst 200,150 people, small and big, male and females, horses, wild asses, donkeys, camels, oxen and sheep without number and I classified (them) as spoil.
>
> (As for) him, I enclosed him like a bird in a cage in the midst of Jerusalem, his royal city. I erected fortresses against him and made it unthinkable for him to go out of the gate of his city. His cities, which I had despoiled, I cut off from his land and gave to Mitinti, king of Ashdod, Padi, king of Ekron, and Sil-Bel, king of Gaza. I (thus) reduced his land. To the earlier tax, their annual payment, I added tribute (and) gifts for my lordship and imposed (these) upon them.
>
> (As for) him, Hezekiah, the fear of the radiant splendor of my lordship overwhelmed him and he sent after me to Nineveh, my capital, ambushers and his select troops whom he had brought in to strengthen Jerusalem, his royal city, and whom he had acquired as auxiliary troops, (as well as) 30 talents of gold, 800 talents of silver, choice antimony, large blocks of carnelian, beds (inlaid) with ivory, armchairs (inlaid) with ivory, elephant hide, ebony, boxwood, garments with multi-colored trim, linen garments, blue-purple wool, red-purple wool, utensils of copper, iron, bronze, tin and iron, chariots, shields, lances, coats of mail, swords on belts, bows and arrows, *tillu*-equipment, instruments of war without number along with his daughters, his palace women, and male and female singers—and, in order to deliver the tribute and to carry out his servitude, he dispatched his messenger.¹⁶

The correspondence between the two accounts, although not exact, is remarkable. Particularly noteworthy is the agreement in a number of details, such as the general terms of the tribute. Both accounts mention the 30 talents of gold;

---

15. Gonçalves, *L'expédition de Sennachérib*, 360. It is true that the person who incorporated the annals extract into the text could have simply used a fragment of the account without the proem, but it would have been more natural for him to have included the statement that introduced the setting for the event.

16. From the Rassam Cylinder (700 B.C.E.). The translation is that of William R. Gallagher, *Sennacherib's Campaign to Judah: New Studies* (SHCANE 18; Leiden: Brill, 1999), 129–30.

and although the silver amount is greater in the Assyrian record, the biblical source seems to indicate that Hezekiah gave more silver than was demanded of him. Did Sennacherib require *all* the silver that was in the temple and in the palace?[17] Some have played down the similarities between the two sources in an attempt to cast doubt on the annalistic origin of the biblical passage,[18] but most scholars accept that the biblical report at 2 Kgs 18:13b–16 was drawn from a contemporary document of equal historical weight with the Assyrian source and believe the two are largely consistent. It thus seems best to take verse 13b as part of the pericope that includes verses 14–16[19] and to consider these three-and-a-half verses to be accessory to the main narrative. (For convenience, we shall follow scholarly convention and refer to verses 13b–16 as segment A throughout the remainder of this discussion.)

Oddly, the Assyrian record agrees *only* with segment A, while the rest of the narrative in chapters 18 and 19 has no parallel in the Assyrian sources. Although the Assyrian report is a typical example of Assyrian propaganda, and it is probable that Sennacherib deliberately omitted any information that would present him in a bad light,[20] little of what is described in Kings would have embarrassed Sennacherib apart from his inglorious defeat at 2 Kgs 19:35, 36. So the omission of a great number of details on the Assyrian side makes for a noteworthy discrepancy between sources.

We are now left to ponder the significance of verse 13a. Although it appears to be written specifically as an introduction to segment A, we might wish to consider the possibility that it was not originally linked to segment A. As has been mentioned above, verse 13a cannot refer to Sennacherib's campaign in his fourth year without disrupting the chronological statement at 2 Kgs 18:1. It simply does not fit where it is currently situated, at least from a historical standpoint. Thus verse 13a has become a notorious crux because no one knows for sure to what the chronological statement "in the fourteenth year of King Hezekiah" applies. Interestingly, there is a passage nearby which is indeed set in that year, the account of Hezekiah's illness in chapter 20. We know that the events of chapter 20 are supposed to have taken

---

17. Cogan and Tadmor, *II Kings*, 229.

18. For example, Christopher R. Seitz, *Zion's Final Destiny: A Reassessment of Isaiah 36–39* (Minneapolis: Fortress, 1991), 47–66, esp. 61–66, whose main purpose is to prove the priority of Isaiah's version over that of Kings. John B. Geyer, "2 Kings XVIII 14–16 and the Annals of Sennacherib," *VT* 21 (1971): 604–6, also, but only in order to point out that there is not an *exact* correspondence between the Assyrian and biblical sources.

19. For a discussion of the issue, see Honor, *Sennacherib's Invasion of Palestine*, 37–40.

20. See the excellent article by Antti Laato, "Assyrian Propaganda and the Falsification of History in the Royal Inscriptions of Sennacherib," *VT* 45 (1995): 198–223.

place in Hezekiah's fourteenth year, because on that occasion he is granted another fifteen years of life, and the total length of his reign is given as 29 years (14 + 15 = 29).[21]

Some have suggested that verse 13a originally introduced chapter 20.[22] But chapter 20 possesses an opening chronological statement of its own ("In those days"), and there is no textual evidence to suggest it is not original. Non-specific temporal expressions such as בימים ההם ("In those days…"), בעת ההיא ("At that time…"), and others, do not introduce major structural units in the narrative but are coordinating clauses that mark *a turning point* within a story and refer back to a previous date formula.[23] The events of chapter 20 are clearly subordinate to a more momentous series of events. Therefore we may view the account in chapter 20 as part of a longer narrative, for which 18:13a provides the temporal setting. We should also expect, between 18:13a and 20:1, a major episode that would recount the principal set of circumstances in which chapter 20 plays a part. So the question is: How much of chapters 18 and 19 are part of the original tale?

The invasion of Sennacherib as described in verses 13b–16 cannot be viewed as the original setting for Hezekiah's illness. I have already pointed out the linguistic dissimilarities between segment A and the narrative in which it is embedded, as well as the chronological problem. But still other factors alienate the passage from its context. The succession of events from verses 13b–16 into verse 17 is unnatural. Why would Sennacherib send his officials to demand unconditional surrender of Jerusalem immediately after Hezekiah made peace with him by way of a substantial tribute?[24] Every indication is that Sennacherib accepted this tribute and was appeased. In a similar vein, why would Hezekiah willingly yield to Sennacherib but decide to resist forthwith? With regard to either king, his actions *after* segment A are incongruous with the behavior that has been displayed *in* segment A. Furthermore, the account from verse 17 forward makes no reference whatsoever to Hezekiah's capitulation and proceeds

---

21. 2 Kgs 18:2. See Cogan and Tadmor, *II Kings*, 228.
22. Cogan and Tadmor, *II Kings*, 228.
23. Hull, "Hezekiah, Saint and Sinner," 220–23.
24. Evans tries to make a case that the Assyrian officials here are not coming to Jerusalem to lay siege to it, but only to collect a part of the tribute that Hezekiah withheld (Paul S. Evans, "Sennacherib's 701 Invasion into Judah: What Saith the Scriptures?" in *The Function of Ancient Historiography in Biblical and Cognate Studies* [ed. Patricia G. Kirkpatrick and Timothy Goltz; LHBOTS 489; New York: T&T Clark, 2008], 57–77). His argument relies on some unusual translations of the Hebrew text and appears to ignore the fact that the Rabshekah is on the outside of the city and demanding that its inhabitants "come out" (2 Kgs 18:31).

as if the events of segment A were never recounted.[25] This is odd, considering the pivotal role of the tribute and its sheer size. The abrupt and problematic transitions, therefore, on either side of segment A probably signal redactional seams. Although it may be possible to conclude that this passage is an *addition* from an entirely different hand, the source citation at 2 Kgs 20:20 seems to indicate that this passage was incorporated into the text from the very beginning, that is, if it is truly derived from the state annals, as many have argued.

I contend that 2 Kgs 13b–16 was deliberately moved to its current position from another location within Kings itself. The motivations for the repositioning of the segment will be addressed hereafter. However, if A's present position is secondary, then its omission should reveal the original sequence of the narrative. The text would have read: "In the fourteenth year of King Hezekiah, the king of Assyria sent the viceroy, the chief eunuch, and the chief attendant from Lachish to King Hezekiah with a large military force to Jerusalem," verse 13a leading directly into verse 17.[26]

At first glance, it would seem that no chronological difficulties are solved by the removal of segment A. However, difficulties remain only if we assume that the account beginning with verse 17 refers to events having to do with Sennacherib's invasion. As we shall see, this may not be the case.

Before I discuss the significance of my last statement, I suggest that we determine whether any other part of chapters 18 and 19 is not original to the Sennacherib story. The remainder of the narrative, often called segment B (18:17–19:37), presents certain difficulties of its own. It has been suggested, and widely accepted, that segment B contains two separate stories. Strand B_1 recounts the appearance of three Assyrian officials at Jerusalem's gates who threaten King Hezekiah. The king turns to Isaiah, who predicts the withdrawal of the Assyrians, and the prophecy comes true when they pull away from Lachish (19:8). In strand B_2, Sennacherib sends a threatening letter to Hezekiah, who prays for assistance and receives a reassuring prophecy from Isaiah. The story concludes with the miracle of the angel of God slaying 185,000 of the Assyrian army. There are several convincing reasons for dividing the account in this way:

---

25. Childs, *Isaiah and the Assyrian Crisis*, 73.

26. Gonçalves' remark (359) that verse 13a could not have been connected to 17ff, because prophetic narratives never contain introductions with such precise dating, is simply not true. The account of 2 Kgs 22:3ff, which describes Josiah seeking an oracle from the prophetess Huldah after the book of the law was found in the temple is one example. In fact, the order of the elements in the date formula at 2 Kgs 22:3 is the same as at 2 Kgs 18:13. (For other examples of precisely dated prophetic narratives written in the third person, see Jer 28:1ff, 32:1ff, and 36:9ff.)

(1) It is difficult to understand how Sennacherib could have expected his letter(s) to frighten the Judahites into surrendering Jerusalem (19:9, 14), when his personal ambassadors had already failed to do so by means of a display of force (18:17, 18), especially when the message of the second threat is merely a repetition of the first.²⁷

(2) Why would Hezekiah pray for Yahweh to turn his attention to the situation and save Jerusalem (19:15–19) after Isaiah had already promised him that Yahweh would not allow Jerusalem to be taken and that the king of Assyria would withdraw to his own land and die there (19:6, 7)? Similarly, Isaiah's prophecy at 19:20–34 is presented as if this were the first time he has provided a reassuring oracle to Hezekiah concerning Sennacherib.

(3) In 19:32–33, the prophet assures Hezekiah that the king of Assyria will not lay siege to the city, the imperfect verb forms indicating that the Assyrians had not yet done so. This seems odd, considering that the king had "sent a heavy military force to Jerusalem" immediately prior to this (18:17).²⁸ That the Assyrians are actually laying siege to the city in chapter 18 is supported by iconographic evidence that suggests that the actions of the Rabshakeh as described in 2 Kings reflect a part of Assyrian siege method.²⁹

A fourth argument used to support the division of segment B, and the most predominant among scholars, calls attention to the similarity in the sequence of events outlined in the two accounts. Both begin with a demand for surrender by Assyrian messengers, and the threats are strikingly similar in both of the narratives. In each account, Hezekiah seeks divine assistance, and Isaiah provides him with a prophecy of hope, which is in turn fulfilled. This has led many to conclude that each strand is merely a different version of the same tale.

Although there are grounds for separating the section into two accounts, the idea of parallel narratives cannot be sustained. To my knowledge, the

---

27. Smelik's argument that the letter was a logical follow-up to the visit of the Rabshakeh is weak (Klaas A. D. Smelik, "Distortion of Old Testament Prophecy: The Purpose of Isaiah XXXVI and XXXVII," in *Crises and Perspectives: Studies in Ancient Near Eastern Polytheism, Biblical Theology, Palestinian Archaeology and Intertestamental Literature* [OtSt 24; Leiden: Brill, 1986], 81). He would have us believe that the letter was "the culmination of Sennacherib's arguments and blasphemy," asserting that "a letter has to convince where spoken words have failed." Even if we were willing to accept the logic of this statement, he simply fails to take into account that the earlier threat was backed by a show of military strength, whereas the later, written threat was not. The approach of Kushite forces would have further reduced the intimidating effect of the letter.

28. Laato, "Hezekiah and the Assyrian Crisis," 63.

29. Yigael Yadin, *The Art of Warfare in Biblical Lands in the Light of Archaeological Study* (trans. M. Pearlman; New York: McGraw-Hill, 1963), 320, 424–25.

only time we find *parallel* adjacent accounts in the Hebrew Bible is when a redactor joins two *preexisting* works that he either is not at liberty to cut or that he finds impractical to do so. Usually the stories are of two different genres (prose and poetry), such as we find at Exodus 14–15 and Judges 4–5. Author-redactors with greater editorial freedom make an effort to blend various accounts into a flowing narrative, as we know the Deuteronomistic Historian has consistently done elsewhere. Both B_1 and B_2 exhibit evidence of Deuteronomistic editing. For example, we can be fairly confident that the second account was put into the history by the Deuteronomistic Historian, since we find typical Deuteronomic phraseology in Hezekiah's prayer (19:15–19).[30] There are also indications that he had a hand in the first story, not only because there are Deuteronomic themes present,[31] but because there are elements in B_1 that anticipate elements in B_2.[32] It does not seem reasonable to conclude that he would add a second version of the same story immediately after the original one without expecting readers to conclude that the latter piece described events that happened *after* the first story.[33]

The similarities between the two accounts of Assyrian invasion are only superficial. The Rabshakeh, the central figure of the first account, does not figure in the second whatsoever. Eliakim, Shebna, and Joah, who participate in the dialogue in the first section, are not even mentioned in the second. Isaiah, who is featured prominently in B_2, has only a minor role in B_1. While in B_1 Egypt is said to be Judah's ally, B_2 speaks of Kush.[34] The content of each

---

30. For example, אתה הוא האלהים לבדך לכל ממלכות הארץ ("You alone are the God for all the kingdoms of the earth"), cf. Deut 4:35, and מעשה ידי אדם עץ ואבן ("human handicraft, wood and stone"), Deut 4:28. See Weinfeld, *Deuteronomy and the Deuteronomic School*, 39.

31. See the article by Ehud Ben Zvi, "Who Wrote the Speech of Rabshakeh and When?" *JBL* 109 (1990): 79–92, esp. 85–86, 88.

32. For example, 18:27, 31 appear to anticipate 19:29, and 18:35 appears to anticipate 19:18. (See Gallagher, *Sennacherib's Campaign to Judah*, 159.)

33. There is always the possibility that the Deuteronomistic Historian, drawing from two separate sources, did not realize that both accounts described the same events, but this could only be true if one of the sources was so damaged that its setting was unclear and if the Historian himself was a bit naïve.

34. Although many historians have argued that these two place-names are almost synonymous, it must be acknowledged that the Assyrian sources differentiate between the two (Anthony J. Spalinger, "The Year 712 B.C. and Its Implications for Egyptian History," *JARCE* 10 [1973]: 100), and so we should be careful to avoid generalizations. Historically, it was during Hezekiah's reign (712 B.C.E.) that Kush gained ascendancy over Egypt (Spalinger, "The Year 712 B.C.," 95–101), and therefore the second story may reflect events from a later period than does the first.

of Isaiah's messages has some noteworthy differences as well. Although both predict the withdrawal of Assyrian forces, the prophecy in B_2 makes no mention of the king of Assyria returning to his homeland after hearing a report of trouble and then being killed there. A further significant variance, which seems odd if both stories are relating the details of the same event, is that Assyrian forces actually come to Jerusalem in B_1, but not in B_2. In fact, B_2 states that a siege will not take place. Another striking difference is that only B_2 recounts the dramatic finale of the angel slaying 185,000 Assyrian soldiers. There is nothing even remotely parallel to this in B_1. The most interesting difference in the players of each drama has to do with the king of Assyria himself. Strand B_1 mentions the Assyrian monarch ten times, but only as מלך אשור "the king of Assyria" (18:17, 19, 23, 28, 30, 31, 33; 19:4, 6, 8). Not once is a name provided.[35] Strand B_2, on the other hand calls the king "Sennacherib" three out of the four times he is mentioned (19:16, 20, 36). It is therefore possible that Sennacherib does not feature at all in the first account. There is, admittedly, an unmistakable parallel between the Rabshakeh's speech in B_1 and Sennacherib's letter in B_2 (cf. 18:33, 34 with 19:12, 13),[36] but in all probability the reason for the correspondence between the Assyrian speeches in each strand is not because both stories go back to a common source, but because both were composed by the same hand. The notion that strands B_1 and B_2 are variants of the same tradition will therefore be rejected in favor of a theory that each strand recounts an independent and distinct series of events and that the second series of events did not ensue immediately after the first.

3. Sargon and Hezekiah

If we accept the datum that Samaria was conquered in Hezekiah's 6th year, then it naturally follows that his 14th year would fall within the reign of Assyrian king Sargon II, rather than that of Sennacherib. As 2 Kgs 18:13a may introduce the account recorded in segment B_1, and as that segment allows for the participation of someone other than Sennacherib as the king of Assyria, it requires no forced understanding of the text to imagine Sargon as that king.[37]

---

35. This was noted by Allan K. Jenkins, "Hezekiah's Fourteenth Year: A New Interpretation of 2 Kings xviii 13 - xix 37," *VT* 26 (1976): 287; 2 Kgs 20:6 also neglects to name the king.

36. For a fuller discussion of this issue, see Gallagher, *Sennacherib's Campaign to Judah*, 153–59.

37. This observation is not new. However, previous attempts to equate the narrative with Sargon have proven unconvincing. For example, Jenkins, accepting the theory of parallel narratives, relates *both* B_1 and B_2 to Sargon, arguing that all references to Sennacherib

Extrabiblical evidence adds weight to this hypothesis. For example, Sargon's army did, in fact, campaign into the Levant in his 10th regnal year (712 B.C.E.). There is every indication that this year coincided with the fourteenth year of King Hezekiah. Gershon Galil has persuasively argued in favor of dating the fall of Samaria to 720 B.C.E., Sargon's 2nd year and Hezekiah's 6th.[38] He bases his argument on several factors: 1) in the Babylonian Chronicle, the Samaria ravaged by Shalmaneser V could be the entire northern kingdom of Israel rather than the city itself, 2) the biblical text, although connecting Shalmaneser to the events associated with the conquest of Samaria, does not explicitly state that he was the king who conquered it, and 3) the numerous testimonies to Samaria's overthrow in the time of Sargon cannot be ignored and all assumed false. By Galil's dating, Sargon's military endeavor on Judah's doorstep in 712 matches Hezekiah's 14th year precisely.

According to Sargon's annalistic and display inscriptions, it was necessary at this time to put down a revolt in the Philistine city of Ashdod led by a certain Yamani. The earliest is Nineveh Prism A, Fragment D.[39] The account breaks off during the description of the Ashdod campaign, and it is impossible to tell how much farther the text went on. In English, the text reads as follows:

> [But these] accursed [Hittites] conceived [the idea] of not delivering the tribute and [started] a rebellion against their ruler; they expelled him ... Yamani, a comm[oner without claim to the throne] to be king over them, they made sit down [on the very throne] of his (former) master and [they prepared?] their city for the at[tack] (lacuna of 3 lines) ...its neighborhood, a moat [they prepared] of a depth of 20+ cubits ... it even reached the underground waters. In order to [...To] the rulers of Philistia, Judah, Ed[om], Moab, (and) those who live by the sea and bring tribute [and] tamartu gifts to my Lord Aššur [he spread] countless evil lies to alienate (them) from me, and sent bribes to Pharaoh the king of Egypt, a prince incapable of saving them, and asked him to be an ally. But I, Sargon, the rightful ruler, devoted to the pronouncements of Nebo and Marduk, who observes

---

in B₂ are a later editor's reinterpretation of the text. Schedl goes one step further and associates 2 Kgs 18:13–16 with Sargon's campaign to Judah following Ashdod's revolt, which fails to account for the passage's similarity with Sennacherib's annals (Claus Schedl, "Textkritische Bemurkungen zu den Synchronismen der Könige von Israel und Juda," *VT* 12 [1962]: 88–119). The theory presented here does not necessitate the rejection of the name Sennacherib in the narratives.

38. Galil, *Chronology of the Kings of Israel and Judah*, 83–97.

39. Original publication by Hugo Winckler, *Die Keilschrifttexte Sargons* (2 vols.; Leipzig: Pfeiffer, 1889), 1:186–89.

the orders of Aššur, led my army over the Tigris and Euphrates, at the[ir] highest water level, the spring high water, as (if it were) dry ground. This Yamani, their king who had put his trust in his own power and who did not bow to my rule, heard about the approach of my expedition (yet) far away, and the terror of my Lord Aššur overwhelmed him and ... of the bank of the river ... in the depth of the waters ... distant ... fled ... Ashdod ... I took [the road]. The city of ... against ... in the midst ... as ...the city of Lu... the city of ... against the land of ... the city of ... the land of Egypt ... his stones ... over the people ...[40]

Sargon claims that Judah received an invitation to join Yamani's anti-Assyrian coalition. Whether or not Yamani was temporarily successful in alienating the states here mentioned from Assyria is not stated, but the biblical text testifies that Hezekiah rebelled against his Assyrian overlords.[41] If this was the context of Judah's rebellion, Sargon may very well have responded with a show of military strength. The text breaks off just as it is getting interesting. It would appear that several cities were engaged by Assyrian forces, but only Ashdod's name is preserved. Another ("Lu...") is partially preserved. Parallel sources mention also Gath and Ashdod-Yam.[42]

---

40. Translation partly from Pritchard, *ANET*, and partly from Luckenbill, *ARAB*.

41. 2 Kgs 18:7. For a full discussion of the evidence, see Paul K. Hooker, "The Kingdom of Hezekiah: Judah in the Geo-Political Context of the Late Eighth Century B.C.E." (Ph.D. diss., Emory University, 1993), 18–32.

42. The other inscriptions describing the Ashdod campaign shed no more light on whether Judah was involved. The Display Inscription on the walls of the Khorsabad palace (first published in Winckler, *Die Keilschrifttexte Sargons*, 1:115–16) reads: "But the[se] Hittites, always planning evil deeds, hated his (their former ruler Ahimiti's) reign and elevated to rule over them Yamani who, without any claim to the throne, had no respect for authority, just as they themselves (did not). In a sudden rage, I did not assemble the full might of my army (or to) prepare the camp(ing equipment), (only) my warriors who, even in friendly areas, never leave my side. But this Yamani heard about the approach of my expedition (yet) far away, and he fled into the territory of Egypt that belongs to Kush; and his (hiding) place could not be detected. I besieged (and) conquered the cities of Ashdod, Gath, Ashdod-Yam; I declared his images, his wife, his children, all his possessions and treasure of his palace, as well as the inhabitants of his country, as booty" (translation partly from Pritchard, *ANET* and partly from Luckenbill, *ARAB*). We are informed that Gath and Ashdod-Yam, both Philistine cities, are among the conquests of Sargon, but Judah is not mentioned. The Khorsabad Annals (II, 21 and H1, lines 249–61, originally published in Arthur G. Lie, *The Inscriptions of Sargon II, King of Assyria, Part I: The Annals* [Paris: Geuthner, 1929], 38–41) also mention the campaign, and their description is very similar to the Display Inscription: "But the[se] Hittites, always planning evil deeds, hated his (Ahimiti's) reign and elevated to rule over them Yamani who, without any claim to the throne, had no respect for authority, just as they themselves (did not). [In a sudden rage],

From the pertinent inscriptions, we are able to ascertain a general order of events relating to the campaign:

(1) The Philistines of Ashdod ("accursed Hittites") depose and expel Sargon's vassal king Ahimiti and elevate Yamani as king in his place.
(2) The Ashdodites begin preparations for invasion, including the digging of a moat and the sending of conspiratorial messages to neighboring kingdoms (Judah, Edom, Moab, and other Philistine cities), and a payment to Egypt for military assistance.
(3) Sargon and his personal guard cross the Tigris and Euphrates (springtime) and approach Ashdod.
(4) Yamani goes to Kush, leaving his family behind.
(5) Sargon besieges and conquers Ashdod, Gath, and Ashdod-Yam.
(6) Other cities, the names of which are not preserved, are apparently conquered or attacked.[43]

Did Judah actually have a military encounter with Assyria at this time? We do have epigraphic evidence to support this conclusion. The text commonly known as the Azekah inscription describes the siege of the fortified city of Azekah in Judah by Assyrian forces. It consists of two fragments (BM 82-3-23, 131 and K 6205), originally published separately,[44] but in 1974 Nadav Na'aman discovered the join and made a preliminary analysis.[45] Na'aman

---

I marched quickly in my state chariot and with my cavalry which, even in friendly areas, never leaves my side against Ashdod, his royal residence. I besieged (and) conquered the cities of Ashdod, Gath, Ashdod-Yam; I declared the gods residing therein, himself, as well as the inhabitants of his country, the gold, silver, and his personal possessions as booty" (translation partly from Pritchard, *ANET*, and partly from Luckenbill, *ARAB*). Again, no mention is made of Judah.

43. Interestingly, a recent study offers evidence that sites destroyed in eighth century southwestern Judah, often attributed to Sennacherib's campaign of 701, should be associated with a slightly earlier Assyrian campaign into that area (Jeffrey A. Blakely and James W. Hardin, "Southwestern Judah in the Late Eighth Century B.C.E.," *BASOR* 326 [2002]: 11–64).

44. K 6205 originally published by Henry C. Rawlinson and George Smith, *The Cuneiform Inscriptions of Western Asia III* (London: Bowler, 1870), 9:2; BM 81-3-23, 131 first appeared in Hugo Winckler, *Altorientalische Forschungen* (3 vols.; Leipzig: Pfeiffer, 1893–1905), 2:570–74.

45. Nadav Na'aman, "Sennacherib's 'Letter to God' on his Campaign to Judah," *BASOR* 214 (1974): 25–39.

dated the inscription to Sennacherib's 701 campaign against Judah;[46] however, his position has been called into question recently by several scholars who prefer to date the events described in the text to Sargon's campaign of 712.[47] Their reasons are as follows: 1) The inscription locates Azekah "between my land and the land of Judah" (line 5).[48] Since the Assyrians turned Ashdod and its environs into a province as a result of the 712 campaign (making it "their land") and since Sennacherib's Annals refer to Ashdod as a vassal kingdom as a result of the 701 campaign (after which it would not be "their land"), the inscription must have been composed between 712 and 701. Furthermore, there is no evidence for any Assyrian campaign against Philistia in this period. Therefore, the events described must refer to Assyria's last venture into the territory. 2) The literary style and lexicon of the inscription are closely akin to that of Sargon's epic description of his campaign against Urartu, the last major campaign Sargon undertook before the Ashdod affair. 3) The composer spells the deity name "Anšar," rather than "Aššur," which is typical of many of Sargon's early inscriptions. For these reasons, the inscription is best dated to the time of Sargon. An English translation of the text reads as follows:

(1) ....
(2) ....
(3) ... and to Ju[dah I approached]. In the course of my campaign, [I received] the tribute of the ki[ng/kings of ...]
(4) [with the power and mi]ght of Anšar, my lord, [I overwhelmed] the district of [Hezek]iah of Judah. L[ike a hurricane]
(5) ... Azekah, his stronghold, which is located between my [la]nd and the land of Judah ...
(6) [...] it is located on a mountain ridge, like pointed daggers without number reaching high to the heaven ...

---

46. And as of 1994 he still held the same opinion. Nadav Na'aman, "Hezekiah and the Kings of Assyria," *Tel Aviv* 21 (1994): 235–54.

47. Gershon Galil, "Judah and Assyria in the Sargonid Period," *Zion* 57 (1992): 111–33 [Hebrew]; Hooker, "Kingdom of Hezekiah," 32–38; Gershon Galil, "A New Look at the 'Azekah Inscription,'" *RB* 102 (1995): 327–28; Jeremy Goldberg, "Two Assyrian Campaigns Against Hezekiah and Later Eighth Century Biblical Chronology," *Bib* 80 (1999): 363, esp. n. 10.

48. Na'aman reads "my border" ([*mi-iṣ*]-*ri-ia*), rather than "my land" ([*áš*]-*ri-ia*), and interprets the "border" to be the military encampment of the king (Na'aman, "Hezekiah and the Kings of Assyria," 246). Both the reading and the interpretation are stretches.

(7) [its walls] were strong and rivaled the highest mountains, to the (mere) sight, as if from the sky [appears its head …]
(8) [I besieged (this city) by means of beaten (earth) ra]mps, (by) great? battering rams brought near (its walls), (and with) the attack by foot soldiers …
(9) … they had seen [the … of my cav]alry, and they had heard the roar of the mighty troops of the god Anšar and [their hea]rts became afraid …
(10) I captured [this stronghold], I carried off its spoil, I destroyed, I devastated, [I burned with fire]
(11) [I approached Ekron], a royal ci[ty] of the Philistines, which [Hezek]iah had captured and strengthened for himself …
(12) … like a vine (planted) [on a peak of a mountain]
(13) … it was surrounded with mighty towers and [its ascent] was very sloping …
(14) … a palace? (huge) like a mountain was barred in front of them and high is [its top …]
(15) [its ascent] was dark and the sun never shone on it; its waters were situated in darkness and [its?] overflow …
(16) … it was cut with axes, and a moat was dug around it(s walls) …
(17) (his) skillful in battle warriors he caused to enter into it; his weapon he bound (on him) …
(18) … all the units of Amurru; I caused them to carry earth …
(19) … against them. In the seventh time, its mighty … [I smashed] like a pot [of clay …]
(20) [… shee]p I carried out from it, [and counted as] spo[il …
(21) ….[49]

The Azekah inscription confirms that Sargon not only settled matters in Ashdod and other Philistine cities, but also punished Judah for its support of Yamani's rebellion. At the very least, the Assyrians besieged Azekah and (apparently) conquered it. There is mention of the siege and conquest of another city. Though unnamed, it is identified as a former Philistine city that Hezekiah had recently taken over. Galil makes a good case for identifying the city as Ekron.[50]

A passage in the book of Isaiah clearly relates to the time of Sargon's attack on Philistia:

---

49. The translation is Galil's ("A New Look at the 'Azekah Inscription,'" 323–24).
50. Galil, "Judah and Assyria in the Sargonid Period," 111–33.

APPENDIX B: YEAR 14 OF HEZEKIAH

¹In the year that the viceroy came to Ashdod, when Sargon the king of Assyria sent him, he fought against Ashdod and captured it.⁵¹ ²At that time, Yahweh spoke by means of Isaiah the son of Amoz, saying, "Go, and loosen the sackcloth from around your waist and take your sandals off your feet." And he did so, walking around naked and barefoot. ³Then Yahweh said, "Just as my servant Isaiah walked naked and barefoot (three years there was a sign and an omen concerning Egypt and Kush),⁵² ⁴so shall the king of Assyria lead the captives of Egypt and the exiles of Kush, young and old, naked and barefoot and with buttocks stripped, [from] the nakedness of Egypt. ⁵And they will be terrified and ashamed of Kush their hope and of Egypt their pride. ⁶And the inhabitants of this coastland will say on that day, 'So this was our hope to which we fled for assistance to be delivered from the face of the king of Assyria. Now how shall we escape?'" (Isa 20:1–6)

This prophecy may be about the "inhabitants of this coastland," that is, the Philistines, but it is surely directed toward a Judahite audience. Isaiah's own

---

51. Many find the grammatical structure of verses 1–3 awkward, chiefly because verse 1 seems to be left hanging and does not appear to continue until verse 3. The most common explanation is that verse 2 is a later additon, or at least a parenthetical statement. To support such an interpretation, some have argued that God's command to Isaiah must have preceded the assault on Ashdod because the explanation of the three-year sign had to have been given at the end of the prophetic activity and when the Philistines were still hoping Egypt would come to their aid (cf. v. 6). Therefore the בעת ההיא ("at that time") of verse 2 would not refer specifically to the event mentioned in verse 1 but to a time at least fourteen months prior (Otto Kaiser, *Isaiah 13–39: A Commentary* [OTL; Philadelphia: Westminster, 1974], 113–14; John N. Oswalt, *The Book of Isaiah: Chapters 1–39* [NICOT; Grand Rapids: Eerdmans, 1986], 384; John H. Hayes and Stuart A. Irvine, *Isaiah the Eighth Century Prophet: His Times and His Preaching* [Nashville: Abingdon, 1987], 270–71). However, verse 2 probably is original to the story because sign-act prophecies customarily follow the pattern: a) command, b) execution, c) interpretation. The command, as a necessary component, would not constitute a later addition (Hans Wildberger, *Isaiah 13–27: A Continental Commentary* [Minneapolis: Fortress, 1997], 286–87; cf. Jer 13:1–14). Recognizing this, others have suggested that verse 1 is an addition and that the original context of verse 2 is lacking (ibid., 287). I do not think such a view is necessary. Grammatically, we may understand verse 1 as a complete sentence, with a preterital prefix verb introducing the apodosis. My translation reflects this interpretation. Naturally, this would indicate that God commisions Isaiah to perform the sign the same year that he explains it.

52. Most commentators consider the three years to be the period that Isaiah walked naked and barefoot; however, the final part of verse 3 can be understood as a parenthetical statement and translated as a verbless clause. The three years would indicate the period in which the prophet had been giving signs and omens against an Egyptian alliance, but not necessarily the time he walked naked and barefoot. The three year figure aids us in determining the time that Yamani's rebellion began. An approximate date of 714 is indicated here.

people would see his signs, and they would be the ones interested in them. The implication is that the Philistine appeal to Egypt was a topic of concern in Judah, no doubt because the Judahites too feared reprisal from the Assyrians. Judah also entertained hopes of Egyptian protection because they were among the rebels. That Isaiah had been speaking out against a Judahite-Egyptian alliance is clear from prophecies in the book bearing his name (cf. Isa 30:1–17, 31:1–4). It is therefore likely that Ashdod and Judah were united against Assyria at this time. That Isaiah was already wearing sackcloth before he was asked to remove it is an indication that he had been in mourning for some period of time.[53] This attire may have been prophetic of what he thought would result from the alliance, namely the destruction of Judahite cities and the death of many of their inhabitants.

An examination of the Rabshakeh's taunts in a Sargonic context proves rather interesting. He calls to Judah's attention how certain other states have fallen to the might of Assyria (2 Kgs 18:33–35). He specifically mentions Arpad, Hamath, Sepharvaim, and Samaria.[54] It may be no coincidence that Sargon, in his annals, boasts of putting down a rebellious coalition from Arpad, Hamath, and Samaria in the second year of his reign. The Rabshakeh's reference to this could not have been more apropos, as now Judah is taking refuge in a similar coalition, and the fate of Samaria and her allies is still fresh in mind.[55] Sepharvaim was probably located in eastern Babylonia[56] and would have been conquered by Sargon when he campaigned against Marduk-apla-iddina. However, it is especially interesting that in B_2 *Sennacherib* makes similar statements (2 Kgs 19:12, 13) but remarks that Arpad, Hamath, Samaria, and Sepharvaim (along with Hena and Ivvah) are among the lands "that *my forefathers* brought to ruin." In strand B_1, the king of Assyria gives due credit, not to his ancestors, but to himself: "Where are the gods of Hamath and Arpad? ... Have any delivered Samaria out of my hand?"[57]

---

53. Joseph Blenkinsopp, *Isaiah 1–39: A New Translation with Introduction and Commentary* (AB 19; New York: Doubleday, 2000), 323.

54. The names Hena and Ivvah, which appear in this verse in MT, are probably later additions to the text, considering that the names are missing in other manuscript traditions. They may have been placed here under the influence of 19:13. See Raymond F. Person, *The Kings-Isaiah and Kings-Jeremiah Recensions* (Berlin: de Gruyter, 1997), 62.

55. See Chaim Cohen, "Neo-Assyrian Elements in the First Speech of the Biblical Rab-šaqê," *IOS* 9 (1979): 36–38.

56. Nadav Na'aman, "New Light on Hezekiah's Second Prophetic Story," *Bib* 81 (2000): 394–95.

57. Na'aman asks the question why Sennacherib would choose to list places that were conquered so long ago (Gozan, Harran, Rezeph, and Eden) or that were "remote and unimportant" (Telassar, Lair, Hena, and Ivvah; Nadav Na'aman, "Updating the Messages:

APPENDIX B: YEAR 14 OF HEZEKIAH

The reference to the appearance of Sargon's viceroy (Hebrew *tartān*; Akkadian *turtanu*) at Jerusalem's gates at 2 Kgs 18:17 is historically possible, because we know that he was in the Levant during the campaign in 712 (Isa 20:1). Thus the *tartān* mentioned in Kings and in Isaiah may be one and the same person.

One must acknowledge, however, that in the Kings account, the king of Assyria is said to be personally involved in the campaign, while in the eponym chronicle for that year, Sargon is reported as staying home. This would seem to be supported by Isa 20:1, which describes the *turtanu*, rather than Sargon, leading the assault on Ashdod. However, in his annals, Sargon depicts himself as personally leading the campaign into the Levant. Likewise, in the Azekah inscription, the king also maintains that he is involved in the siege. Although we can easily dismiss his claims as self-aggrandizement, we should at least consider the possibility that Sargon participated in the campaign.

Where does strand B_1 end? The account would logically conclude with the king fighting against the Philistine city of Libnah (19:8) but would not include the reference to Tirhakah (mentioned in the next verse), as he would not have been alive at that time.[58] Although Sennacherib is credited with capturing Lachish, it is not anachronistic to find Sargon there in 712. He too may have attempted to take the city—perhaps with success, perhaps not.

The reference to Sennacherib's death in 2 Kgs 19:37 has usually been taken as the fulfillment of Isaiah's prophecy in 19:6–7 that the Assyrian king would fall by the sword in his own country. However, the phrase "fall by the sword" (נפל בחרב) in the Bible refers to casualties of war, not to assassination (cf. Lev 26:7–8; Num 14:43; 2 Sam 1:12; Ezek 11:9–10). As Sargon was killed in battle in 705 B.C.E. near the eastern Assyrian border, this prophecy applies more fittingly to him.

Hezekiah's Second Prophetic Story [2 Kings 19.9b–35] and the Community of Babylonian Deportees," in Grabbe, ed., *"Like a Bird in a Cage,"* 2003, 201–20). His answer is that these places were significant to the Jewish exiles in Babylon, and this, for him, is an indication that account B_2 was written during the exile. Though this is possible, we simply do not know enough about the history of these places and their relationship with Assyria to make such a judgment. From what we can tell, Telassar, Lair, Hena, and Ivvah were all in a region known to have been conquered by Sennacherib's father Sargon. Is it not possible that the other places were also recently of note in Assyrian current events?

58. The historicity of Tirhakah's involvement in the second account is substantiated by Kenneth A. Kitchen in *The Third Intermediate Period in Egypt (1100–650 B.C.)* (Warminster: Aris & Phillips, 1986), 157–61.

4. Sennacherib and Hezekiah

The second tale, strand B_2, begins with the statement, "When he heard it said about Tirhakah, the king of Kush, 'He is now coming out to fight against you,' he sent messengers again to Hezekiah" (2 Kgs 19:9). The "he" referred to is no longer Sargon, but Sennacherib. However, one must note that the pronoun "he" has no antecedent, and the word וישב indicates a previous correspondence between Sennacherib and Hezekiah. B_2, therefore, would seem to require a proper opening. As Antii Laato has pointed out, the narrative beginning with Tirhakah's advance "presupposes some kind of introduction, for which purpose Tirhakah's planned campaign is eminently suitable."[59] However, the opening need not be segment B_1. Surely the withdrawal of the Assyrian king to Libnah (19:8) constitutes the conclusion of an episode rather than an introduction. It is at this point that we should again take note of segment A. We have not, as of yet, determined its original context in Kings, and it is evident that it cannot stand on its own. Some continuation of A must be assumed, as it does not contain a conclusion. What was Sennacherib's reaction after Hezekiah paid the tribute? Was the attack on Judah halted?[60] In this case, the simplest solution works best: segment A is the most suitable prologue to B_2. This conclusion is supported by the remarkable affinity between B_2 and A. The usage of epithets for the kings corresponds to the suggested divisions (see Table B.1). The formula *"x, the king of y"* is common in both A and B_2, but is not found in B_1. Moreover, the title *"King Hezekiah"* is used in B_1, but not in either A or B_2. A personal name by itself is found in all three segments.

I believe the manner in which the names are used is an indication that the Deuteronomistic Historian drew from two sources, one that described Sargon's campaign of 712 and one that recounted Sennacherib's invasion of 701. This interpretation is reinforced by the fact that segments A and B_2 both feature Sennacherib as the antagonist, whereas B_1 does not mention him at all. Furthermore, the sequence of events from A through B_2 flows smoothly and better fits the extrabiblical evidence for Sennacherib's invasion of Judah in the fourth year of his reign. Likewise, as we have seen, the account in B_1 best fits a historical context in the reign of Sargon.

If indeed segments A and B_2 were once connected as part of a separate narrative, and if the Deuteronomistic Historian was aware that each invasion story was distinct, then B_2, like A, was not in its present position in an early edition of the Deuteronomic History. Without B_2, the story in B_1, set in

---

59. Laato, "Hezekiah and the Assyrian Crisis," 53.
60. Ibid., 56–57.

TABLE B.1. NAME PATTERNS IN 2 KINGS 18–19

A (18:13b–16)	B_1 (18:13a; 18:17–19:8)	B_2 (19:9–37)
Sennacherib, the king of Assyria (13b)	King Hezekiah (13a)	Tirhakah, the king of Kush (9)
	King Hezekiah (17)	
Hezekiah, the king of Judah (14)	Hezekiah (19)	Hezekiah (9)
		Hezekiah, the king of Judah (10)
Hezekiah, the king of Judah (14)	Hezekiah (22)	
	Hezekiah (29)	Hezekiah (14)
Hezekiah (15)		
	Hezekiah (30)	Hezekiah (14)
Hezekiah (16)		
	Hezekiah (31)	Hezekiah (15)
	Hezekiah (32)	Sennacherib (16)
	Hezekiah (37)	Hezekiah (20)
	King Hezekiah (19:1)	Sennacherib, the king of Assyria (20)
	Hezekiah (3)	
	King Hezekiah (5)	Sennacherib, the king of Assyria (36)

Note: All references to kings in the text that are unaccompanied by a personal name are omitted from this table.

Hezekiah's fourteenth year, leads neatly into chapter 20, which also recounts events of that very year. Hence, the narrative sequence may once have run as follows: 18:13a; 18:17–19:8; 20:1–19. These events all are set in Hezekiah's fourteenth year, and since the Babylonian king Merodach-baladan (Marduk-apla-iddina) mentioned in chapter 20 reigned from 721–710, there is further reason for accepting 712 B.C.E. as Hezekiah's fourteenth regnal year.

If all mentioned portions of the text were put into chronological order, segments A and B_2 would be positioned after 2 Kgs 20:19. Such an order would account for the apparent discrepancy of Isaiah predicting Hezekiah's deliverance (20:6) *after* the deliverance is recounted (19:35). It would additionally explain how it happened that Hezekiah showed off his great treasures (20:13) *after* he had given them all away (18:15–16). It seems sensible to conclude that the Sennacherib story once followed upon the heels of the narratives found in chapter 20.

5. Who Reordered the Narrative, and When?

Ascertaining the person responsible for restructuring the Hezekiah narratives and the date of his editing is extremely difficult. Of note is that *both* the Kings and Isaiah versions of this text are out of order and agree in their disorder. If it is true that the Isaiah version is based on a text of Kings earlier than MT, as textual analysis appears to indicate,[61] we must presume an early date for the reorganized text. The layout of the reordering is simple and clear:

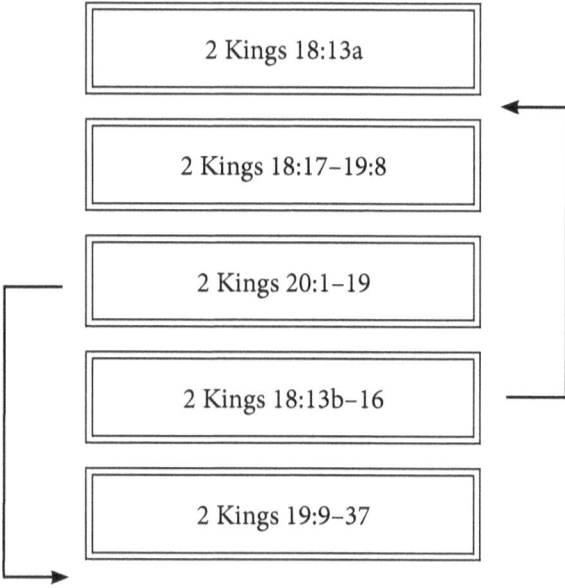

Figure B.1: The Reordering of 2 Kings 18–20

This sort of restructuring of a narrative sequence by ancient editors of texts is by no means uncommon and is usually done for thematic or ideological

---

61. Person, *The Kings-Isaiah and Kings-Jeremiah Recensions*, 8–79; Raymond F. Person, "II Kings 18–20 and Isaiah 36–39: A Text Critical Case Study in the Redaction History of the Book of Isaiah," *ZAW* 111 (1999).

reasons, or simply to "correct" a text that is seen to be inaccurate or problematic.[62]

With all of the difficulties involved, I can only present a possible scenario: both the prexilic and exilic editions of the Deuteronomic History had the material in the proper sequence, but the redactor of the Primary History (Genesis–2 Kings), perhaps under the influence of the Chronicler's version of the story, altered the sequence; an editor of the book of Isaiah copied the later version.

Other scenarios could also be conjectured. What seems certain, however, is that editorial activity in both 2 Kings 18–20 and Isaiah 36–39 has obscured an original story about a Sargonic invasion of Judah in 712 B.C.E. and created a historical misunderstanding that has lasted until today.

---

62. See David A. Glatt, *Chronological Displacement in Biblical and Related Literatures* (SBLDS 139; Atlanta: Scholars Press, 1993).

Bibliography

Ackroyd, Peter R. "The Meaning of Hebrew דור Considered." *JSS* 13 (1968): 3–10.
Albrektson, B. *History and the Gods: An Essay on the Idea of Historical Events as Divine Manifestations in the Ancient Near East and in Israel*. Lund: Gleerup, 1967.
Albright, William Foxwell. "Abram the Hebrew: A New Archaeological Interpretation." *BASOR* 163 (1961): 36–54.
———. "The Gezer Calendar." *BASOR* 92 (1943): 16–26.
André, G. "מחר." *TDOT* 8:237–41.
Auerbach, Elias. "Die babylonische Datierung im Pentatuech und das Alter des Priester-Kodex." *VT* 2 (1952): 334–42.
Barnes, William Hamilton. *Studies in the Chronology of the Divided Monarchy of Israel*. HSM 48. Atlanta: Scholars Press, 1991.
Barthélemy, Dominique. *Les devanciers d'Aquila*. VTSup 10. Leiden: Brill, 1963.
Beckwith, Roger T. *Calendar and Chronology, Jewish and Christian: Biblical, Intertestamental, and Patristic Studies*. Leiden: Brill, 1996.
Ben Zvi, Ehud. "Malleability and Its Limits: Sennacherib's Campaign Against Judah as a Case-Study." Pages 73–105 in *"Like a Bird in a Cage": The Invasion of Sennacherib in 701 BCE*. Edited by Lester L. Grabbe. London: Sheffield, 2003.
———. "Who Wrote the Speech of Rabshakeh and When?" *JBL* 109 (1990): 79–92.
Bickerman, Elias J. *Chronology of the Ancient World*. Ithaca, N.Y.: Cornell University Press, 1968.
Bin-Nun, Shoshana R. "Formulas from Royal Records of Israel and of Judah." *VT* 18 (1968): 414–32.
Blakely, Jeffrey A., and James W. Hardin. "Southwestern Judah in the Late Eighth Century B.C.E." *BASOR* 326 (2002): 11–64.
Blenkinsopp, Joseph. *Isaiah 1–39: A New Translation with Introduction and Commentary*. AB 19. New York: Doubleday, 2000.
Boling, Robert G. "Some Conflate Readings in Joshua-Judges." *VT* 16 (1966): 293–98.
Borchardt, Ludwig. *Die Altägyptische Zeitmessung*. Berlin: de Gruyter, 1920.
Borowski, Oded. *Agriculture in Iron Age Israel*. Winona Lake, Ind.: Eisenbrauns, 1987.
Bottéro, Jean. *Mesopotamia: Writing, Reasoning, and the Gods*. Chicago: University of Chicago Press, 1992.
Brin, Gershon. *The Concept of Time in the Bible and the Dead Sea Scrolls*. Edited by F. Garcia Martinez. STDJ 34. Leiden: Brill, 2001.

Britton, John P. "Calendars, Intercalations and Year-Lengths in Mesopotamian Astronomy." Pages 115–32 in *Calendars and Years: Astronomy and Time in the Ancient Near East*. Edited by J. M. Steele. Oxford: Oxbow, 2007.
Buis, Pierre. "Rois (Livres des)." Pages 695–739 (1/4 pages) in vol. 10 of *Supplément au Dictionnaire de la Bible*. 1982.
Childs, Brevard S. *Isaiah and the Assyrian Crisis*. SBT 3. London: SCM, 1967.
Clagett, Marshall. *Calendars, Clocks and Astronomy*. Vol. 2 of *Ancient Egyptian Science: A Source Book*. Independence Square, Pa.: American Philosophical Society, 1995.
Clements, R. E. "ירח." *TDOT* 6:355–62.
Clines, David J. A. "The Evidence for an Autumnal New Year in Pre-exilic Israel Reconsidered." *JBL* 93 (1974): 22–40.
Cogan, Mordechai. "Chronology, Hebrew Bible." *ABD* 1:1002–11.
———. *1 Kings: A New Translation with Introduction and Commentary*. AB 10. New York: Doubleday, 2001.
——— and Hayim Tadmor. *II Kings: A New Translation with Introduction and Commentary*. AB 11. Garden City: Doubleday, 1988.
Cohen, Chaim. "Neo-Assyrian Elements in the First Speech of the Biblical Rab-šaqê." *IOS* 9 (1979): 32–48.
Cohen, Mark E. *The Cultic Calendars of the Ancient Near East*. Bethesda, Md.: CDL, 1993.
Cooper, Alan, and Bernard R. Goldstein. "The Development of the Priestly Calendars (I): The Daily Sacrifice and the Sabbath." *HUCA* 74 (2004): 1–20.
Cortese, E. "Problemi attuali circa l'opera deuteronomistica." *Rivista biblica italiana* 26 (1978): 341–52.
Cross, Frank Moore. *Canaanite Myth and Hebrew Epic*. Cambridge, Mass.: Harvard University Press, 1973.
———. "A Fragment of a Monumental Inscription from the City of David." *IEJ* 51 (2001): 44–47.
———. "The Structure of the Deuteronomic History." Pages 9–24 in *Perspectives in Jewish Learning*. Annual of the College of Jewish Studies 3. Chicago: Spertus College of Judaica, 1968.
Depuydt, Leo. "Calendars and Years in Ancient Egypt: The Soundness of Egyptian and West Asian Chronology in 1500–500 BC and the Consistency of the Egyptian 365-Day Wandering Year." Pages 35–81 in *Calendars and Years: Astronomy and Time in the Ancient Near East*. Edited by J. M. Steele. Oxford: Oxbow, 2007.
Eliade, Mircea. *Cosmos and History: The Myth of the Eternal Return*. Translated by Willard K. Trask. New York: Harper & Row, 1959.
Etz, Donald V. "The Numbers of Genesis V 3–31: A Suggested Conversion and Its Implications." *VT* 43 (1993): 171–89.
Evans, Paul S. "Sennacherib's 701 Invasion into Judah: What Saith the Scriptures?" Pages 57–77 in *The Function of Ancient Historiography in Biblical and Cognate Studies*. Edited by Patricia G. Kirkpatrick and Timothy Goltz. LHBOTS 489. New York: T&T Clark, 2008.

Finegan, Jack. *Handbook of Biblical Chronology: Principles of Time Reckoning in the Ancient World and Problems of Chronology in the Bible*. 2nd ed. Peabody: Hendrickson, 1998.
Fleming, Daniel E. *Time at Emar: The Cultic Calendar and the Rituals from the Diviner's Archive*. Winona Lake, Ind.: Eisenbrauns, 2000.
Forsdyke, John. *Greece before Homer: Ancient Chronology and Mythology*. New York: Norton, 1964.
Frankfort, Henri. *Kingship and the Gods*. Chicago: University of Chicago Press, 1948.
Freedman, David Noel. "The Babylonian Chronicle." *BA* 19 (1956): 50–60.
———. "Kingly Chronologies: Then and Later." Pages 41*–65* in *ErIsr* 24, *Avraham Malamat Volume*. Jerusalem: Israel Exploration Society, 1993.
———. "Pentateuch." *IDB* 3:711–27.
——— and Jack R. Lundbom. "דור." *TDOT* 3:169–81.
Fried, Lisbeth S. and David Noel Freedman. "Was the Jubilee Year Observed in Preexilic Judah?" Pages 2257–70 in Jacob Milgrom, *Leviticus 23–27: A New Translation and Commentary*. New York: Doubleday, 2001.
Friedman, Richard Elliott. *The Bible with Sources Revealed*. San Francisco: HarperSanFrancisco, 2003.
———. "The Deuteronomistic School." Pages 70–80 in *Fortunate the Eyes That See: Essays in Honor of David Noel Freedman in Celebration of His Seventieth Birthday*. Edited by Astrid B. Beck, Andrew H. Bartelt, Paul R. Raabe, and Chris A. Franke. Grand Rapids: Eerdmans, 1995.
———. *The Exile and Biblical Narrative: The Formation of the Deuteronomistic and Priestly Works*. Chico, Calif.: Scholars Press, 1981.
———. "From Egypt to Egypt: Dtr1 and Dtr2." Pages 167–92 in *Traditions in Transformation: Turning Points in Biblical Faith*. Edited by Baruch Halpern and Jon D. Levenson. Winona Lake, Ind.: Eisenbrauns, 1981.
———. *The Hidden Book in the Bible*. San Francisco: HarperSanFrancisco, 1998.
———. "Torah." *ABD* 6:605–22.
———. *Who Wrote the Bible?* Englewood Cliffs, N.J.: Prentice Hall, 1987.
Galil, Gershon. *The Chronology of the Kings of Israel and Judah*. SHANE 9. Leiden: Brill, 1996.
———. "Judah and Assyria in the Sargonid Period [Hebrew]." *Zion* 57 (1992): 111–33.
———. "A New Look at the 'Azekah Inscription.'" *RB* 102 (1995): 321–29.
Gallagher, William R. *Sennacherib's Campaign to Judah: New Studies*. SHCANE 18. Leiden: Brill, 1999.
Gandz, Solomon. "The Calendar of Ancient Israel." *Homenaje a Millás Vallicrosa* 1 (1954): 623–46.
———. "The Origin of the Planetary Week or the Planetary Week in Hebrew Literature." *PAAJR* 18 (1949): 213–54.
Garbini, Giovanni. "Le Fonti Citate nel 'Libro dei Re.'" *Henoch* 3 (1981): 26–46.
Geoghegan, Jeffrey C. "Until Whose Day? A Study of the Phrase 'Until This Day' in the Deuteronomistic History." Ph.D. diss., University of California, San Diego, 1999.

Geyer, John B. "2 Kings XVIII 14–16 and the Annals of Sennacherib." *VT* 21 (1971): 604–6.
Glassner, Jean-Jacques. *Mesopotamian Chronicles*. SBLWAW 19. Atlanta: Society of Biblical Literature, 2004.
Glatt, David A. *Chronological Displacement in Biblical and Related Literatures*, SBLDS 139. Atlanta: Scholars Press, 1993.
Goldberg, Jeremy. "Two Assyrian Campaigns Against Hezekiah and Later Eighth Century Biblical Chronology." *Bib* 80 (1999): 360–90.
Goldstein, Bernard R., and Alan Cooper. "The Festivals of Israel and Judah and the Literary History of the Pentateuch." *JAOS* 110 (1990): 19–31.
Gonçalves, F. J. *L'expédition de Sennachérib en Palestine dans la littérature hébraïque ancienne*. Louvain-la-Neuve: Université catholique de Louvain, Institut orientaliste, 1986.
Goudoever, J. van. *Biblical Calendars*. 2nd rev. ed. Leiden: Brill, 1961.
Gray, John. *I and II Kings*. 2nd ed. OTL. Philadelphia: SCM Press, 1970.
Halpern, Baruch. *The Constitution of the Monarchy in Israel*. Chico, CA: Scholars Press, 1981.
———. *The First Historians: The Hebrew Bible and History*. San Francisco: Harper & Row, 1988.
——— and David S. Vanderhooft. "The Editions of Kings in the 7th–6th Centuries B.C.E." *HUCA* 62 (1991): 179–244.
Hannah, Robert R. *Time in Antiquity*. New York: Routledge, 2009.
Haran, Menahem. "Behind the Scenes of History: Determining the Date of the Priestly Source." *JBL* 100 (1981): 321–33.
———. *Temples and Temple Service in Ancient Israel: An Inquiry into the Character of Cult Phenomena and the Historical Setting of the Priestly School*. Oxford: Clarendon, 1978.
Hayes, John H. "The Beginning of the Regnal Year in Israel and Judah." Pages 92–95 in *The Land That I Will Show You: Essays on the History and Archaeology of the Ancient Near East in Honour of J. Maxwell Miller*. Edited by John A. Dearman and Matt P. Graham. JSOTSup 343. Sheffield: Sheffield Academic Press, 2001.
——— and Paul K. Hooker. *A New Chronology for the Kings of Israel and Judah and Its Implications for Biblical History and Literature*. Atlanta: John Knox Press, 1988.
——— and Stuart A. Irvine. *Isaiah the Eighth Century Prophet: His Times and His Preaching*. Nashville: Abingdon, 1987.
Hendel, Ronald S. *The Text of Genesis 1–11: Textual Studies and Critical Edition*. New York: Oxford University Press, 1998.
Honor, Leo L. *Sennacherib's Invasion of Palestine: A Critical Source Study*. COHP 12. New York: Columbia University Press, 1926.
Hooker, Paul K. "The Kingdom of Hezekiah: Judah in the Geo-Political Context of the Late Eighth Century B.C.E." Ph.D. diss., Emory University, 1993.
——— and John H. Hayes. "The Year of Josiah's Death: 609 or 610 BCE?" Pages 96–103 in *The Land That I Will Show You: Essays on the History and Archaeology of the Ancient Near East in Honour of J. Maxwell Miller*. Edited by J. A. Dearman

and M. P. Graham. Vol. 343 of *JSOT Supplement Series*. Sheffield: Sheffield Academic Press, 2001.

Hornung, Eric, Rolf Krauss, and David A. Warburton, "Methods of Dating and the Egyptian Calendar." Pages 45–51 in *Ancient Egyptian Chronology*. Edited by E. Hornung. HO 1.83. Leiden: Brill, 2006.

Hughes, Jeremy. *Secrets of the Times: Myth and History in Biblical Chronology*. JSOTSup 66. Sheffield: JSOT Press, 1990.

Hull, John H. "Hezekiah, Saint and Sinner: A Conceptual and Contextual Narrative Analysis of 2 Kings 18–20." Ph.D. diss., Claremont Graduate School, 1994.

Hurvitz, Avi. "Dating the Priestly Source in Light of the Historical Study of Biblical Hebrew a Century after Wellhausen." *ZAW* 100 (1988): 88–100.

———. "The Evidence of Language in Dating the Priestly Code." *RB* 81 (1974): 24–56.

———. *A Linguistic Study of the Relationship Between the Priestly Source and the Book of Ezekiel*. Paris: Gabalda, 1982.

Iwry, Samuel. "The Qumran Isaiah and the End of the Dial of Ahaz." *BASOR* 147 (1957): 27–33.

Jacobsen, Thorkild. "Mesopotamian Gods and Pantheons." Pages 16–38 in *Toward the Image of Tammuz and Other Essays on Mesopotamian History and Culture*. Edited by William L. Moran. Cambridge, Mass.: Harvard University Press, 1970.

Jenkins, Allan K. "Hezekiah's Fourteenth Year: A New Interpretation of 2 Kings xviii 13 - xix 37." *VT* 26 (1976): 284–98.

Jenks, A. W. *The Elohist and North Israelite Traditions*. SBLMS 22. Missoula, Mont.: Society of Biblical Literature, 1977.

———. "Elohist." *ABD* 2:478–82.

Jepsen, Alfred. "Zur Chronologie des Priesterkodex." *ZAW* 47 (1929): 252–55.

Kahle, Paul. *The Cairo Geniza*. 2nd ed. New York: Praeger, 1959.

———. "Die Septuaginta: Principielle Erwägungen." Pages 161–80 in *Festschrift Otto Eissfeldt zum 60. Geburtstage*. Edited by Johann Fück. Halle: Niemeyer, 1947.

———. "Untersuchungen zur Geschichte des Pentateuchtextes." *TSK* 88 (1915).

Kaiser, Otto. *Isaiah 13–39: A Commentary*. OTL. Philadelphia: Westminster, 1974.

Kitchen, Kenneth A. "The Historical Chronology of Ancient Egypt, A Current Assessment." Pages 39–52 in *The Synchronisation of Civilisations in the Eastern Mediterranean in the Second Millennium B.C.* Edited by Manfred Bietak. Vienna: Verlag der Österreichischen Akademie der Wissenschaften, 2000.

———. *The Third Intermediate Period in Egypt (1100–650 B.C.)*. 2nd ed. Warminster: Aris & Phillips, 1986.

Klein, Ralph W. "Archaic Chronologies and the Textual History of the Old Testament." *HTR* 67 (1974): 255–63.

Knohl, Israel. *The Sanctuary of Silence: The Priestly Torah and the Holiness School*. Minneapolis: Augsburg Fortress, 1995.

Kugler, Franz X. *Von Moses bis Paulus: Forschungen zur Geschichte Israels*. Münster: Aschendorff, 1922.

Kutsch, E. "'…am Ende des Jahres': Zur Datierung des israelitischen Herbstfestes in Ex 23,16." *ZAW* 83 (1971): 15–21.

Laato, Antti. "Assyrian Propaganda and the Falsification of History in the Royal Inscriptions of Sennacherib." *VT* 45 (1995): 198–223.

———. "Hezekiah and the Assyrian Crisis in 701 B.C." *SJOT* 2 (1987): 49–68.

Lagarde, Paul de. *Ankündigung einer neuen Ausgabe der griechischen Übersetzung des alten Testaments*. Göttingen, 1882.

Langdon, Stephen S. *Babylonian Menologies and the Semitic Calendars*. London: Oxford University Press, 1935.

Larsson, Gerhard. "The Chronology of the Pentateuch: A Comparison of the MT and LXX." *JBL* 102 (1983): 401–9.

Lemaire, André. "Vers l'histoire de la rédaction des livres des Rois." *ZAW* 98 (1986): 221–36.

Lie, Arthur G. *The Inscriptions of Sargon II, King of Assyria, Part I: The Annals*. Paris: Geuthner, 1929.

Lohfink, Norbert. *Rückblick im Zorn auf den Staat, Vorlesungen zu ausgewählten Schlüsseltexten der Bücher Samuel und Könige*. Frankfurt: Privatdruck, 1984.

Lundbom, Jack R. *Jeremiah: A Study in Ancient Hebrew Rhetoric*. 2nd ed. Winona Lake, Ind.: Eisenbrauns, 1997.

———. "Jeremiah, Book of." *ABD* 3:706–21.

———. *Jeremiah 1–20: A New Translation with Introduction and Commentary*. AB 21A. New York: Doubleday, 1999.

———. *Jeremiah 21–36: A New Translation with Introduction and Commentary*. AB 21B. New York: Doubleday, 2004.

Macalister, Robert A. S. *The Excavation at Gezer*. 2 vols. London: Palestine Exploration Fund, 1912.

Malalae, Ioannis. *Chronographia; ex recensione Ludovici Dindorfii*. Bonnae: Weber, 1831.

Malena, Sarah, and David Miano, eds. *Milk and Honey: Essays on Ancient Israel and the Bible in Appreciation of the Judaic Studies Program at the University of California, San Diego*. Winona Lake, Ind.: Eisenbrauns, 2007.

Meyer, Eduard. "Herodots Chronologie der griechischen Sagengeschichte." Pages 151–88 in *Forschungen zur alten Geschichte*. Halle: Niemeyer, 1892.

———. "Principien der rechnung nach Königsjahren." Pages 440–53 in *Forschungen zur alte Geschichte*. Halle: Niemeyer, 1899.

Miano, David. "The Twelve Sepharim of the Torah." *The Biblical Historian* 1 (2004): 10–19.

Milgrom, Jacob. "The Antiquity of the Priestly Source." *ZAW* 111 (1999): 10–22.

———. *Leviticus 1–16: A New Translation with Introduction and Commentary*, AB 3. New York: Doubleday, 1991.

———. *Leviticus 23–27: A New Translation with Introduction and Commentary*. AB 3B. New York: Doubleday, 2001.

Millard, Alan. *The Eponyms of the Assyrian Empire 910–612 BC*. SAA 2. Helsinki: Neo-Assyrian Text Corpus Project, 1994.

Möller, Astrid, and Nino Luraghi. "Time in the Writing of History: Perceptions and Structures." *Storia della Storiografia* 28 (1995): 3–15.

Momigliano, Arnaldo. "Time in Ancient Historiography." Pages 1–23 in *History and the Concept of Time*. History and Theory 6. Middletown, Conn.: Wesleyen University Press, 1966.
Montgomery, James A. *A Critical and Exegetical Commentary on the Books of Kings*. ICC. New York: Scribner's Sons, 1951.
Moor, Johannes C. de. *New Year with Canaanites and Israelites*. 2 vols. Kampen: Kok, 1972.
Morganstern, Julian. "The New Year for Kings." Pages 439–56 in *Occident and Orient: Being Studies in Semitic Philology and Literature, Jewish History and Philosophy and Folklore in the Widest Sense*. Edited by Bruno Schindler. London: Taylor's Foreign Press, 1936.
———. "Supplementary Studies in the Calendars of Ancient Israel." *HUCA* 10 (1935): 1–148.
Mosshammer, Alden A. *The Chronicle of Eusebius and Greek Chronographic Tradition*. Lewisburg, Pa.: Bucknell University Press, 1979.
——— ed. *Georgii Syncelli: Ecloga Chronographica*. Leipzig: Teubner, 1984.
Mowinckel, Sigmund. *Zum israelitischen Neujahr und zur Deutung der Thronbesteigungspsalmen*. Oslo: Dybwad, 1952.
———. *Psalmenstudien*. 2 vols. Amsterdam: Schippers, 1966.
Na'aman, Nadav. "Hezekiah and the Kings of Assyria." *Tel Aviv* 21 (1994): 235–54.
———. "Historical and Chronological Notes on the Kingdoms of Israel and Judah in the Eighth Century B.C." *VT* 36 (1986): 71–92.
———. "New Light on Hezekiah's Second Prophetic Story." *Bib* 81 (2000): 393–402.
———. "Sennacherib's 'Letter to God' on his Campaign to Judah." *BASOR* 214 (1974): 25–39.
———. "Updating the Messages: Hezekiah's Second Prophetic Story (2 Kings 19.9b–35) and the Community of Babylonian Deportees." Pages 201–20 in *"Like a Bird in a Cage": The Invasion of Sennacherib in 701 BCE*. Edited by Lester L. Grabbe. London: Sheffield Academic Press, 2003.
Nelson, Richard D. *The Double Redaction of the Deuteronomistic History*. JSOTSup 18. Sheffield: JSOT Press, 1981.
Neuberg, Frank J. "An Unrecognized Meaning of Hebrew *dôr*." *JNES* 9 (1950): 215–17.
Nicholson, Ernest. *The Pentateuch in the Twentieth Century: The Legacy of Julius Wellhausen*. Oxford: Clarendon, 1998.
Niehr, H. "ערב." *TDOT* 11:335–41.
Noll, Kurt L. "The Evolution of Genre in the Book of Kings: The Story of Sennacherib and Hezekiah as Example." Pages 30–56 in *The Function of Ancient Historiography in Biblical and Cognate Studies*. Edited by Patricia G. Kirkpatrick and Timothy Goltz. LHBOTS 489. New York: T&T Clark, 2008.
Norin, S. "An Important Kennicott Reading in 2 Kings XVIII 13." *VT* 32 (1982): 337–38.
North, F. S. "Four-Month Seasons of the Hebrew Bible." *VT* 11 (1961): 446–48.
North, J. L. "חדש." *TDOT* 4:225–44.
Northcote, Jeremy. "The Lifespans of the Patriarchs: Schematic Orderings in the Chrono-genealogy." *VT* 57 (2007): 243–57.

———. "The Schematic Development of Old Testament Chronography: Towards an Integrated Model." *JSOT* 29 (2004): 3–36.
Oswalt, John N. *The Book of Isaiah: Chapters 1–39*. NICOT. Grand Rapids: Eerdmans, 1986.
Otto, Eckart. "שׁבע." *TDOT* 14:336–67.
Parker, Richard A. *The Calendars of Ancient Egypt*. SAOC 26. Chicago: University of Chicago Press, 1950.
———. "The Beginning of the Lunar Month in Ancient Egypt." *JNES* 29 (1970): 217–20.
——— and Waldo H. Dubberstein. *Babylonian Chronology, 626 B.C. - A.D. 75*. 3rd ed. Providence: Brown University Press, 1956.
Person, Raymond F. *The Kings-Isaiah and Kings-Jeremiah Recensions*. Berlin: de Gruyter, 1997.
———. "II Kings 18–20 and Isaiah 36–39: A Text Critical Case Study in the Redaction History of the Book of Isaiah." *ZAW* 111 (1999): 373–79.
Polzin, Robert. *Late Biblical Hebrew: Toward an Historical Typology of Biblical Hebrew Prose*. Atlanta: Scholars Press, 1976.
Prakken, Donald Wilson. *Studies in Greek Genealogical Chronology*. Lancaster, Pa.: Lancaster, 1943.
Propp, William H. C. *Exodus 1–18: A New Translation with Introduction and Commentary*. AB 2. New York: Doubleday, 1999.
Pury, Albert de. "Yahwist ("J") Source." *ABD* 6:1012–20.
Rawlinson, Henry C., and George Smith. *The Cuneiform Inscriptions of Western Asia III*. London: Bowler, 1870.
Rendsburg, Gary A. "Late Biblical Hebrew and the Date of P." *JANES* 12 (1980): 65–80.
Richter, Wolfgang. *Die Bearbeitung des "Retterbuches" in der deuteronomistischen Epoche*. Bonn: Hanstein, 1964.
———. *Traditionsgeschichtliche Untersuchungen zum Richterbuch*. Bonn: Hanstein, 1963.
Roberts, J. J. M. "Mowinckel's Enthronement Festival: A Review." Pages 97–115 in *The Book of Psalms: Composition and Reception*. Edited by Peter W. Flint and Patrick D. Miller Jr. VTSup 99. Leiden: Brill, 2005.
Rochberg-Halton, Francesca. "Calendars, Ancient Near East." *ABD* 1:810–14.
Rochberg, Francesca. "Astronomy and Calendars in Ancient Mesopotamia." Pages 1925–40 in *Civilizations of the Ancient Near East*. Edited by Jack M. Sasson. New York: Scribner's Sons, 1995.
Saggs, Henry W. F. *The Greatness That Was Babylon*. New York: Mentor, 1968.
Samuel, Alan E. *Greek and Roman Chronology: Calendars and Years in Classical Antiquity*. Munich: Beck, 1972.
Schedl, Claus. "Textkritische Bemurkungen zu den Synchronismen der Könige von Israel und Juda." *VT* 12 (1962): 88–119.
Schlauri, I. "W. Richters Beitrag zur Redaktionsgeschichte des Richterbuches." *Bib* 54 (1973): 367–403.

Schwyzer, E., ed. *Dialectorum Graecarum Exempla Epigraphica Potiora*. Hildescheim: Olms, 1960.
Segal, J. B. "Intercalation and the Hebrew Calendar." *VT* 7 (1957): 250–307.
Seitz, Christopher R. *Zion's Final Destiny: A Reassessment of Isaiah 36–39*. Minneapolis: Fortress, 1991.
Seow, C. L. *Myth, Drama, and the Politics of David's Dance*. HSM 44. Atlanta: Scholars Press, 1989.
Sethe, Kurt. "Die Zeitrechnung der alten Ägypter im Verhältnis zu der der andern Völker." Pages 130–38 in *Nachrichten von der Königlichen Gesellschaft der Wissenschaften zu Göttingen, Philologisch-historische Klasse aus dem Jahre 1920*. Berlin: Weidmann, 1920.
Sewell, J. W. S. "The Calendars and Chronology." Pages 1–15 in *The Legacy of Egypt*. Edited by Stephen R. K. Glanville. London: Oxford, 1942.
Shenkel, James Donald. *Chronology and Recensional Development in the Greek Text of Kings*. Cambridge, Mass.: Harvard University Press, 1968.
Shortland, A. J. "Shishak, King of Egypt: The Challenges of Egyptian Calendrical Chronology." Pages 43–54 in *The Bible and Radiocarbon Dating*. Edited by Thomas E. Levy and Thomas Higham. London: Equinox, 2005.
Smelik, Klaas A. D. "Saul, de voorstelling van Israëls eerste koning in de Masoretische tekst van het Oude Testament." Ph.D. diss., Universiteit van Amsterdam, 1977.
———. "Distortion of Old Testament Prophecy: The Purpose of Isaiah XXXVI and XXXVII." Pages 70–93 in *Crises and Perspectives: Studies in Ancient Near Eastern Polytheism, Biblical Theology, Palestinian Archaeology and Intertestamental Literature*. OtSt 24. Leiden: Brill, 1986.
Snaith, Norman H. *The Jewish New Year Festival*. London: S.P.C.K., 1947.
Soggin, J. Alberto. *Judges: A Commentary*. Philadelphia: Westminster, 1981.
Spalinger, Anthony J. "The Year 712 B.C. and Its Implications for Egyptian History." *JARCE* 10 (1973): 95–101.
Stendebach, F. J. "שנה." *TDOT* 15:323–39.
Steele, John M. "The Length of the Month in Mesopotamian Calendars of the First Millennium BC." Pages 133–48 in *Calendars and Years: Astronomy and Time in the Ancient Near East*. Edited by J. M. Steele. Oxford: Oxbow, 2007.
Stern, Sacha. *Calendar and Community: A History of the Jewish Calendar, Second Century BCE–Tenth Century CE* Oxford: Oxford University Press, 2001.
Stott, Katherine M. *Why Did They Write This Way? Reflections on Reference to Written Documents in the Hebrew Bible and Ancient Literature*. London: T&T Clark, 2008.
Stroes, H. R. "Does the Day Begin in the Evening of Morning? Some Biblical Observations." *VT* 16 (1966): 460–75.
Tadmor, Hayim. "The Chronology of the First Temple Period: A Presentation and Evaluation of the Sources." Pages 44–60, 318–20 in *Age of the Monarchies: Political History*. Edited by Abraham Malamat and Israel Eph'al. Jerusalem: Massada, 1979.
———. *The Inscriptions of Tiglath-pileser III, King of Assyria*. Jerusalem: Israel Academy of Sciences and Humanities, 1994.

Talmon, Shemaryahu. "Divergences in Calendar-Reckoning in Ephraim and Judah." *VT* 8 (1958): 48–74.

———. "»400 Jahre« oder »vier Generationen« (Gen 15,13–15): Geschichtliche Zeitangaben oder literarische Motive?" Pages 13–25 in *Die Hebräische Bibel und ihre zweifache Nachgeschichte*. Neukirchener: Neukirchener Verlag, 1990.

———. "The Gezer Calendar and the Seasonal Cycle of Ancient Canaan." Pages 89–112 in *King, Cult and Calendar in Ancient Israel*. Jerusalem: Magnes, 1963.

———. "Whence the Day's Beginning in the Biblical Period and in the Beginning of the Second Temple Period?" Pages 109–29 in *The Bible as Reflected in Its Commentators*. Edited by Sara Japhet. Jerusalem: Magnes, 1994.

Taylor, Jeremy Graeme. "Framing the Past: The Roots of Greek Chronography." Ph.D. diss., University of Michigan, 2000.

Tetley, M. Christine. *The Reconstructed Chronology of the Divided Kingdom*. Winona Lake, Ind.: Eisenbrauns, 2005.

Thiele, Edwin R. *The Mysterious Numbers of the Hebrew Kings*. 3rd edition. Grand Rapids: Zondervan, 1983.

Tov, Emanuel. *Textual Criticism of the Hebrew Bible*. 2nd rev. ed. Minneapolis: Augsburg Fortress, 2001.

VanderKam, James C. "Calendars, Ancient Israelite and Early Jewish." *ABD* 1:814–20.

———. "Weeks, Feast of." *ABD* 6:895–97.

Vaux, Roland de. *Ancient Israel: Its Life and Institutions*. London: Darton, Longman, & Todd, 1961.

Verbrugghe, Gerald P., and John M. Wickersham. *Berossus and Manetho, Introduced and Translated*. Ann Arbor: University of Michigan Press, 1996.

Wacholder, Ben Zion. "Biblical Chronology in the Hellenistic World Chronicles." *HTR* 61 (1968): 451–81.

Waerden, Bartel L. van der. *Science Awakening II: The Birth of Astronomy*. New York: Oxford University Press, 1974.

Wagenaar, Jan A. *Origin and Transformation of the Ancient Israelite Festival Calendar*. Wiesbaden: Harrassowitz, 2005.

Weinfeld, Moshe. *Deuteronomy and the Deuteronomic School*. London: Oxford University Press, 1972.

Weippert, Helga. "Die 'deuteronomistischen' Beurteilungen der Könige von Israel und Juda und das Problem der Redaktion der Königsbücher." *Bib* 53 (1972): 301–39.

Weippert, Manfred. "Fragen des israelitischen Geschichtsbewusstseins." *VT* 23 (1973): 415–42.

Wildberger, Hans. *Isaiah 13–27: A Continental Commentary*. Minneapolis: Fortress, 1997.

Williamson, H. G. M. "The Death of Josiah and the Continuing Development of the Deuteronomic History." *VT* 32 (1982): 242–47.

Wilson, Robert R. *Genealogy and History in the Biblical World*. New Haven: Yale University Press, 1977.

Winckler, Hugo. *Die Keilschrifttexte Sargons*. 2 vols. Leipzig: Pfeiffer, 1889.

———. *Altorientalische Forschungen*. 3 vols. Leipzig: Pfeiffer, 1893–1905.

Wright, Richard M. *Linguistic Evidence for the Pre-exilic Date of the Yahwistic Source.* New York: T&T Clark, 2005.

Yadin, Yigael. "מעלות אחז." *ErIsr* 5 (1958): 91–96.

———. *The Art of Warfare in Biblical Lands in the Light of Archaeological Study.* Translated by M. Pearlman. New York: McGraw-Hill, 1963.

Zevit, Ziony. "Converging Lines of Evidence Bearing on the Date of P." *ZAW* 94 (1982): 502–9.

Ancient Sources Index

Hebrew Bible/Old Testament

Genesis
1:1–31	11
1:5	51
1:14	26, 33, 48
2:4	83
4:17–26	75, 95 n. 46
4:24	75
5:1	83
5:1–32	61, 65, 67–76, 77, 80, 82, 83–86, 88, 94 n. 46, 95, 96
5:12	80
5:22	66
5:29	76
6:3	60
6:5–8	76
7:1	76
7:6	52, 64, 71, 82, 84–85, 92, 95
7:11	22, 24, 25, 52, 64, 84–85
7:17	85 n. 28
7:23	69
8:3–4	26
8:4–5	22, 24, 64
8:13–14	22, 24, 64, 84–85
8:22	29, 31, 37
9:28	71, 82
9:28–29	84–85, 88, 95
10:1–32	86
11:10–11	92
11:10–32	65, 67, 74 n. 14, 76–86, 88, 96
11:32	93
12:4	63 n. 1
12:4–5	81, 93
14:4	52
15:13–16	59–62
16:15	63 n. 1
16:16	96
17:1	63 n. 1
17:17	93
17:21	29
19:33–34	9
21:5	63 n. 1, 96
23:1	88–89
24:55	33
25:7	88–89, 93, 96
25:20	63 n. 1
25:20–21	93
25:26	63 n. 1, 96
26:34	63 n. 1
29:26–27	29
29:27–28	29
30:33	9 n. 6
30:36	51
31:22	51
35:28–29	89, 96
37:2	63 n. 1
38:24	20 n. 35
40:4	33
40:19–20	51
41:46	63 n. 1
42:17–18	51
45:6	31
47:7–9	58, 64
47:28	88–89, 96
50:23	62, 88–89
50:26	88–89

Exodus		23:5	12, 22
2:2	19	23:6	22
6:14–27	90	23:15–16	29, 52, 58
6:16	88–89	23:23–25	41
6:16–20	59	23:24	22
6:18	89	23:27	13, 22
6:20	89	23:32	12, 13, 22
7:7	63 n. 1	23:39–41	42
9:31–32	20 n. 37	23:39	22, 34, 39
12:2	36, 37 n. 79, 40	23:41	22, 34, 39
12:2–6	22, 24	25:1–22	31, 41
12:4–5	79	25:8	29
12:6	12	25:9	22
12:15	52	25:10	58
12:18	22	25:29	33
12:18–19	12	26:5	33
12:40–41	58, 59, 62, 79, 81 n. 22	26:7–8	239
13:4	20		
14:24	13	Numbers	
16:1	22–23	1:1	22, 24
16:23–25	11	1:18	22, 24
19:1	22–24	9:1	22, 24
19:15–16	51	9:3	12, 22
20:5	59	9:5	12, 22
20:6	61 n. 20	9:11	12, 22
23:10–11	31	9:22	33
23:15	20, 40	10:11	22–23
23:16	34–35, 41	11:19–20	50
29:39	12	11:32	10
29:41	12	13:6	64 n. 2
30:8	12	13:22	64 n. 2
34:6–7	62	13:30–31	64 n. 2
34:18	20, 40	13:33	64 n. 2
34:21	31	14:6–9	64 n. 2
34:22	29, 41	14:12	64 n. 2
40:2	22, 24	14:32–34	94 n. 43
40:17	22, 24	14:34	50, 58, 84
		14:43	239
Leviticus		20:1	22–23
7:15	11	28–29	23
13:4–6	52	28:16	22
16:29	22	28:17	22
22:30	11	29:1	22
23	23	29:1–6	42
23:4–8	40	29:7	23

29:12	23, 34, 39	14:10	54, 57, 64, 102, 105 n. 17, 106 n. 19, 210, 212
33:1–49	23–24, 90		
33:3	11 n. 10, 22	24:2–5	214
33:38	23	24:29	89
33:39	89		

Judges

Deuteronomy		2:6–23	100–01
1:2	50	2:10	105 n. 17, 212
1:3–4	23–24	2:11–19	101 n. 9
4:28	230 n. 30	3:3	57, 210
4:35	230 n. 30	3:8	57, 102, 210, 212
5:10	61 n. 20	3:11	57, 105, 210, 212
11:12	31, 37 n. 80	3:12	101 n. 10
11:14	37 n. 80	3:14	57, 102, 210
12–26	5	3:30	101
14:28	51	3:31	101
15:1	51	4:1	101 n. 10, 105
15:9	51	4:3	57, 102, 210
16:1–9	10	5:31	57, 210, 212
16:1	20	6:1	57, 101 n. 10, 102, 210
16:4	10 n. 9	6:34–40	10
16:6	10 n. 9	7:2–11	10
16:7	11	7:13–25	10
16:8	11	7:19	13
16:9–12	29	8:28	57, 210, 212
16:13	34	8:30	103
21:13	19	8:32	103
23:2–3	61 n. 20	8:48	105
23:12 [11]	10 n. 9	9:22	57, 102, 105, 210
26:12	51	10:1–4	57
31:2	64	10:1–5	103
33:14	19	10:2	105 n. 17, 210, 212
34:4	214	10:3	105 n. 17, 210, 213
34:7	89	10:6	101 n. 10
		10:8	57, 102, 105, 210
		11:26	102, 105, 213
Joshua		12:7	210, 213
4:19	23–24	12:7–15	57, 103
5:6–7	59	12:8	210, 213
5:10–12	10	12:11	210, 213
8:29	10 n. 9	12:14	210, 213
9:16–17	51	13:1	57, 101 n. 10, 102, 105, 106 n. 20, 210
10:26–27	10 n. 9		
11:23	105	14:14–15	51
14:7	55, 64	14:17	51

Judges (cont.)	
15:20	57 n. 10, 106 n. 20
16:31	106 nn. 19–20, 213
17:10	33
19:2	33
19:9	9
21:4	9

1 Samuel	
5:2–4	9 n. 7
6:1	50
7:2	50
7:13	57 n. 10
11:11	13
13:1	57, 117, 210
19:10–11	9
20:5	25
20:24	25
25:38	50
27:7	20 n. 35, 33, 54
29:3	33
30:13	50

2 Samuel	
1:12	239
5:4–5	117
11:1	40
14:26	33
24:8	20 n. 35

1 Kings	
1–2	125
2:11	57, 106 n. 19, 211, 213
4:7–19	48
5:7 [4:27]	20 n. 35
5:27–28	34
6:1	20, 21, 38, 56, 57, 106 n. 19, 108, 211
6:37–38	19, 20, 21, 38, 45, 53, 108
7:1	53
8:1–66	40
8:2	19, 20, 21, 34, 38, 108
8:16	115 n. 31
11:32	115 n. 31
11:41	108
11:42	117, 211, 213
12:5	51
12:12	51
12:32–33	21, 34 n. 71, 38–40, 108
14:19	108, 223 n. 7
14:19–20	118
14:20	119
14:21	112, 115 n. 31
14:25	110, 111, 152, 156
14:29	108
15:1	111, 154, 159
15:1–2	112, 114
15:7	108
15:9	154, 160
15:9–10	112, 114, 128–29
15:23	108
15:25	119, 152, 160
15:31	108
15:33	119, 152, 160
16:5	108
16:8	119, 129–30, 132 n. 48, 152, 164
16:10	120–21, 141, 165
16:14	108
16:15	119, 121, 131–33, 152, 165
16:16	165
16:20	108
16:21–22	130
16:23	119, 130–32, 152, 166
16:27	108
16:29	119, 133–34, 152, 167
20:22	40
20:26	40
22:1–2	51
22:39	108
22:41	154, 168
22:41–42	112
22:45	108
22:51	171
22:52	119, 153
24:8	50

2 Kings	
1:17	120, 141
1:18	108
1:18 (LXX)	120, 135

2:11	117	15:26	108, 223 n. 7
3:1	119, 120, 153, 172	15:27	119, 153, 194
4:23	25	15:30	120–21, 140, 141, 154 n. 67
8:16	125, 136, 154, 172	15:31	108, 223 n. 7
8:16–17	112, 135	15:32	154, 193
8:23	108	15:32–33	112
8:25	136, 137, 154, 174	15:36	108
8:25–26	112	16:1	140, 154, 194
9:27–28	122	16:1–2	113
9:29	136, 154	16:17–18	15
10:30	62	16:19	108
10:34	108	17:1	119, 121, 140, 150, 153, 196
10:34–36	118	18:1	154, 197, 222 n. 6, 224 n. 12, 226
10:36	119		
11:1	122	18:1–2	113
11:1–3	174	18:2	227 n. 21
11:21–12:1	112	18:7	233 n. 41
12:2	122, 154, 175	18:9a	224 n. 14
12:7	110, 153	18:9–10	51, 110, 141, 153, 154, 197–98
12:20 [19]	108		
13:1	119, 153, 179	18:10	144, 150, 221, 224 n. 12
13:8	108	18:13	110, 145, 153, 221, 228 n. 26
13:10	119, 153, 182	18:13–17a	222–23
13:12	108	18:13a	224, 226–27, 231, 241–42
14:1	154, 182	18:13b–16	224–28, 241–42
14:1–2	112	18:14–16	223–24
14:15	108	18:15–16	242
14:17	137–39, 141, 153 n. 62, 154 n. 67, 183	18:17	227–29, 231, 239
		18:17–19:8	241–42
14:18	108	18:17–19:37	228
14:23	119, 139, 153	18:17–18	229
14:28	108	18:19	231
15:1	137–38, 153 n. 62, 154, 185	18:23	231
15:1–2	112	18:27	230 n. 32
15:5	125	18:28	231
15:6	108	18:30	231
15:8	46, 119, 153, 191	18:31	227 n. 24, 230 n. 32, 231
15:10	46	18:33	231
15:11	108, 223 n. 7	18:33–35	238
15:12	62	18:35	230 n. 32
15:13	19, 119, 153	19:4	231
15:15	108, 223 n. 7	19:6	231
15:17	50, 119, 153, 191	19:6–7	229, 239
15:21	108	19:8	228, 231, 239, 240
15:23	119, 153, 193	19:9	229, 240

2 Kings (cont.)		Isaiah	
19:9–37	241–42	1:13	25
19:12–13	231, 235	7:8	141, 145
19:14	229	14:28	122
19:15–19	229, 230	14:28–32	145
19:16	231	20:1	239
19:20	231	20:1–6	237–38
19:20–34	229	30:1–17	238
19:29	230 n. 32	31:1–14	238
19:32–33	229	32:10	33
19:35	242	36:1–2	224 nn. 11 and 14
19:35–36	226	38:7–8	14, 205
19:36	231	38:8	17
19:37	239	38:22	14, 205
20:1	145, 227		
20:1–19	242	Jeremiah	
20:6	145, 242	1:2	98 n. 4
20:8–11	14, 205	2:23–24	20 n. 35
20:12–19	145	5:24	37 n. 80
20:13	242	8:20	31
20:19	241	25:1–3	98 n. 4
20:20	108, 223 n. 7, 228	25:3	52
21:1	113	26:1	99
21:17	108	27:1	99, 100
21:19	113	28:1	99–100, 228 n. 26
21:25	108	32:1	44, 228 n. 26
22–23	43	36:1–32	98
22:1	113	36:9	228 n. 26
22:3	153, 228 n. 26	36:22	38, 43
23:12	15	46:2	142
23:23	153	49:34	99
23:28	108	52:12	43
23:29	143		
23:31	20 n. 35, 113	Ezekiel	
23:36	113	11:9–10	239
24:5	108	31:1–18	43
24:8	113	45:18	42
24:10–11	143		
24:12	143	Hosea	
24:18	113, 150	2:13	25
25:1–30	21, 38, 97, 100, 108–09		
25:2	44, 143	Amos	
25:8	21, 38, 43, 44, 143, 150	5:8	36–37 n. 79
25:26	98	8:1–2	31
25:27	99 n. 6	8:5	25

9:13	33	ANCIENT NEAR EASTERN TEXTS	
Zechariah		Enuma Elish	
11:8	19	V:12–22	28
14:16	43		
		GRECO-ROMAN LITERATURE	
Psalms			
47	43	Herodotus, *Histories*	
63:6	14	2.143.1–144.2	87
74:7–8	37	7.204	87
74:17	37	8.131.2	87
81:4[3]	25		
90:4	14	Hesiod, *Works and Days*	
93	43	109–201	91
95–100	43	383–688	31, 33
119:147–148	14		
		Homer, *Iliad*	
Job		2.484–93	66
3:6	19	2.494–759	66
7:3	19	2.816–77	66
29:2	19	10.253	14
39:2	19		
42:16	59	Homer, *Odyssey*	
		12.312	14
Lamentations			
2:19	14	Josephus, *Against Apion*	
		1.14	80
Daniel			
9:24–27	73 n. 13	Josephus, *Antiquities*	
12:7	26	9.216	138
12:11	26	9.227	138
Ezra		Marcellinus, *Life of Thucydides*	
4:2	141, 145	2–4	87
2 Chronicles			
12:13	115 n. 31		
13:1–2	115 n. 31		
14:1–2	116		
21:15	33		
21:19	33		
29:1	115 n. 31		

Modern Authors Index

Ackroyd, Peter R.   58 n. 13
Albrektson, B.   50 n. 2
Albright, William Foxwell   35 n. 73, 59 n. 16
André, G.   9 n. 6
Auerbach, Elias   20 n. 37
Barnes, William Hamilton   113 n. 27
Barthélemy, Dominique   127
Beckwith, Roger T.   9 n. 5
Ben Zvi, Ehud   207 n. 3, 230 n. 31
Bickerman, Elias   8 n. 3, 13 n. 16, 14 n. 18
Bin-Nun, Shoshana R.   113 n. 27
Blakely, Jeffrey A.   234 n. 43
Blenkinsopp, Joseph   238 n. 53
Boling, Robert G.   103 n. 14, 217 n. 2
Borchardt, Ludwig   17 n. 24
Borowski, Oded   32, 34 n. 71, 34 nn. 74–76
Bottéro, Jean   66 n. 5
Brin, Gershon   8 n. 1, 9 n. 5, 29 n. 55, 59 n. 14,
Britton, John P.   26 n. 48, 47 n. 103
Buis, Pierre   5 n. 10
Childs, Brevard S.   222 n. 4, 223 n. 8, 228 n. 25
Clagett, Marshall   8 n. 2, 17 nn. 23 and 25, 18 n. 29, 25 n. 45, 27 n. 51, 28 n. 52, 33 n. 68, 48 n. 104
Clements, R. E.   19 n. 31
Clines, David J. A.   36 n. 77, 52 nn. 4 and 6, 53 n. 7
Cogan, Mordecai   97 n. 2, 99 n. 7, 221 n. 2, 224 n. 13, 226 n. 17, 227 nn. 21–22
Cohen, Chaim   238 n. 55
Cohen, Mark E.   20 n. 34, 30 n. 61, 36 n. 78, 37 n. 81, 47 n. 102
Cooper, Alan   25 n. 43, 26 n. 47, 36 n. 79, 37 n. 82, 43 n. 93
Cortese, E.   5 n. 10
Cross, Frank Moore   5 n. 10, 21 n. 38, 23 n. 40, 84 n. 26, 110 n. 24
Depuydt, Leo   30 n. 60, 205 n. 1
Dubberstein, Waldo H.   8 n. 3
Eliade, Mircea   49 n. 1
Etz, Donald V.   68, 69
Evans, Paul S.   227 n. 24
Finegan, Jack   121 n. 37
Fleming, Daniel E.   30 n. 63, 47 n. 103, 50 n. 2
Forsdyke, John   94 n. 45
Frankfort, Henri   42 n. 91
Freedman, David Noel   2 n. 3, 41 n. 90, 45 n. 97, 58 n. 13, 59 n. 17, 62 n. 22, 116 n. 33, 143 n. 52
Fried, Lisbeth S.   41 n. 90, 45 n. 97
Friedman, Richard Elliott   3 nn. 6–8, 5 n. 10, 6 n. 11, 9 n. 4, 23 n. 39, 83 n. 25, 90 n. 40, 98 n. 3
Galil, Gershon   43 n. 94, 222 nn. 5–6, 232, 235 n. 47, 236
Gallagher, William R.   225 n. 16, 230 n. 32, 231 n. 36
Gandz, Solomon   25 n. 44, 26 n. 48, 28 n. 54
Garbini, Giovanni   209 n. 5
Geoghegan, Jeffrey C.   103 n. 14, 217 n. 2
Geyer, John B.   226 n. 18

Glassner, Jean-Jacques 50 n. 2, 60 n. 19, 87 n. 31, 107 n. 22, 110 n. 23, 207 n. 4
Glatt, David A. 243 n. 62
Goldberg, Jeremy 235 n. 47
Goldstein, Bernard R. 25 n. 43, 26 n. 47, 36 n. 79, 37 n. 82, 43 n. 93
Gonçalves, F. J. 223 nn. 8–9, 225 n. 15, 228 n. 26
Goudoever, J. van 40 n. 85
Gray, John 5 n. 10
Halpern, Baruch 42 n. 91, 43 n. 93, 101 n. 9, 115 n. 31, 116 n. 32
Hannah, Robert R. 18 n. 28, 28 n. 53, 33 n. 66, 47 n. 103
Haran, Menahem 3 n. 7
Hardin, James W. 234 n. 43
Hayes, John H. 45 n. 98, 111 n. 25, 125 n. 41, 143 n. 52, 237 n. 51
Hendel, Ronald S. 68–69, 72, 74–77, 82
Honor, Leo L. 223 n. 7, 226 n. 19
Hooker, Paul K. 111 n. 25, 125 n. 41, 143 n. 52, 233 n. 41, 235 n. 47
Hornung, Eric 8 n. 2
Hughes, Jeremy 20 n. 36, 31 n. 64, 39 n. 84, 41 n. 90, 48 n. 105, 68–69, 74–75, 102, 125 n. 41
Hull, John H. 223 n. 7, 227 n. 23
Hurvitz, Avi 3 n. 7
Iwry, Samuel 15 n. 21, 17 n. 27
Jacobsen, Thorkild 42 n. 91
Jenkins, Allan K. 231 nn. 35 and 37
Jenks, A. W. 6 n. 11
Jepsen, Alfred 83 n. 24
Kahle, Paul 127
Kaiser, Otto 237 n. 51
Kitchen, Kenneth A. 146 n. 55, 239 n. 58
Klein, Ralph W. 68–69, 74–77, 81 n. 23
Knohl, Israel 4 n. 8, 23 n. 39, 24 n. 42
Krauss, Rolf 8 n. 2
Kugler, Franz X. 20 n. 35
Kutsch, E. 41 n. 88
Laato, Antti 224 n. 14, 226 n. 20, 240
Lagarde, Paul de 127
Langdon, Stephen S. 19 n. 30, 29 n. 57
Larsson, Gerhard 72 n. 11
Lemaire, André 116 n. 32
Lie, Arthur G. 233 n. 42
Lohfink, Norbert 5 n. 10
Lundbom, Jack R. 58 n. 13, 59 n. 17, 62 n. 22, 98 nn. 3–4, 99 n. 5, 100 n. 8
Luraghi, Nino 50 n. 2
Macalister, Robert A. S. 35 n. 72
Malalae, Ioannis 73 n. 13
Meyer, Eduard 94, 121 n. 37
Miano, David 84 n. 26
Milgrom, Jacob 4 n. 7, 12 nn. 13 and 15, 40 n. 86, 42 nn. 90 and 92
Millard, Alan 221 n. 2
Möller, Astrid 50 n. 2
Momigliano, Arnaldo 50 n. 2, 206 n. 2
Montgomery, James A. 5 n. 10
Moor, Johannes C. de 34 n. 70, 41 n. 87
Morganstern, Julian 9 n. 5, 11 n. 11, 31 n. 64, 45 n. 97
Mosshammer, Alden A. 73 n. 13, 87 n. 37, 94 n. 45
Mowinckel, Sigmund 25 n. 44, 43 n. 93
Na'aman, Nadav 222 n. 6, 234–35, 238 nn. 56–57
Nelson, Richard D. 5 n. 10, 114
Neuberg, Frank J. 58 n. 13
Nicholson, Ernest 3 n. 5, 4 n. 8
Niehr, H. 10 n. 9
Noll, Kurt L. 207 n. 3
Norin, S. 224 n. 14
North, F. S. 33 n. 67
North, J. L. 20 n. 33
Northcote, Jeremy 80 n. 20, 82 n. 23
Oswalt, John N. 237 n. 51
Otto, Eckart 29 n. 55
Parker, Richard A. 8 nn. 2–3, 27 n. 51, 30 n. 60, 47 n. 103
Person, Raymond F. 238 n. 54, 242 n. 61
Polzin, Robert 3 n.7
Prakken, Donald Wilson 94 n. 44
Propp, William H. C. 12 nn. 14–15, 16, 18, 40 n. 86, 60
Pury, Albert de 3 n. 5

MODERN AUTHORS INDEX

Rawlinson, Henry C.   234 n.44
Rendsburg, Gary A.   4 n. 7
Richter, Wolfgang   5 n. 10, 57 n. 9
Roberts, J. J. M.   43 n. 93
Rochberg, Francesca   27 n. 50, 44 n. 96, 47 n. 103
Saggs, Henry W. F.   43 n. 91
Samuel, Alan E.   8 n. 3, 26 n. 49, 27 n. 50, 94 n. 45
Schedl, Claus   232 n. 37
Schlauri, I.   5 n. 10
Schwyzer, E.   87 n. 33
Segal, J. B.   48 n. 105
Seitz, Chrisopher R.   226 n. 18
Seow, C. L.   43 n. 93
Sethe, Kurt   8 n. 2
Sewell, J. W. S.   30 n. 62
Shenkel, James Donald   120 n. 35, 127, 137 n. 49
Shortland, A. J.   146 n. 55
Smelik, Klaas A. D.   57 n. 11, 229 n. 27
Smith, George   234 n. 44
Snaith, Norman H.   40 n. 86
Soggin, J. Alberto   10 n. 8, 101 n. 10, 103 n. 12
Spalinger, Anthony J.   230 n. 34
Stendebach, F. J.   29 n. 58
Steele, John M.   27 n. 50
Stern, Sacha   25 n. 45
Stott, Katherine M.   209 n. 5
Stroes, H. R.   9 n. 5
Tadmor, Hayim   46 n. 101, 146 n. 54, 221 n. 2, 224 n. 13, 226 n. 17, 227 nn. 21–22
Talmon, Shemaryahu   9 n. 5, 34 n. 69, 35 n. 73, 36 n. 74, 39 n. 84, 61 n. 21
Taylor, Jeremy Graeme   66 nn.4 and 6–7, 67 n. 8, 87 n. 35, 88 n. 38
Tetley, M. Christine   107 n. 21
Thiele, Edwin R.   44 n. 95, 46 n. 100, 107 n. 21, 111 n. 25, 123 n. 38, 124 n. 39, 146 n. 54
Tov, Emanuel   137 n. 49
Vanderhooft, David S.   115 n. 31, 116 n. 32
VanderKam, James C.   2, 29 n. 56
Vaux, Roland de   48 n. 105
Verbrugghe, Gerald P.   73 n. 13, 81 n. 21
Wacholder, Ben Zion   73 n. 12
Waerden, Bartel L. van der   19 n. 30, 33 n. 66, 36 n. 78
Wagenaar, Jan A.   20 n. 35, 41 nn. 88–89
Warburton, David A.   8 n. 2
Weinfeld, Moshe   3 n. 7, 230 n. 30
Weippert, H.   116 n. 32
Weippert, M.   116 n. 32
Wickersham, John M.   73 n. 13, 81 n. 21
Wildberger, Hans   237 n. 51
Williamson, H. G. M.   5 n. 10
Wilson, Robert R.   86 n. 30, 87 n. 31, 94 n. 46
Winckler, Hugo   232 n. 39, 233 n. 42, 234 n. 44
Wright, Richard M.   3 n. 5
Yadin, Yigael   15, 17, 229 n. 29
Zevit, Ziony   4 n. 7

www.ingramcontent.com/pod-product-compliance
Lightning Source LLC
Chambersburg PA
CBHW031708230426
43668CB00006B/150